AF599073

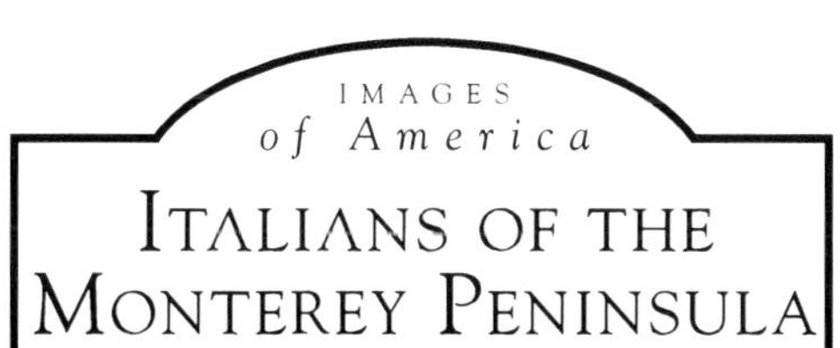
IMAGES
of America
ITALIANS OF THE
MONTEREY PENINSULA

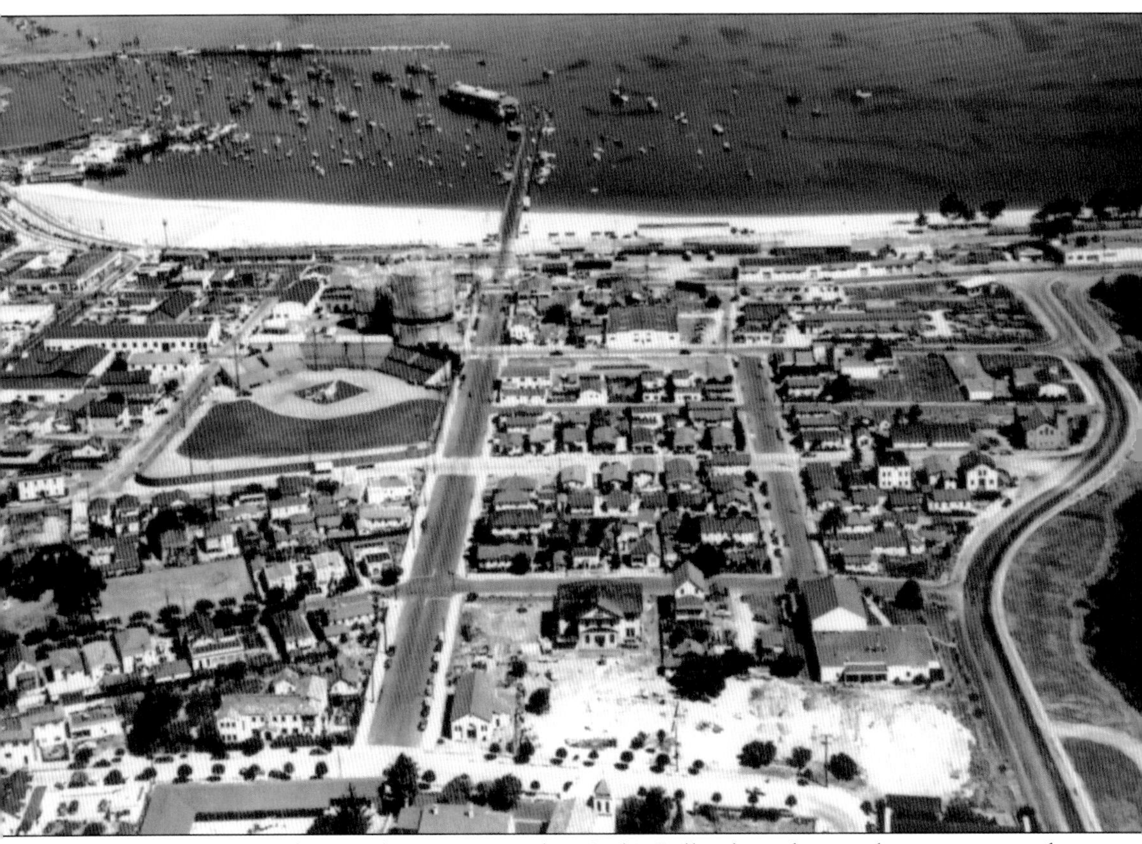

This is a 1950 aerial view of Monterey Harbor, Jack's Ballpark, and natural gas storage tanks. Jack's Ballpark was a wooden stadium where the Oakland Seals, a minor league baseball team, conducted spring training. The city reduced the size of the ballpark and created the Monterey Tennis Center. Alongside the wharf is the Booth Cannery pier, but the cannery was torn down as it presented a hazard to the public. To the left of the natural gas tanks is the site where the Monterey Sports Center is now located. At lower right is the USO building, which was the place to go during World War II. It provided dancing for the armed service members, and is now the home of the YMCA. (Courtesy of Monterey Public Library's California Historic Room.)

**On the Cover:** Pictured here is the christening of *San Giovanni*, a purse seiner fishing boat, on August 12, 1939; family and friends rode along to celebrate the occasion. Boat christening was always a big event, as it gave the owner the opportunity to introduce his friends and family to the boat. Ben Compagno was listed as the boat's owner in the 1939–1940 fishing season, and he fished for the San Carlos Canning Company. The *San Giovanni* has survived over the years and still operates today. Many a young teenager has worked on this boat, learning how to fish and finding out whether or not they have what it takes to become a fisherman. (Photograph by William L. Morgan, courtesy of the Monterey Public Library's California Historic Room.)

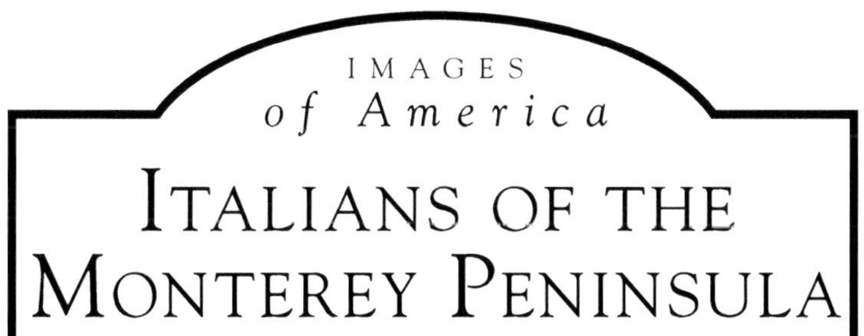


Mike Ventimiglia

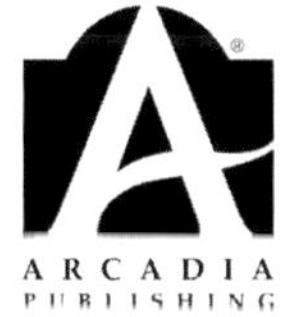

ISBN 978-1-4671-3306-7

Published by Arcadia Publishing
Charleston, South Carolina

Printed in the United States of America

Library of Congress Control Number: 2014949021

For all general information, please contact Arcadia Publishing:
Telephone 843-853-2070
Fax 843-853-0044
E-mail sales@arcadiapublishing.com
For customer service and orders:
Toll-Free 1-888-313-2665

Visit us on the Internet at www.arcadiapublishing.com

*To the Sicilian Italians who migrated to Monterey during the years of the "Silver Harvest," and their families.*

# Contents

# ACKNOWLEDGMENTS

This book would not have been possible if it were not for the work of William L. Morgan and other photographers capturing on film the early Sicilian Italian fishermen who migrated to Monterey, California, to reap the "Silver Harvest." The Pittsburg Historical Society, Vince Ferrante of Pittsburg, Amici Club of Monterey, Peter Torrente, Anne Castaldo Jay, Mary D'Agui Wells, the Bert Cutino family, Cathy Ventimiglia Gomez, and many more families opened their photograph albums and shared their memories with us. Without their assistance, many of the early images in this book could not have been included. Salvatore Ventimiglia, who came to Monterey at the age of 19 in 1912, captured his memories on paper. Phyllis Belleci, his wife, did the same; these minute details of how they lived were priceless. Dennis Copeland, the Monterey Museum director and archivist, provided invaluable aid in the publishing of this book. The early photographs and research material in the archives of the California Historic Room at the Monterey Public Library allowed this story to be told. A big thank-you to Monterey Library volunteers who have the task of preserving the historical documents and photographs in safekeeping for all generations to enjoy. They help us remember the early Sicilian and Italian families who came to Monterey to fish and rear their families and bring to the forefront the hardships that they endured to create a better life. I hope to inspire the younger generations who have benefited from the hard work of their grandparents and great-grandparents to not let the memories die, but to search out their family history and pass it on.

# INTRODUCTION

The Monterey Peninsula was first discovered in 1602, when Phillip III of Spain dispatched Don Sebastian Vizcaino with three vessels on a voyage of discovery up the coast of California. On December 10, 1602, Vizcaino anchored in Monterey Bay. He took possession of the land in the name of the king of Spain and named it Monterey Bay. It would be another 166 years after that first visit before Monterey Bay would be rediscovered, and Father Junipero Serra would found Mission San Carlos.

Father Junipero Serra bonded with the local Indians along the coast, converting them to Christianity. They helped him establish the missions along the central coast and throughout California. The local Indians took advantage of the fish and abalone that were found in Monterey Bay, as the water was one of their major sources of food.

On January 24, 1848, James Marshall found gold in a stream near John Sutter's sawmill in northern California. This led to the Gold Rush of 1849, which brought an influx of many nationalities to the United States to prospect for gold. The Italians had set up fishing communities along the Sacramento and San Joaquin Rivers at Collinsville and New York Landing (Black Diamond), now known as Pittsburg, California. Black Diamond was known for its coal mines, which provided work for Italians as well as access to the Sacramento and San Joaquin Rivers for salmon fishing. In 1886, Frank E. Booth and his family had established a canning company on the Sacramento River, named the River Packing Association.

Chinese migrated south from San Francisco to Monterey and set up a fishing village at Point Alones, off what is known as Cannery Row. Commercialized fishing in Monterey began in 1853, when the Chinese fished for squid and harvested abalone from the Monterey Bay. The squid and abalone were dried and shipped to San Francisco. The smell of the squid and fish drying upset the townspeople, sparking prejudice and animosity. The fishing village caught fire in 1906 and burned to the ground. Very little effort was made to extinguish the fire, and the citizens would not allow the village to be rebuilt.

In 1882, J. Parker Whitney introduced the trolling line for salmon fishing. He would take guests from the luxurious Del Monte Hotel to sport fish for salmon. In 1902, Otosaburo Noda and Harry Malpas established Monterey Fishing and Canning on Ocean View Avenue (Cannery Row); they are credited with one of the first canneries in the area. Japanese fishermen capitalized on the abundance of salmon and prized abalone in the bay.

Frank E. Booth purchased a cannery, reduction plant, and equipment from H.R. Robbins. Booth experimented in the processing and canning of sardines, which were abundant in Monterey Bay. In 1902, Booth's cannery was turning out 3,000 cans of sardines a year. His cannery was mainly canning sardines, reducing the amount of salmon he was purchasing from the local fishermen, and in 1903 his cannery caught fire and burned down. It could not be proven, but the general feeling was that the fire was started by angry salmon fishermen, upset over not being able to sell their fish to Booth. Booth rebuilt his cannery on the same location, doubling the size of the business, and renamed it the Monterey Packing Company.

In 1905, Knut Hovden, a Norwegian and a graduate of Norway's National Fisheries College, began working for Booth. Hovden was astonished at the backwards fishing and canning practices at the cannery. He made tremendous innovations in the canning industry while working for Booth. The improvements introduced by Hovden were so effective that the demand for more fish and improved fishing techniques were evident. Booth contacted Pietro Ferrante, who was working in Black Diamond, California, at Booth's salmon cannery, to come to Monterey in hope that Ferrante could improve the fishing operations and harvest more fish to keep up with the canning process. Ferrante relied on his fishing experience from Sicily and convinced Booth to purchase *lampara* nets from Tangier, Morocco. The lampara net was used instead of gill nets to catch sardines in the Mediterranean Sea. Pietro Ferrante enlisted his family and friends in Black Diamond, Pittsburg, and Sicily. Fishermen also came to Monterey from the islands off the coast of Sicily, such as Isola Egadi, Isola Levanzo, Marettimo, Isola delle Femmine, and Isola Favignana to reap the Silver Harvest.

Canning production increased between 1918 and 1928, as the European fish supplies were cut off during World War I. The canneries in Monterey turned out over four million cases of fish during this time. During this 10-year period, the canneries continued to flourish, creating jobs for hundreds if not thousands of people. Cannery Row became the hub of the city. Reduction plants would become the primary source of revenue for the cannery owners, as the market was more diverse. The fish oils, meal, and fertilizer were in high demand. The reduction plants also created a new problem as they grew. Residents complained about the pungent odors they created. The city council established an odor patrol, which would investigate the canneries responsible and levy fines against them.

Fishing boats were essential to these Italian fishermen, as ownership allowed them to provide for their families. As more sardines were needed, larger and bigger fishing boats were designed that could go farther out to sea for longer periods and could carry tons of fish.

The Italians who settled in Monterey have a rich traditional history, demonstrating an exemplary work ethic and love of family. They came to Monterey with the hope of building a new future and had little money. Those who could afford it rented houses or an apartment, while some lived on their boats or were taken in by relatives until they could afford their own place. Rents for homes in 1917 ranged between $10 and $35 a month.

Religion is an important part of the Italian culture, and most were Roman Catholic. The church provided the families with their spiritual needs, performing baptisms, Holy Communion, confirmations, and marriage ceremonies, all reasons for celebrations with family and friends. These early Italian families were a part of an era that has become known as the Silver Harvest, when the abundant silvery fish made Monterey the "Sardine Capital of the World."

# *One*

# Italians Migrate to Monterey

Italians began migrating to the United States before 1850, during the 1848 discovery of gold in California at Sutter's Mill. Ships would stop at Collinsville on their way to San Francisco and Sacramento. Italian fishermen established themselves in the small communities of Collinsville and New York's Landing, later renamed Black Diamond and now known as Pittsburg, California. Black Diamond, Collinsville, and Martinez were right on the water and home for the Sicilian fishermen who fished the Sacramento and San Joaquin Rivers. The migration of Sicilian Italians began when Pietro Ferrante was summoned by Frank E. Booth to Monterey to resolve the sardine supply problem.

Pietro Ferrante realized that the net being used to catch sardines was insufficient. The introduction of the lampara net changed the sardine fishing industry. Experienced fishermen were needed to handle and deploy the lampara nets. Pietro knew that by bringing the experienced Sicilian fishermen to Monterey, the learning curve in deploying the lampara nets would be reduced, which meant more sardines. This gave the Sicilian fishermen a new opportunity to provide for their families. As the new fishing industry was just beginning, they would have the opportunity to establish themselves, and many families left Pittsburg for Monterey. There is a deep connection between the families of Monterey and Pittsburg still today. The Italian word lampara was derived from the word *lampa*, which means "lightning fast." The lampara net caused some controversy, as local fishermen were worried that it would deplete the fish too rapidly. The nets provided the quantity of sardines that Booth needed for his cannery, and the era known as the Silver Harvest began.

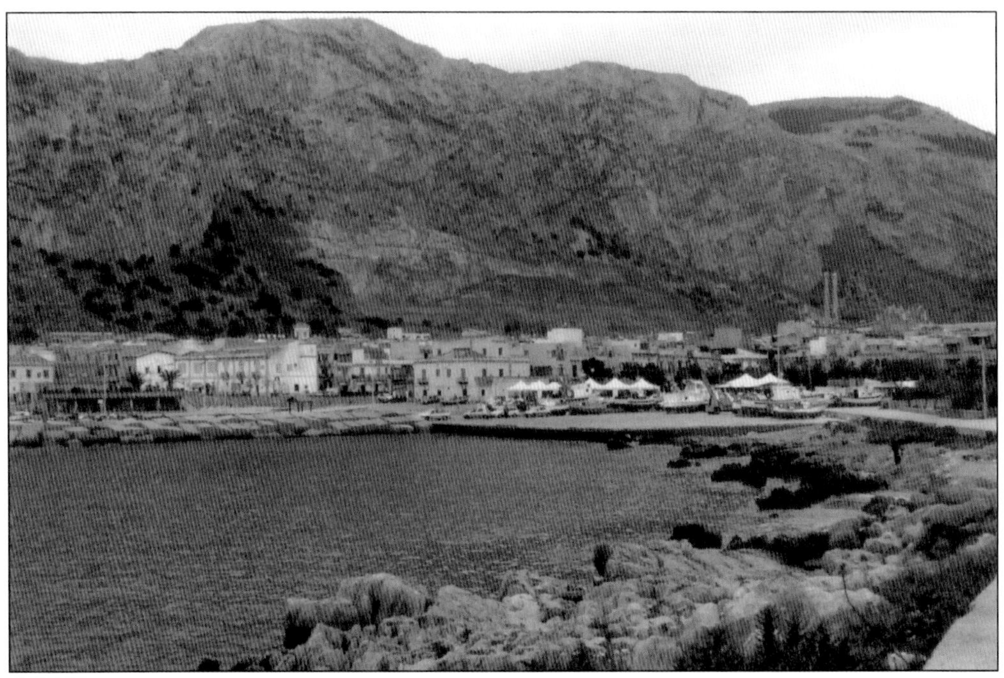

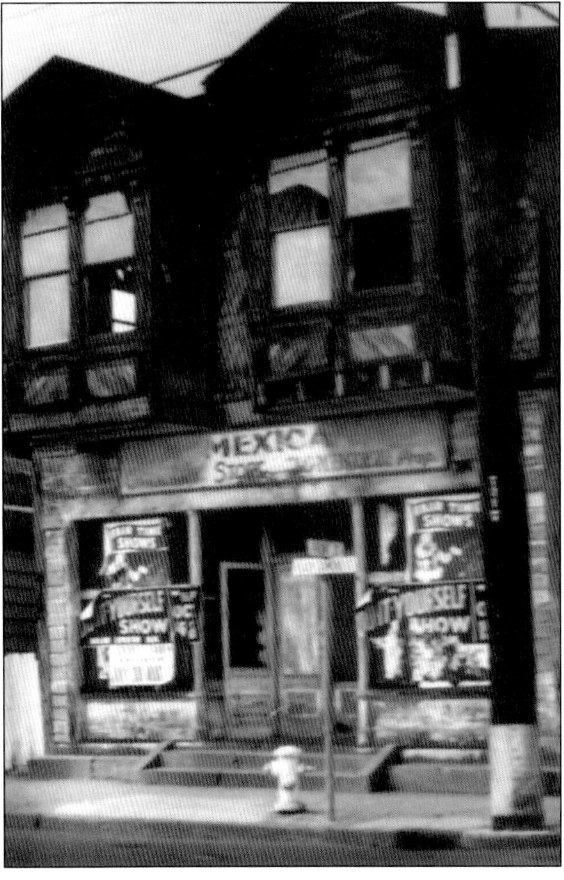


This is the modern-day Isola delle Femmine village in Sicily, from which many Sicilian fishermen migrated when they came to New York Landing, Pittsburg, Collinsville, and Martinez, California. The immigrants took steerage passage in steamship freighters for a cost of $38. They endured the 13-to-14-day ocean voyage at the bottom of the ship, with no windows and little ventilation. Pictured at left is the Mexican store in the town of Black Diamond, named after the coal mines in the area. The town would later be renamed Pittsburg for the steel industry that had emerged in the area. (Above, photograph by Cosmo Tilly; left, courtesy of Pittsburg Historical Society.)

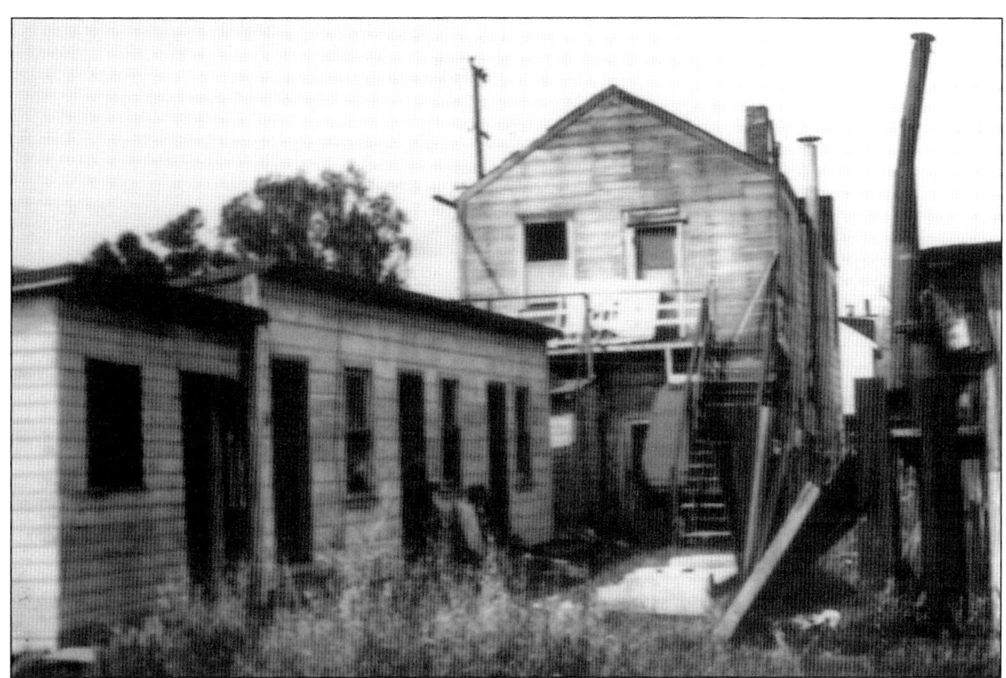

Two-story houses with smaller units to the rear housed fishing families. These structures provided shelter for many immigrants, who would share their home with family members. Sometimes as many as a dozen people would live in the same house. The homes were constructed to provide only the basic needs, but the families were better off than they had been in Italy. At right, the simple square design of this house made it easy to construct and cost less to build. There was electricity in the homes, but it was mainly used for lighting. Each room was normally equipped with one light bulb in the ceiling, and heat was provided by a wood-burning stove. (Both, courtesy of Pittsburg Historical Society.)

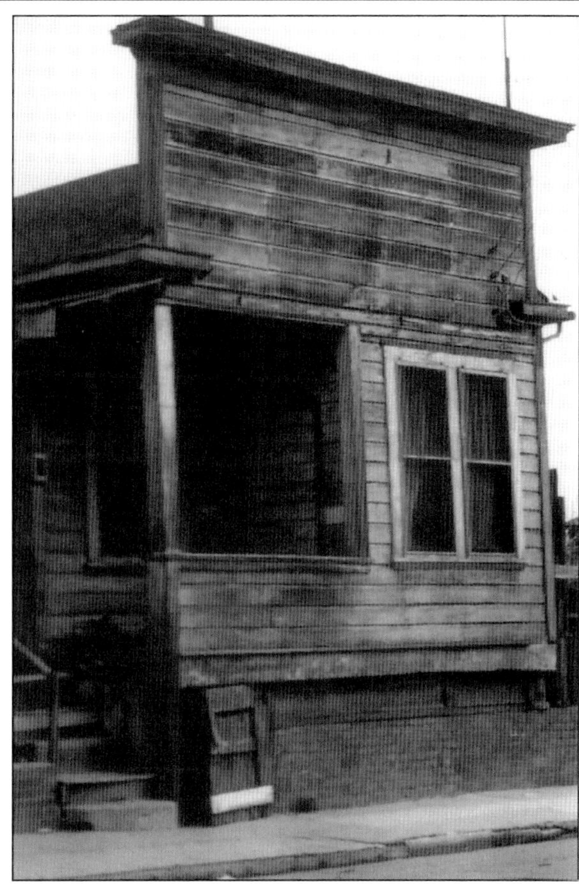

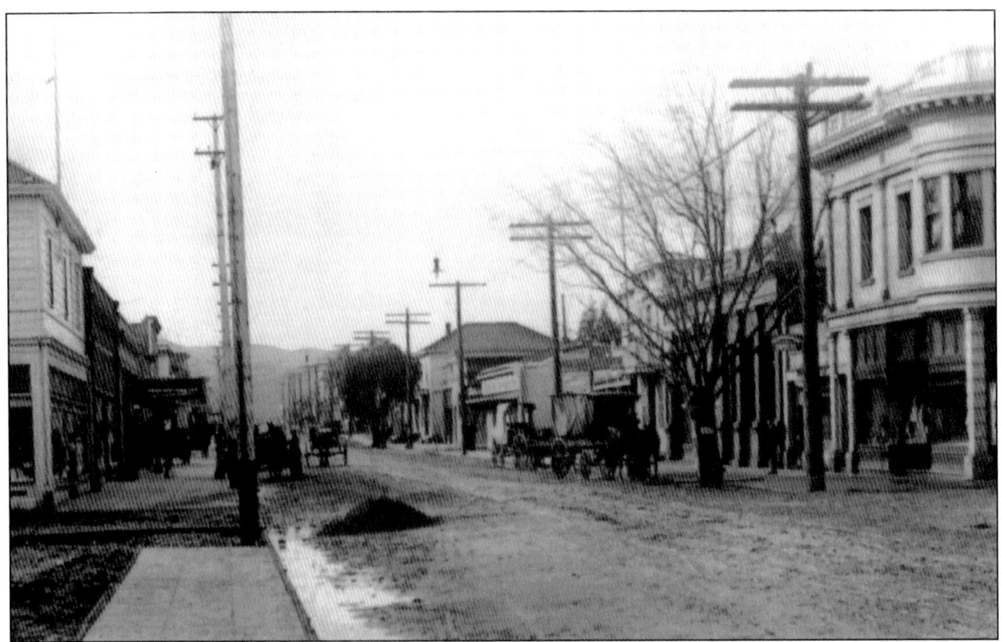

Black Diamond's Main Street was dirt, and the primary mode of transportation was horse and wagon. During the winter months, the streets became mired with mud when the rains came, making travel difficult. A large Sicilian Italian fishing community was established in Black Diamond, and they often went without power. Wood and coal were the primary fuel sources. A wood-burning stove provided heat for cooking and comfort. When ironing needed to be done, a heavy steel iron was placed on the stove and heated. Pictured below are some of the businesses located in downtown Black Diamond: Buggies Wagon Printer and Lettering, Diamond Garage, and Bay View Saloon. In the early 20th century, utility poles carried telephone lines and limited electrical power for stores and street lighting. (Both, courtesy of Pittsburg Historical Society,)

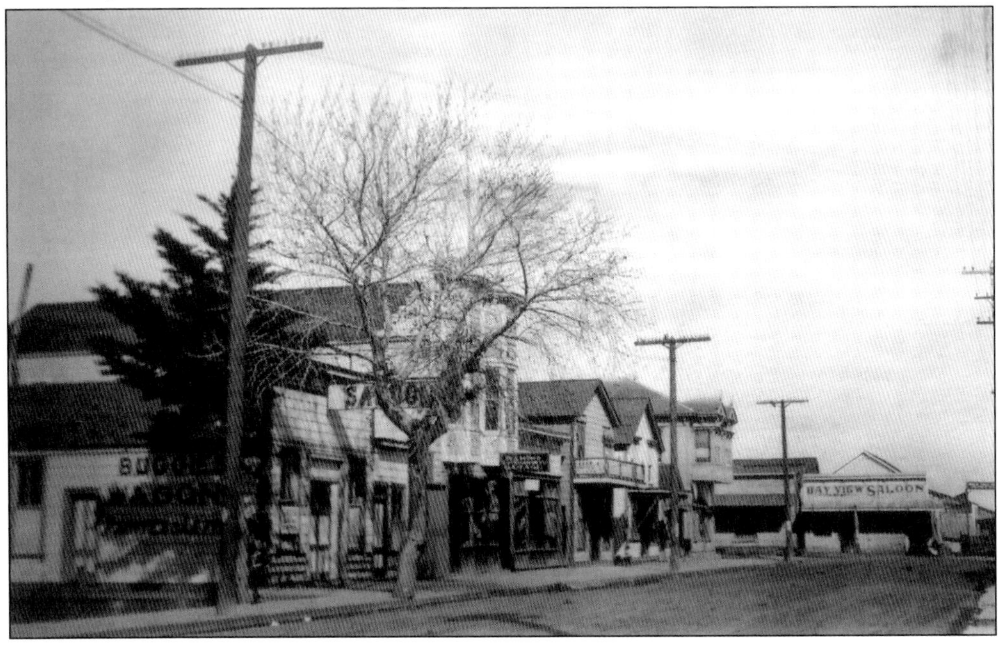

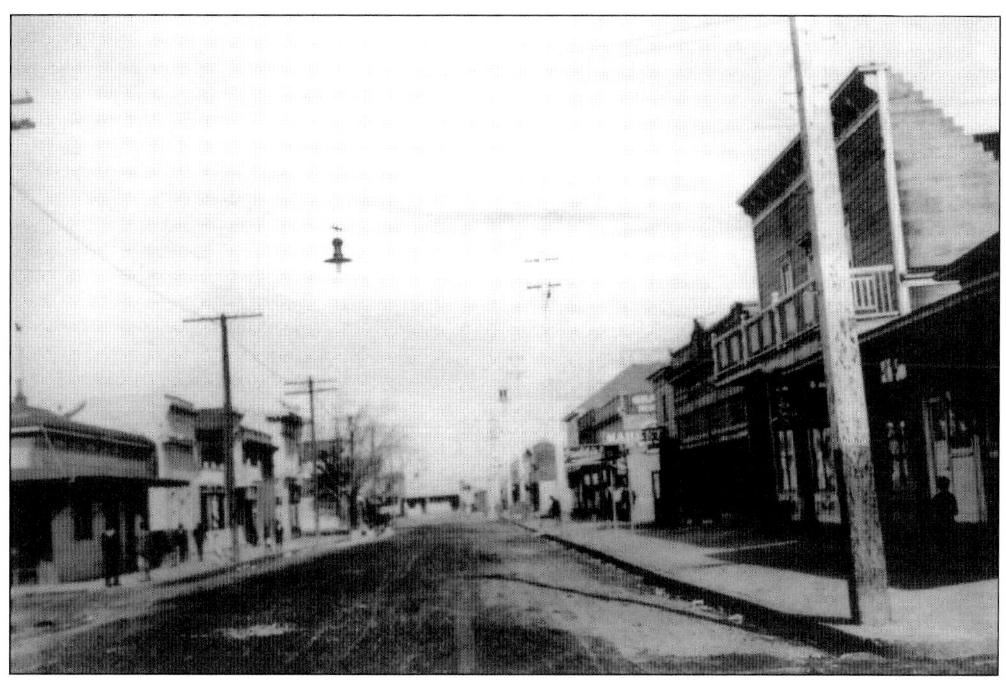

The early town shows signs of progress as concrete sidewalks with curbs are beginning to appear along the street. Street lights are seen hanging over the center of Main Street, and electrical wires are suspended from the utility poles on the sidewalk. Below, children are playing on the sidewalk as the street is a slurry of mud. During the rainy season, the streets were almost impassable, and the mire made it difficult for the children to play. (Both, courtesy of Pittsburg Historical Society.)

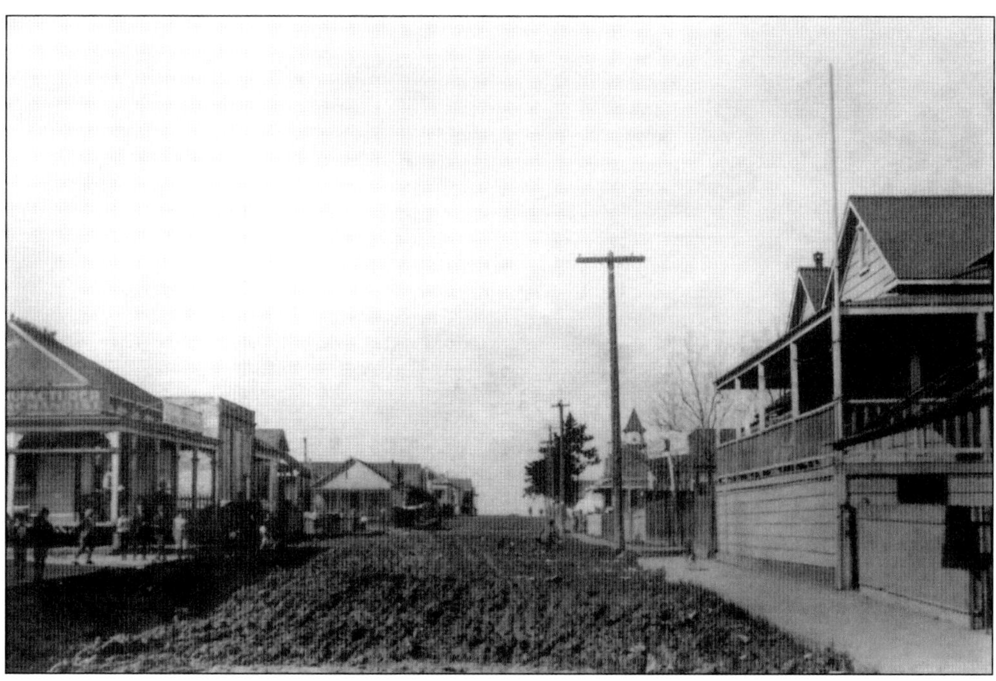

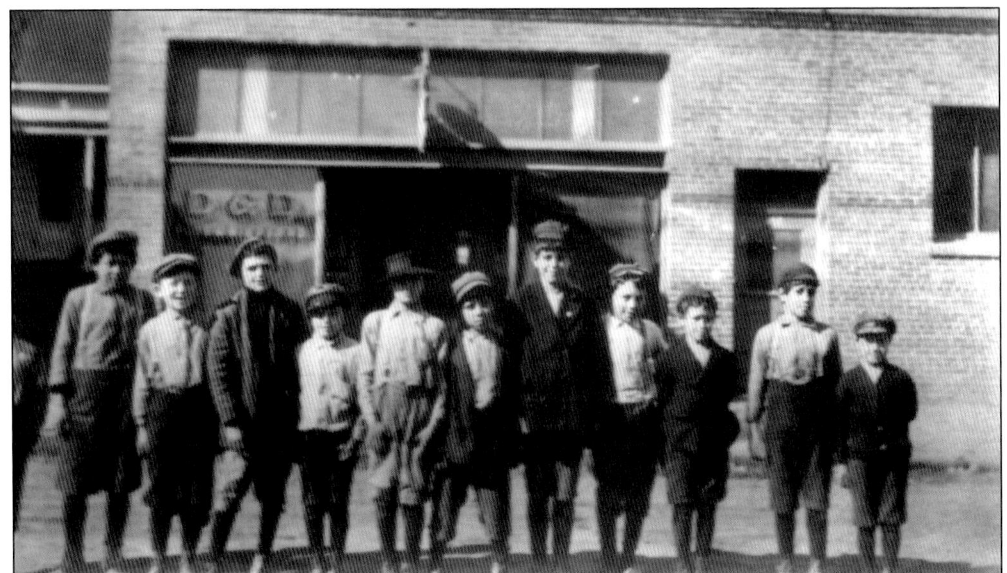

Many of these Black Diamond boys lined up downtown were the children of "Capachuties," a term used to refer to fishermen who hailed from the town of Capaci near Isola delle Femmine, Sicily. Below is a map of Martinez, California, where a large number of Sicilian fisherman lived and fished at Granger's Wharf. Alhambra Creek ran through the city to a slough that emptied into Suisun Bay, and many of the fishermen lived a few blocks up from the wharf on Foster, Buckley, and Howard Streets, to name a few. A number of the homes have historical plates naming the Italian families and the dates they lived there. (Above, courtesy of Pittsburg Historical Society; below, author's collection.)

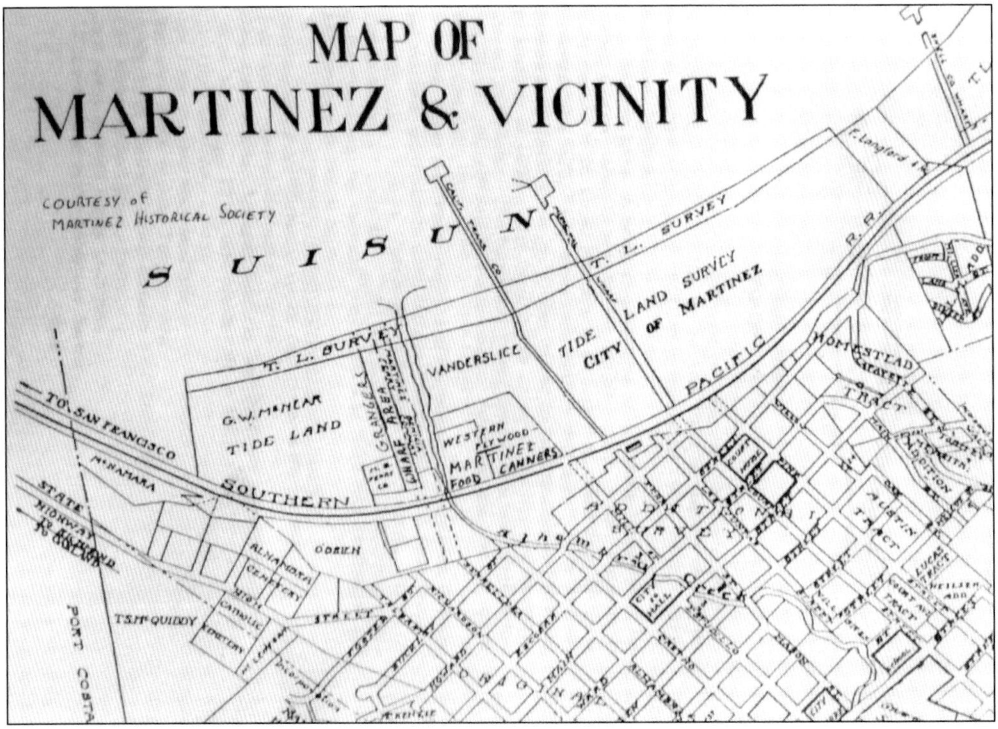

MAP OF
MARTINEZ & VICINITY

COURTESY of
MARTINEZ HISTORICAL SOCIETY

SUISUN
T. L. SURVEY
LAND SURVEY OF MARTINEZ
TIDE CITY
VANDERSLICE
G.W. McNEAR TIDE LAND
GRANGERS WHARF AREA
WESTERN PLYWOOD
MARTINEZ FOOD CANNERS
TO SAN FRANCISCO
SOUTHERN PACIFIC R.R.
McNAMARA
STATE HIGHWAY
O'BRIEN
ALHAMBRA CEMETERY
CATHOLIC CEMETERY
TS.McQUIDDY
PORT COSTA
HOMESTEAD TRACT
AUSTIN TRACT
LUCAS TRACT
Alhambra Creek
CITY HALL

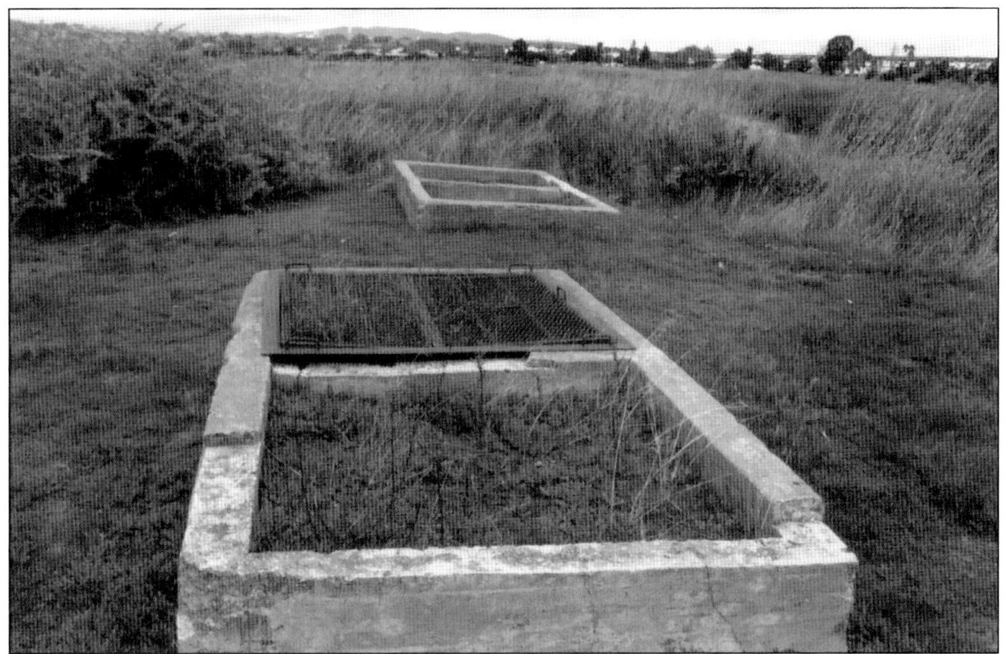

Granger's Wharf, located in Martinez, California, was located about half a mile below Richardson Street in Old Town Martinez. This section of town was predominately made up of Sicilians, with families like Costanza, Lucido, Bellecci, Russo, Enea, and Ferrante living within walking distance of Granger's Wharf. Below is a view of Mussel Point in 1898; the village was built directly on the rocks of the seashore. The living conditions were not the greatest, and the smell of drying fish permeated the air. Chinese junks would sail from China and anchor in Monterey Bay off Cannery Row, exchanging goods and loading their cargo holds with dried squid for the return trip. (Above, courtesy of Contra Costa Historical Society; below, Monterey Public Library's California Historic Room.)

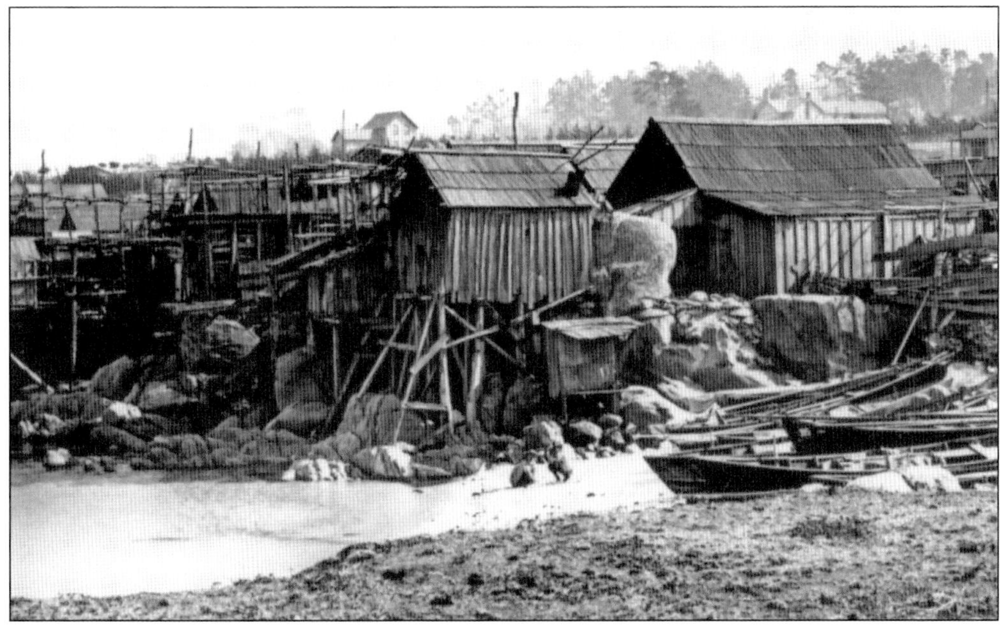

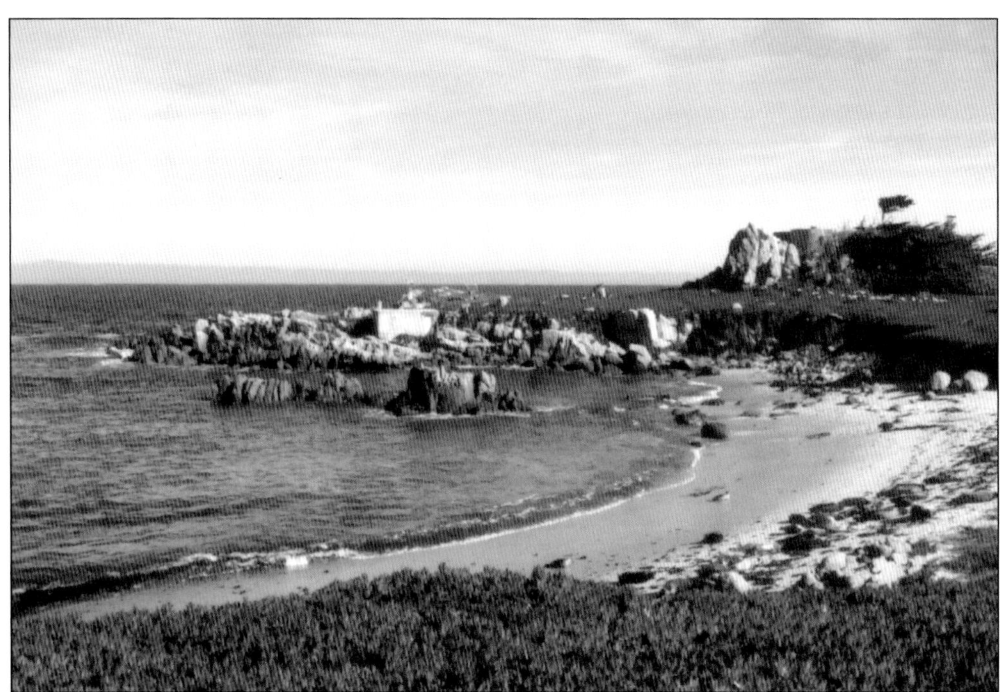

Pictured above is Point Alones as it stands today. Gone are the Chinese fishing shacks and the drying rack that once filled the air with the smell of fish. Point Alones is now the home of Hopkins Marine Laboratory. Below is Robb Ricketts laboratory on Cannery Row. Ed Ricketts, as he liked to be called, was a marine biologist, ecologist, and philosopher. He is best known for his 1939 book *Between Pacific Tides*, a pioneering study of intertidal ecology. His laboratory is about a half mile from Point Alones. (Both, author's collection.)

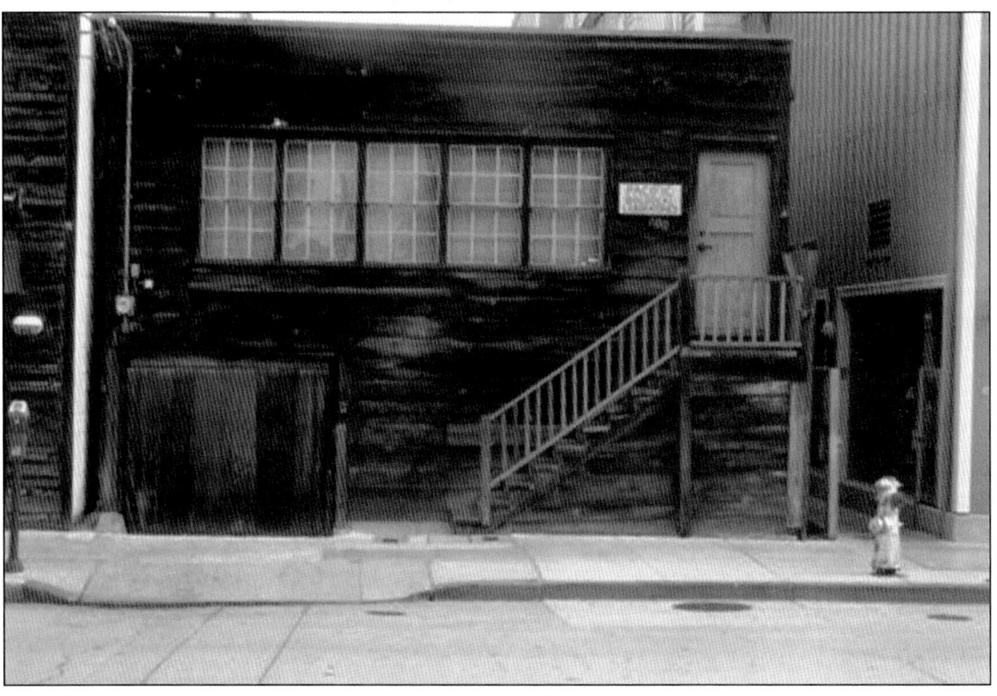

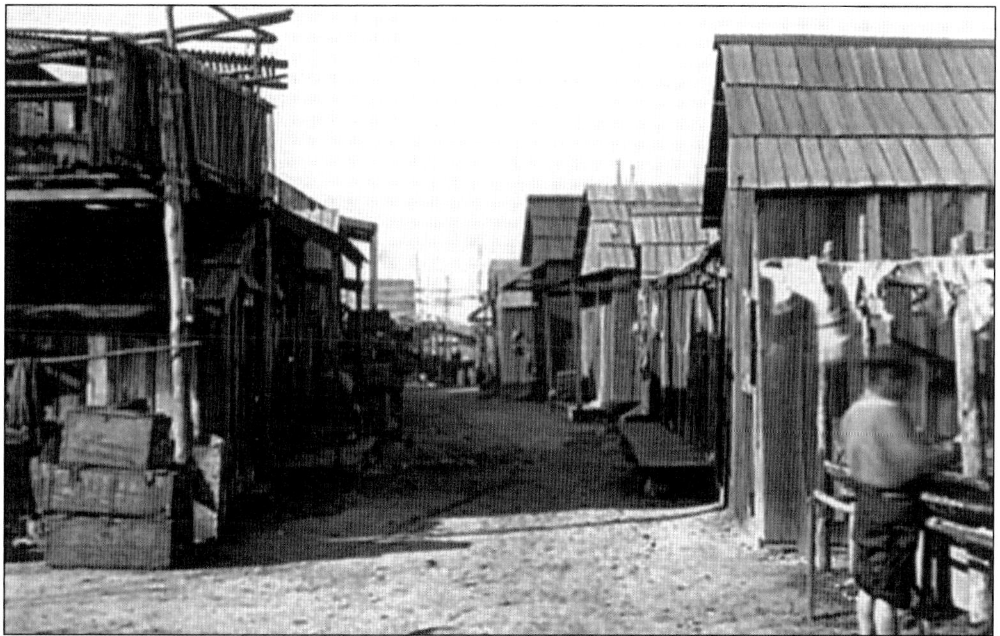

A Chinese fisherman rotates the fish and tends the drying racks along the narrow street that runs through the village. The village caught fire in 1906, and it spread rapidly, destroying the settlement. The citizens of Monterey would not allow the village to be rebuilt after the fire, as the smell that was created by the drying fish was offensive. The Chinese families relocated to the city or moved out of the area. Pictured below is a Sanborn map of Monterey from 1885; the population was at 1,500, and prevailing winds would come out of the northwest bringing storms that had a devastating effect on boats anchored in the bay. (Above, courtesy of Monterey Public Library's California Historic Room; below, author's collection.)

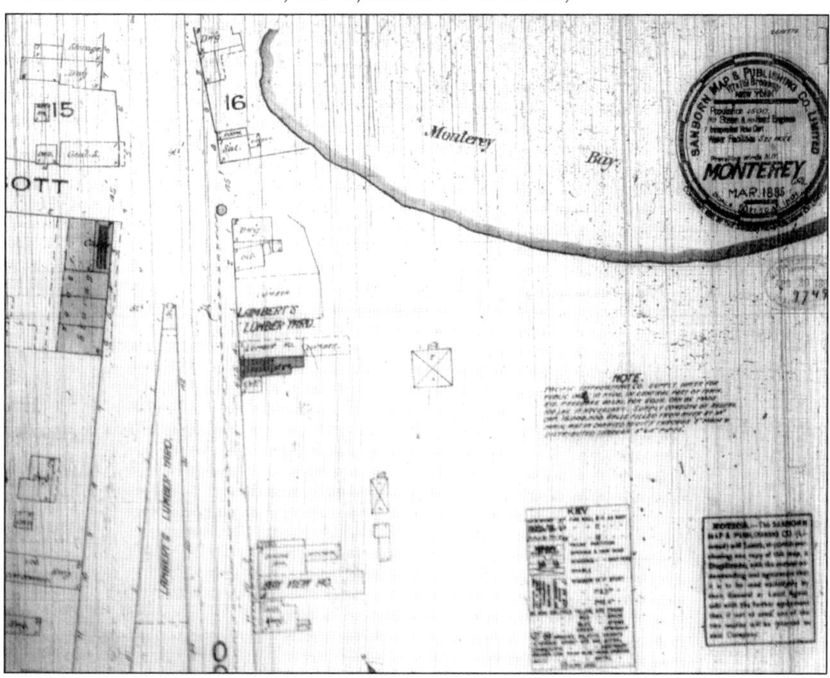

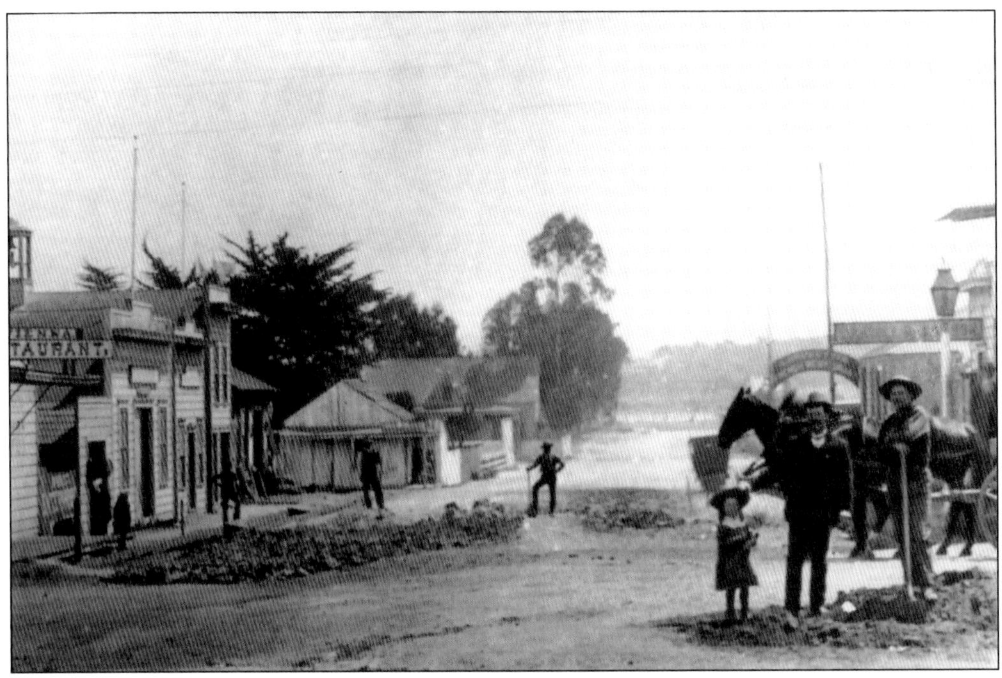

A father and daughter pose in front of men working with shovels on Alvarado Street in 1887. The building on the left is the Vienna Restaurant, and on the roof is an alarm bell that would alert the people in times of trouble. An early gas lamppost can be seen, which gave light to the dark street at night. Pictured below is an early Monterey house, said to be one of the first, in a state of collapse. The pipe lying in front of the home is most likely part of a water main pipe, as the city was extending its water system. (Above, photograph by Charles Wallace Jacob Johnson; both courtesy of Monterey Public Library's California Historic Room.)

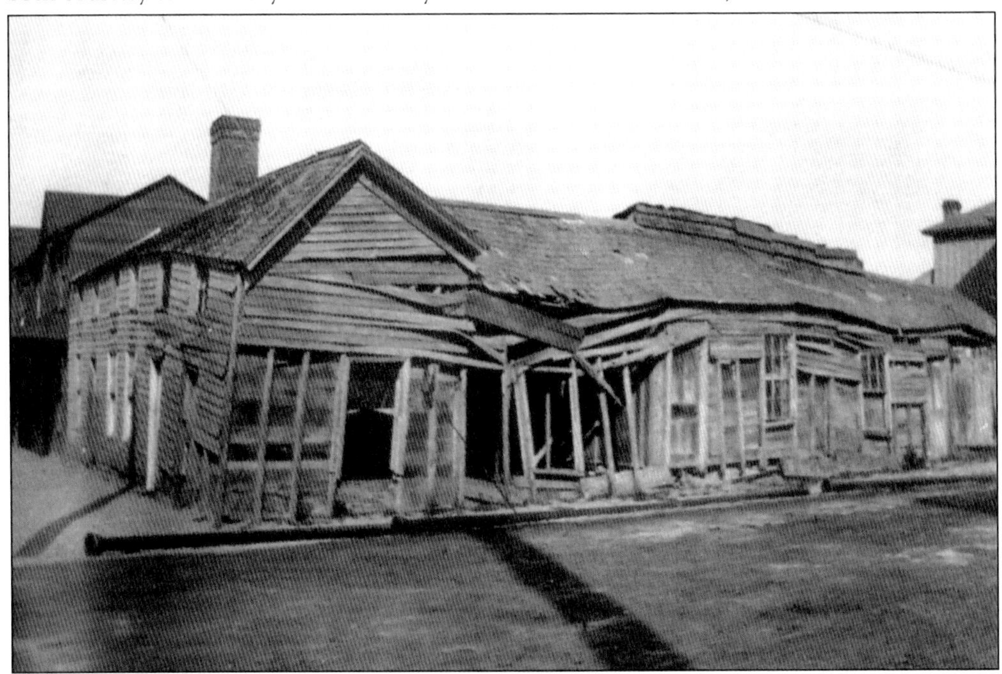

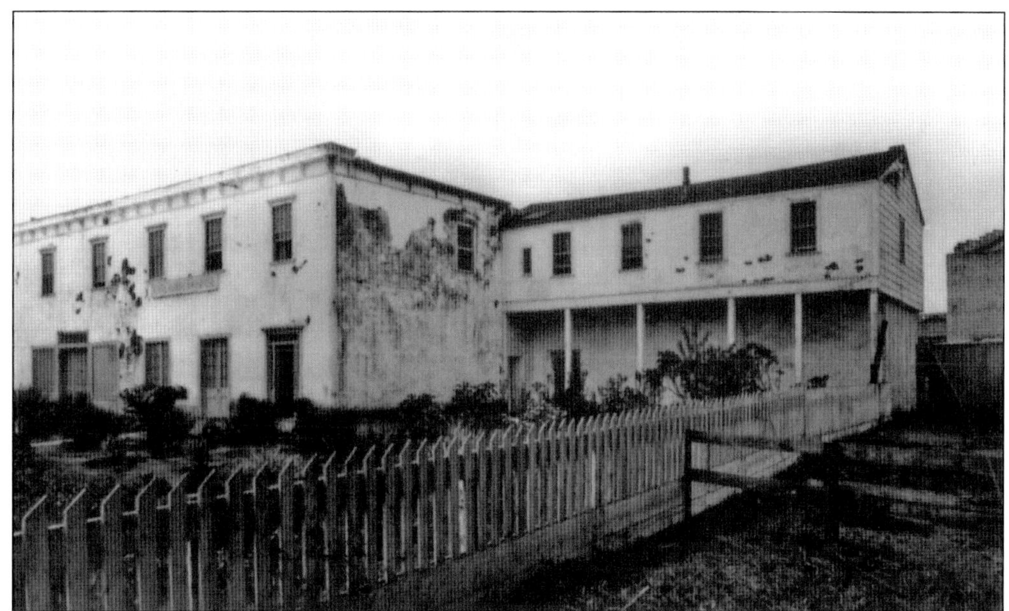

Robert Louis Stevenson's house was first owned by Don Rafael Gonzalez, and was reportedly built in the 1830s. This two-story home is located at 530 Houston Street. Stevenson stayed here while successfully courting Fanny Osbourne. He wrote *The Old Pacific Capital* about Monterey in 1879 and gathered inspiration for his great novel *Treasure Island*. As the Sicilian Italians filtered into Monterey, these historical buildings were already established. Pictured below on March 8, 1849, Colton Hall was completed some 56 years before Pietro Ferrante came to Monterey to work for Frank E. Booth in his cannery. The surrounding buildings with their Spanish architecture would soon become the homes of the Italian and Sicilian families. (Both, courtesy of Monterey Public Library's California Historic Room.)

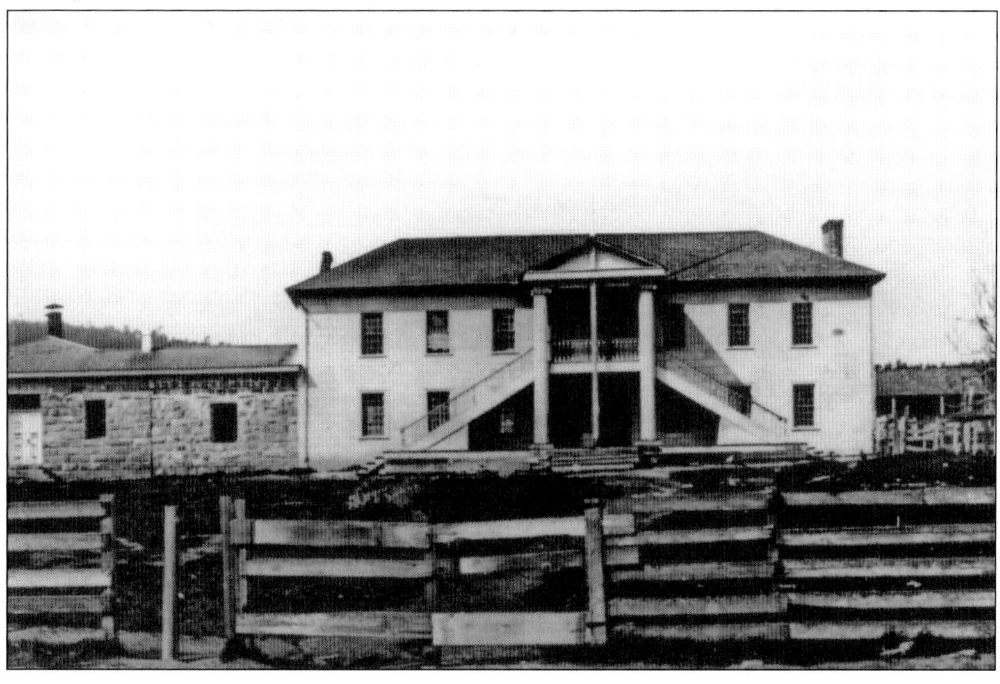

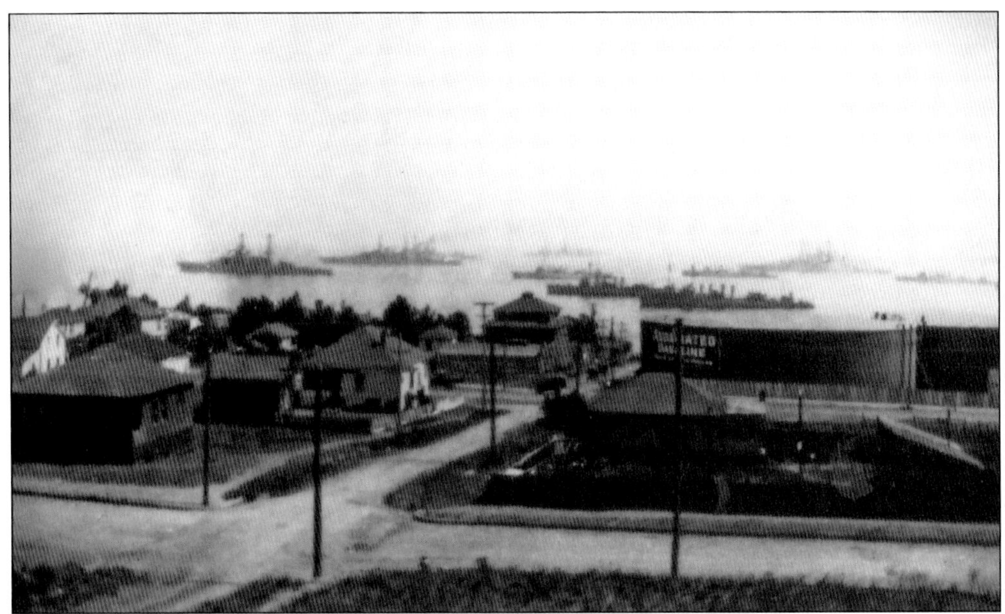

In 1919, the Associated Oil tank farm and company housing was located off Presidio Curve, before Cannery Row. Oil tankers would dock at the Associated Oil Company pier and offload petroleum oil used in the canning industry on Cannery Row. The ships in the background are the US Navy's Pacific Fleet visiting Monterey Harbor in 1919. In 1924, the oil tanks were struck by lightning, destroying most of the company housing and some boats in the harbor; the fire raged for over 72 hours before it burned itself out. Below are some Italian fishermen in front of the custom house in Monterey, working on their fishing nets. The custom house was built around 1827 by the Mexican government at the foot of Monterey Bay, some 78 years before the Italian migration to Monterey. (Both, courtesy of Monterey Public Library's California Historic Room.)

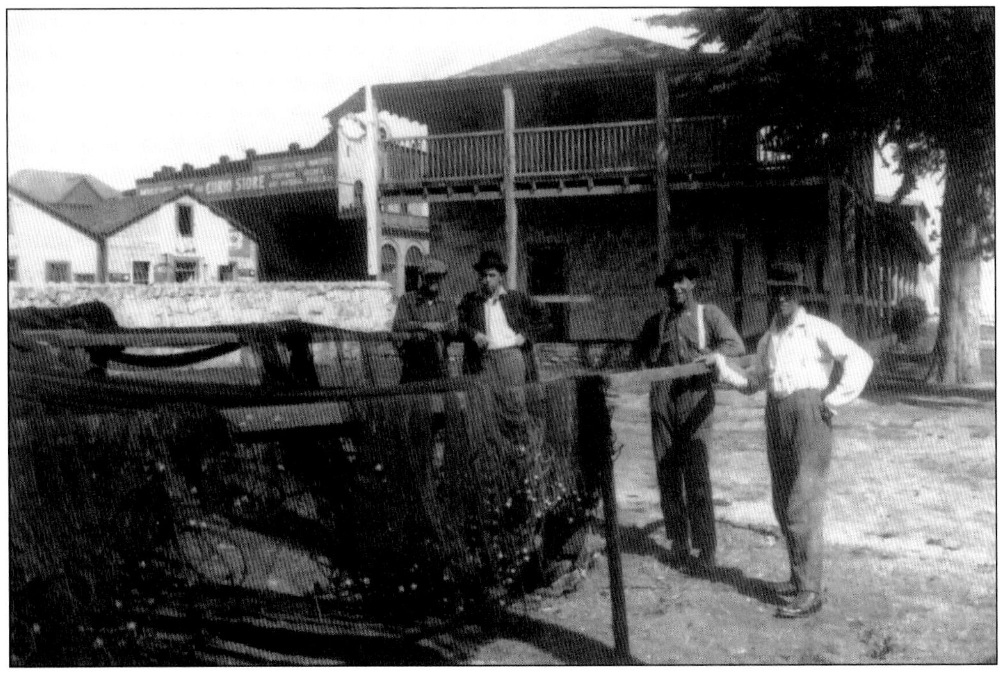

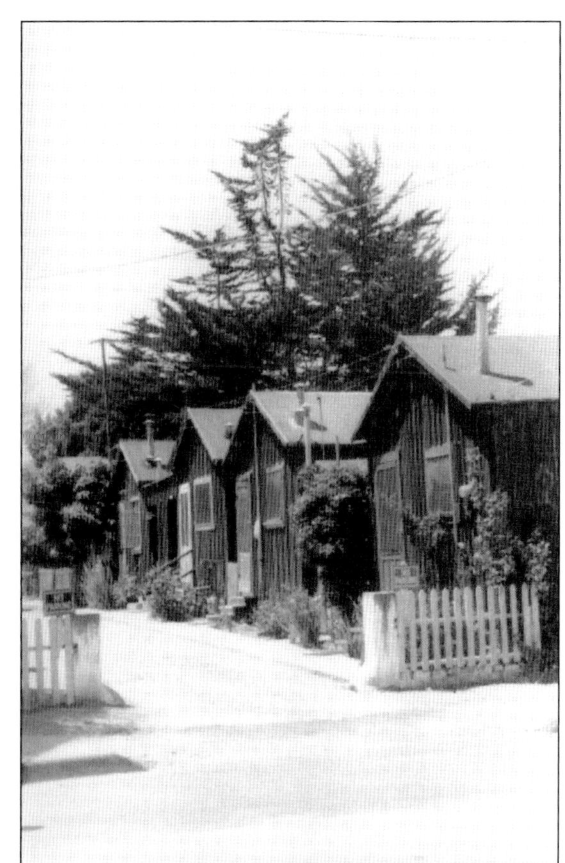

Pictured here are two-room shanties located along Wave Street, one block up from Cannery Row. Fishermen and cannery workers would rent these shanties, which provided for their basic needs. The shanties were moved and preserved and are now located on Bruce Ariss Way between Wave Street and Cannery Row. (Right, courtesy of Pamela Furman Chrislock; below, courtesy of Monterey Public Library's California Historic Room.)

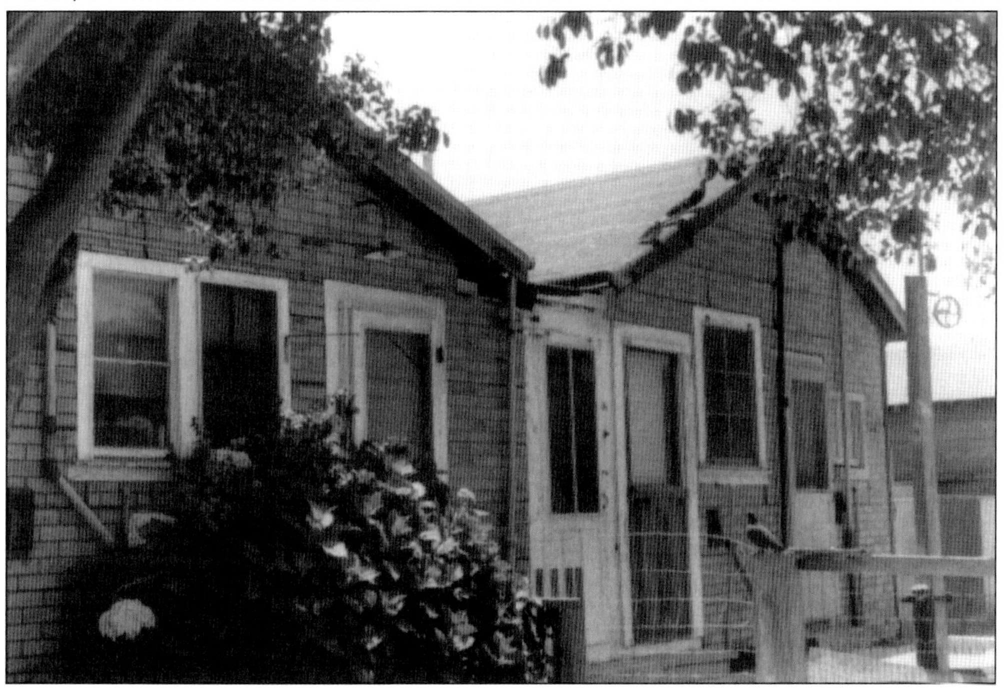

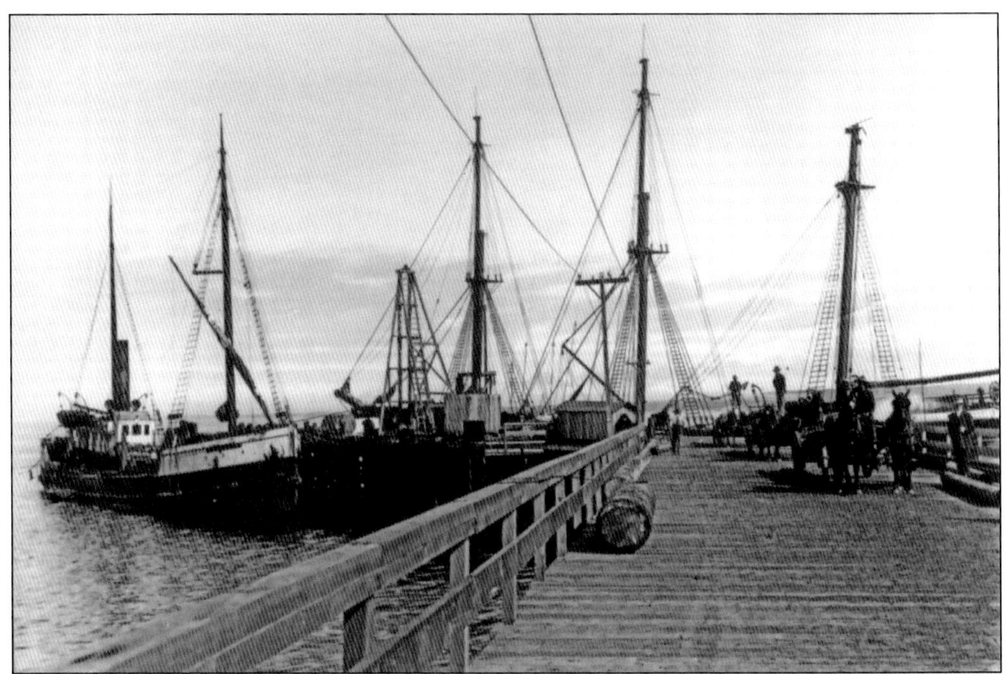

In 1906, several steamships offload supplies and oil to the company oil tank at the Associated Oil pier located just off Presidio Curve in Monterey. Thomas Albert Work, a prominent businessman in Monterey, is standing off to the right of the team of horses. Pictured below in the foreground is Wharf I, with the Pacific Coast Steam Ship Company at the end of the wharf. In the background is the Associated Oil pier. Just behind the pier is a rocky peninsula that would become the anchoring point for the breakwater and a present-day Coast Guard pier. (Above, photograph by J.K. Oliver; both courtesy of Monterey Public Library's California Historic Room.)

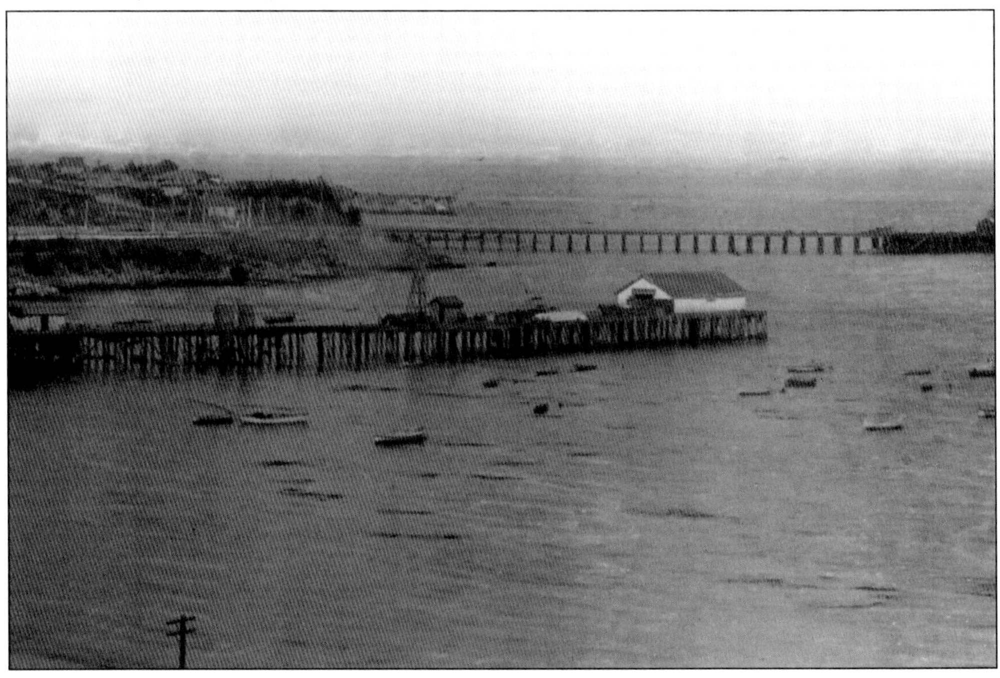

## *Two*

# Canneries and Wharves

The canneries and wharves were the focal points of the fishing industry in Monterey. In 1902, little did Otosaburo Noda and Harry Malpas realize that their establishment of one of the first canneries would set in motion all that followed. The lives of the Sicilian Italian community revolved around these areas of the city. During the years of the Silver Harvest, these areas were essential to the city's economy, providing food and jobs. The early years along Cannery Row were bustling with cannery workers who would be summoned to work by the cannery whistles. As the whistles blew, the workers walked down from their homes to work their shift. It is ironic that some 60 years after the depletion of the sardines, the demise of the fishing industry, and the closure of the canneries, these areas are still the strong economic centers that make the city viable. Cannery Row has transformed itself from an industrial area to a tourist attraction millions of people visit each year. The Old Fisherman's Wharf attracts thousands of visitors to sample the fine food from its many restaurants, embark on whale watching tours, and peruse curio shops. Present now instead of the freighters that once docked at Wharves I and II are the large cruise ships that now make Monterey Bay a port of call. These ships bring in hundreds of tourists, and it was the hard work of the Sicilian Italian community that helped weave the fabric that made Monterey a tourist destination.

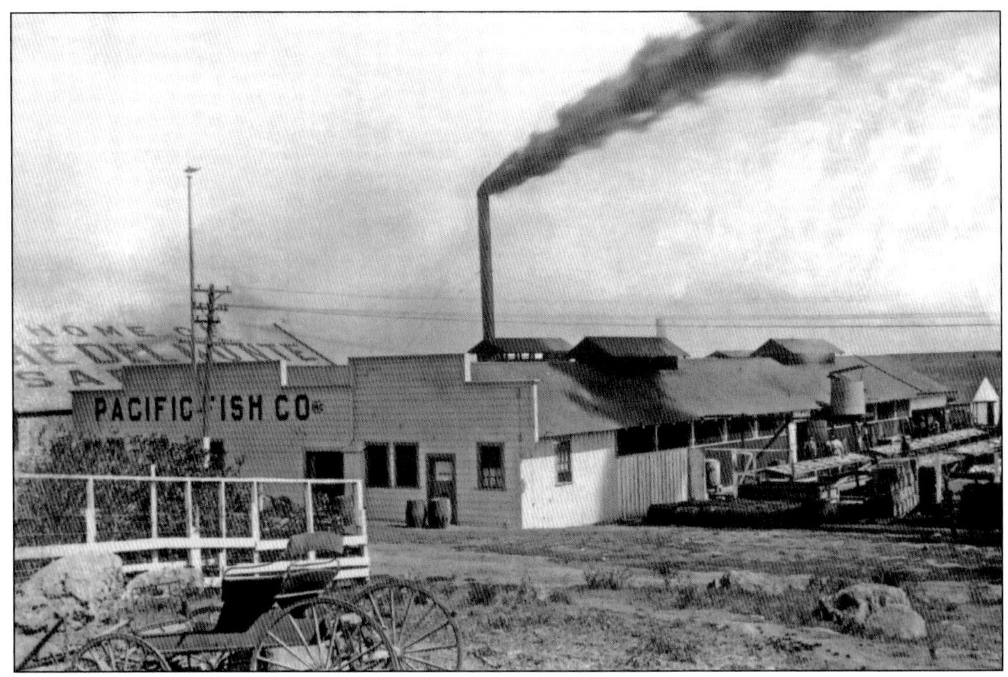


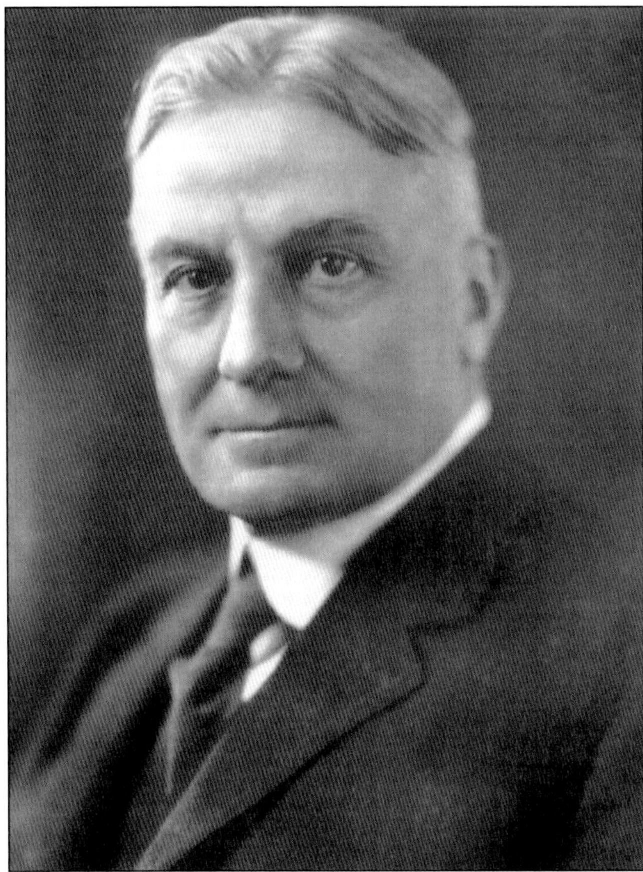

Pictured here in 1909 is the Pacific Fish Company, originally the Monterey Fishing and Canning Company, the first fish canning company on what was later to be called Cannery Row. It was started by Otosuburo Noda and Harry Malpas. In 1908, Pacific Fish became the first major cannery, and California Packing Corporation bought it in 1926. Frank E. Booth (left), a pioneer in the canning industry, owned and operated several canneries in California. He was well liked by the local fishermen in Monterey, as he was fair minded in his dealings. Booth was born in 1863 and died in 1941, the founder of the sardine industry in Monterey. (Both, courtesy of Monterey Public Library's California Historic Room.)

Knut Hovden (right), a Norwegian and a graduate of Norway's National Fisheries College, began working for Frank E. Booth in 1905. Hovden made tremendous innovations in the canning industry, including a machine to solder the oval-shaped tin cans. This invention saved time, as cans were previously soldered by hand. Hovden is also credited for automatic cookers and a machine cutter that cleaned and cut the fish. Pictured below, Pietro Ferrante is credited with organizing the fishing industry in Monterey. Ferrante was born in Sicily in 1867 and immigrated to the United States in 1888. He worked for Booth's cannery on the Sacramento River and implemented the ancestral lampara nets from Tangier, Morocco. (Right, courtesy of Monterey Public Library's California Historic Room; below, courtesy of Vince Ferrante.)

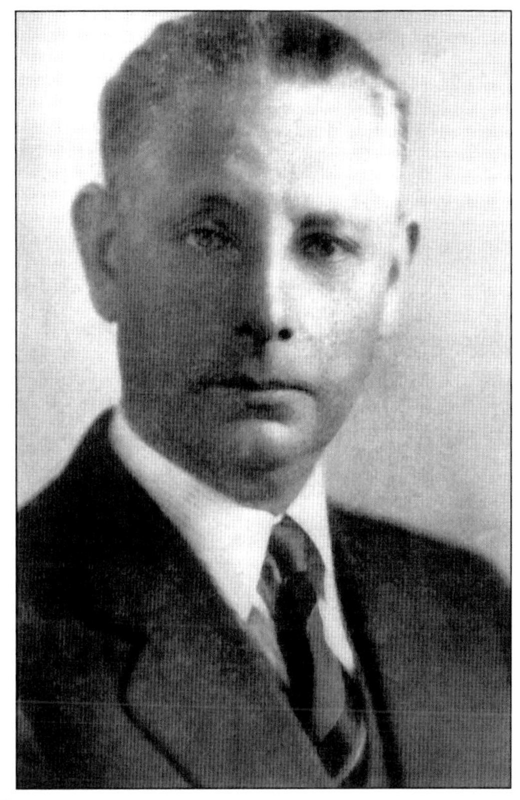

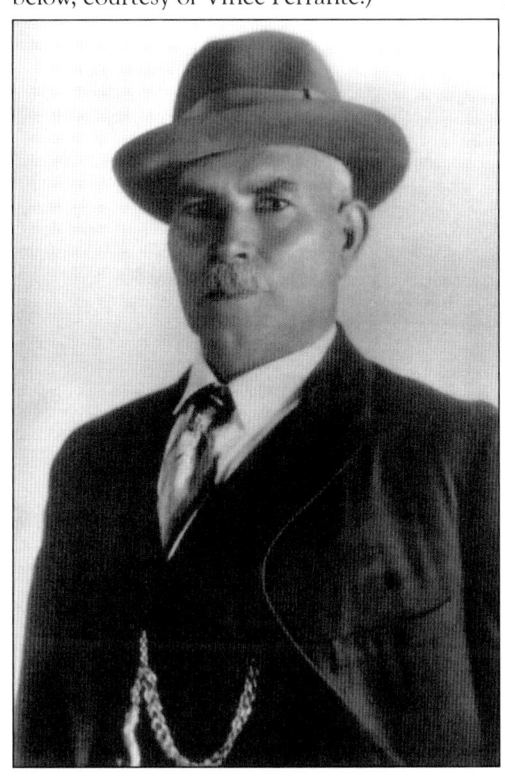

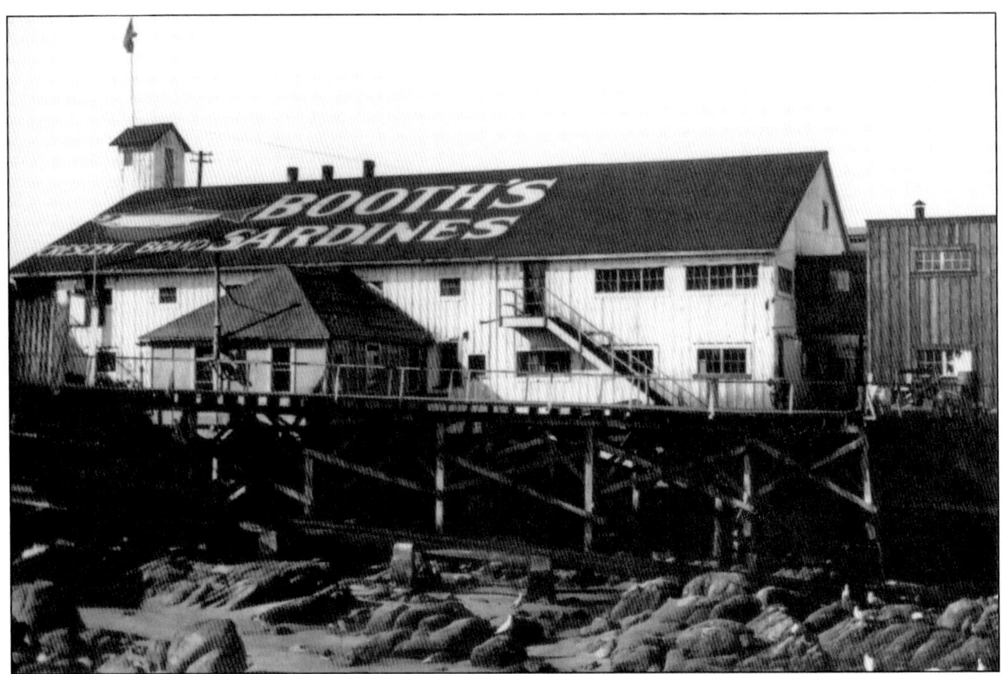


In 1910, Booth Cannery was expanded after it burned down. Booth improved his canning methods and his operations, with the cannery selling sardines under the Crescent brand. The cannery was adjacent to Wharf I. Below, Japanese sailboats tie up at the end of Wharf I to unload salmon in 1910. Most of the fishing was done with gill nets; note the size of the salmon at right center, hanging over the wharf railing. The Japanese fishermen would give way to the Italians and sardine fishing, and the lampara net and motorized lampara boats would replace the sailboat. (Both, courtesy of Monterey Public Library's California Historic Room.)

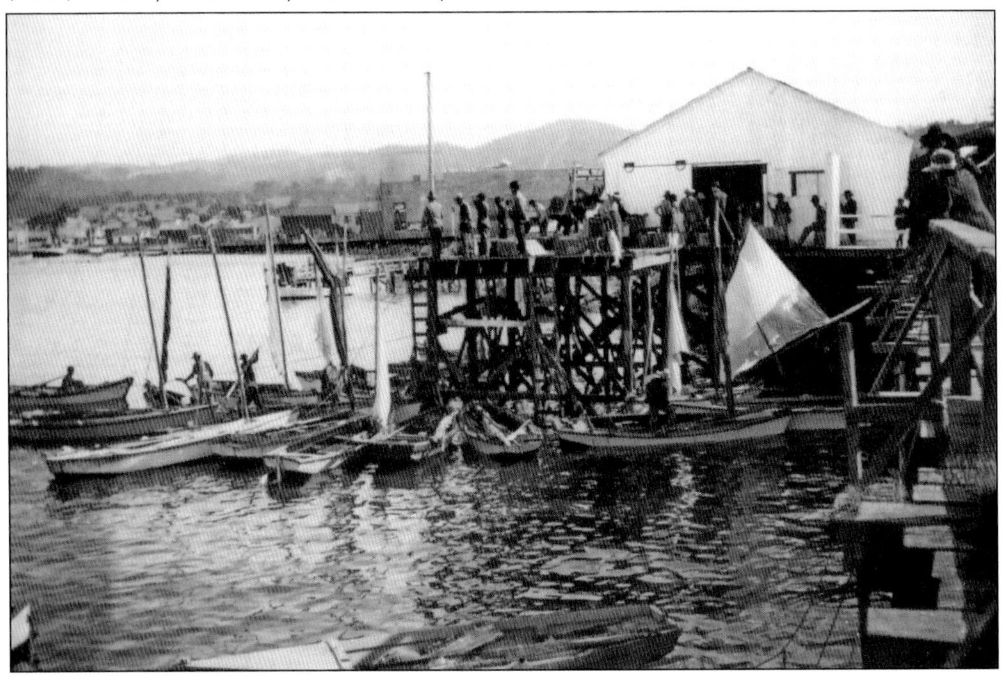

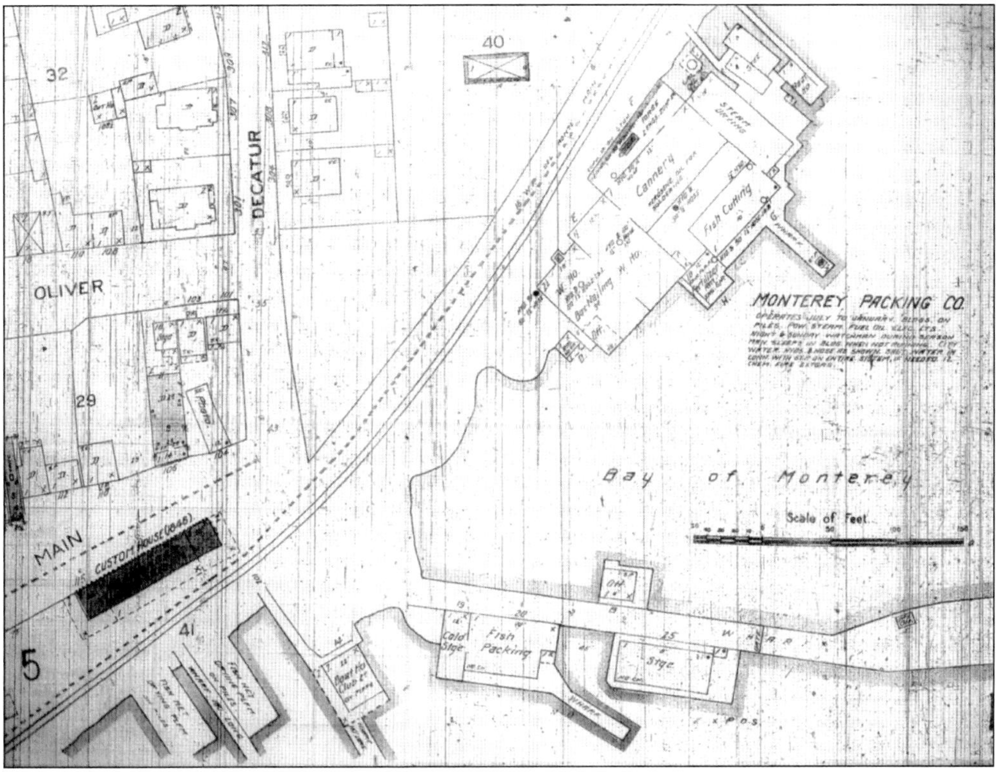

Pictured above is a map showing the location of Booth's Cannery in relationship to Wharf I after it was rebuilt after suspected arson in 1903. It was said that the amount of sardines that Booth's Cannery was producing was cutting into the amount of salmon he was purchasing, which angered the local salmon fishermen. The cannery was self-sufficient, with a box nailing room, warehouse storage, forge area, steam-drying room, fish-cutting room, and cannery and fertilizer room. In operation from July to January, the cannery was powered by steam fuel oil and had electric lights. Booth's Cannery (below) was photographed on September 11 after the storm of 1919, during surveying for a location for a new breakwater. (Both, courtesy of Monterey Public Library's California Historic Room.)

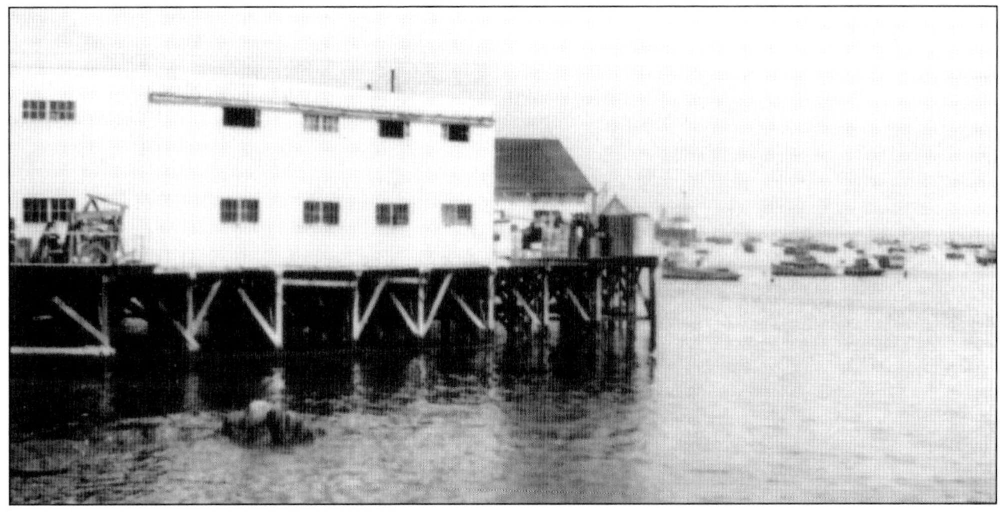

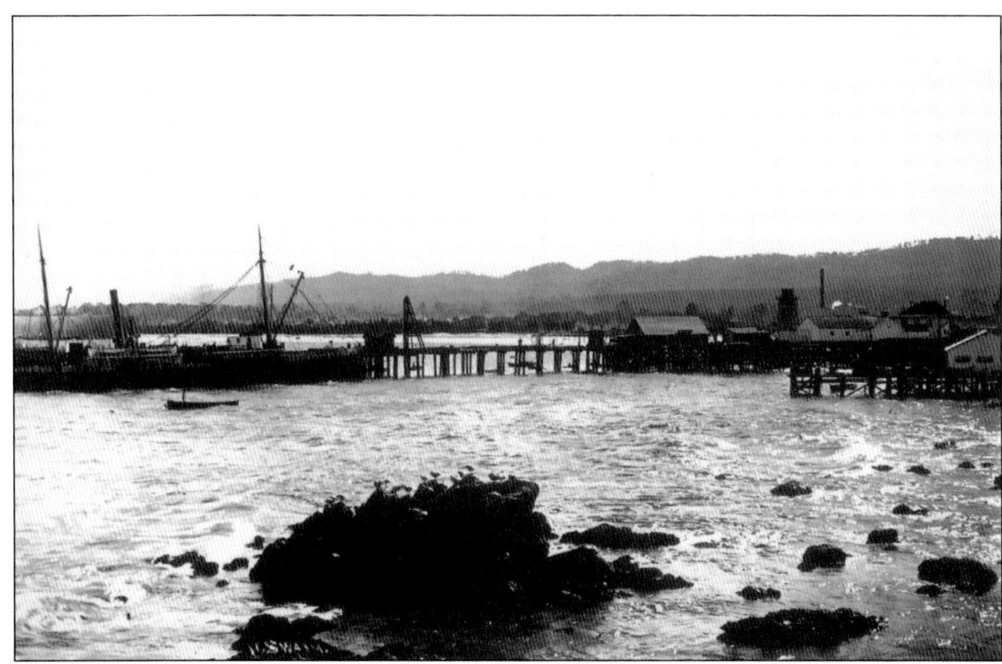

In 1913, a steamship freighter loads at Wharf I, which was later known as Fisherman's Wharf, now a major tourist attraction in Monterey and home to some of the finest restaurants. Pictured below is Booth Cannery in Pittsburg, California, about 1903. This cannery was built on the Sacramento River and canned salmon; improvements were made over the years, increasing its size and capacity. The cannery was supplied with sardines and other types of fish from the Pacific Ocean from Big Sur to Point Reyes. (Above, photograph by F.C. Swain, courtesy of Monterey Public Library's California Historic Room; below, courtesy of Pittsburg Historical Society.)

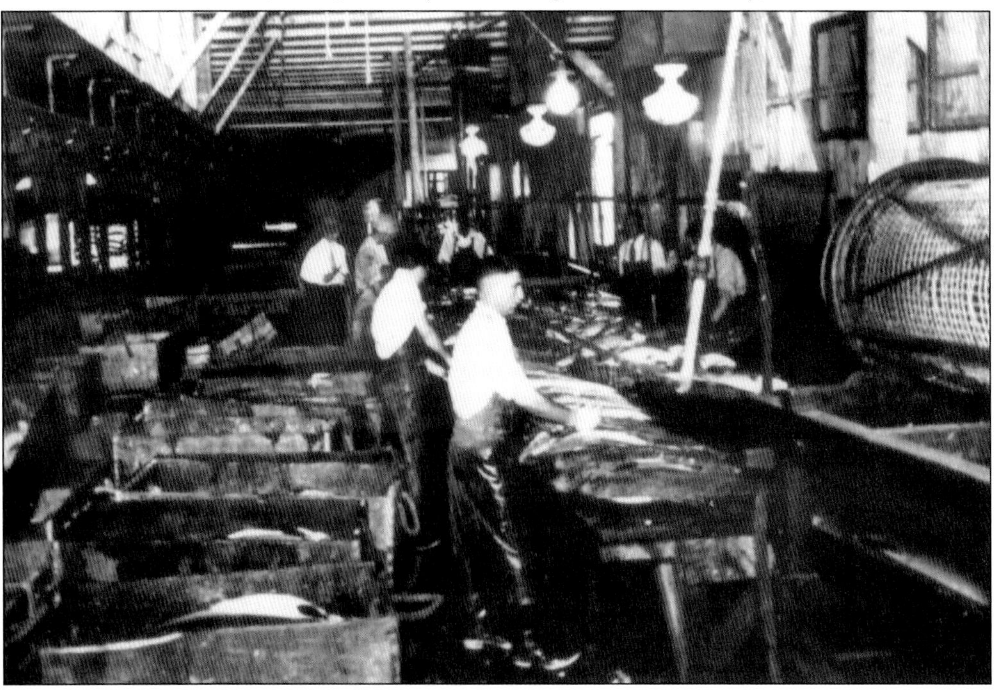

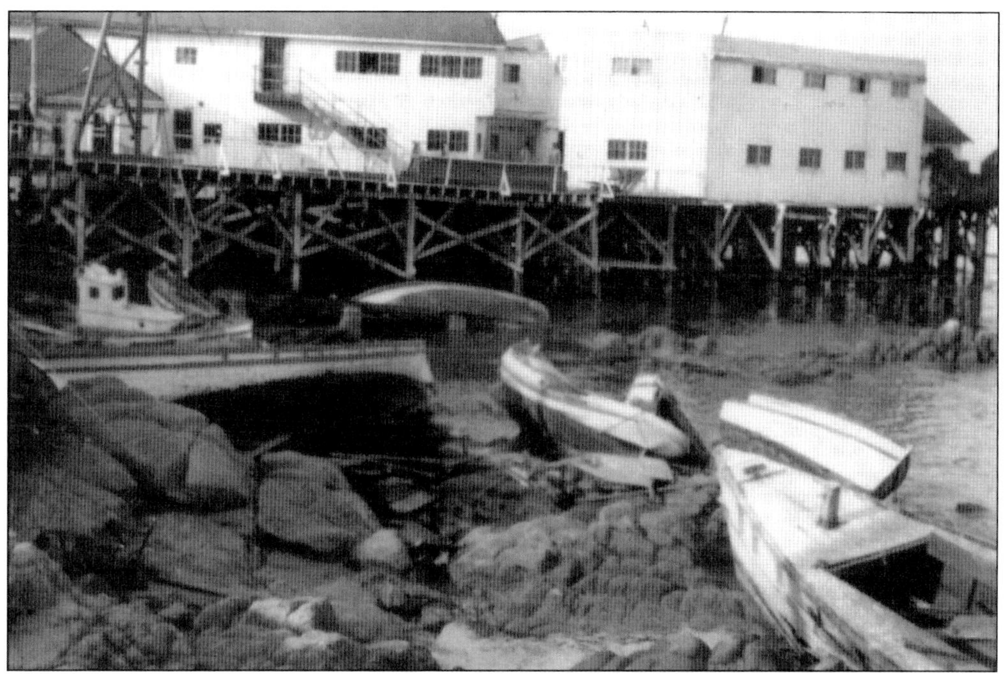

Two cannery workers survey the devastation from the deck of the cannery on November 29, 1919. The storms that came out of the northwest were some of the most violent, as there was no breakwater to protect the fishing boats. The boats broke loose from their moorings due to the intensity of the winds, devastating the fishing fleet. Pictured below is Municipal Wharf I on September 11, 1919. Lou's Pacific Mutual Fish Company was located at No. 50, which is now the address of Domenico's Restaurant. (Above, photograph by William L. Morgan, courtesy of Amici Club Monterey; below, courtesy of Monterey Public Library's California Historic Room.)

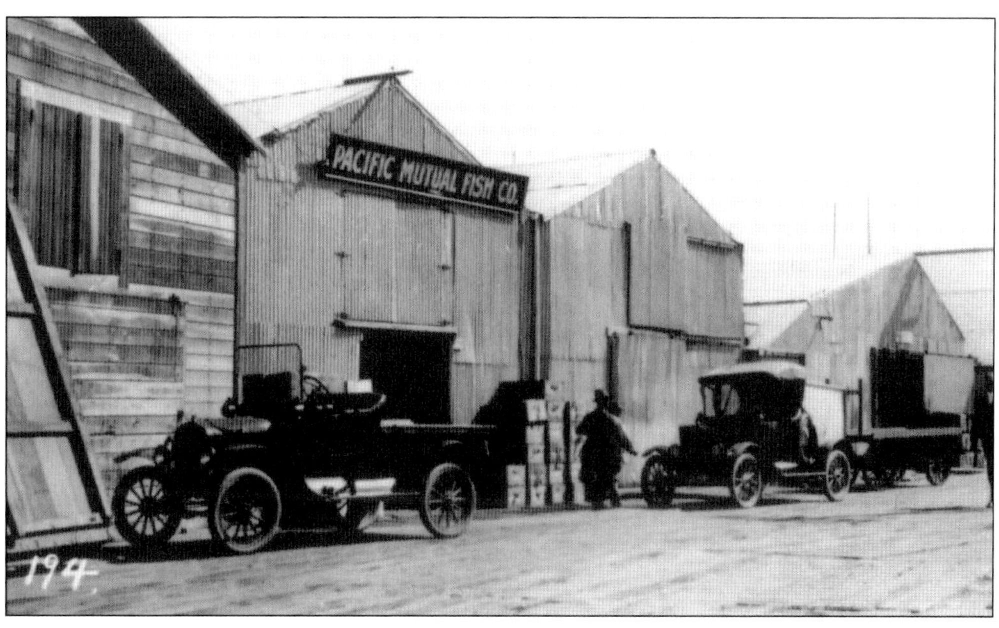

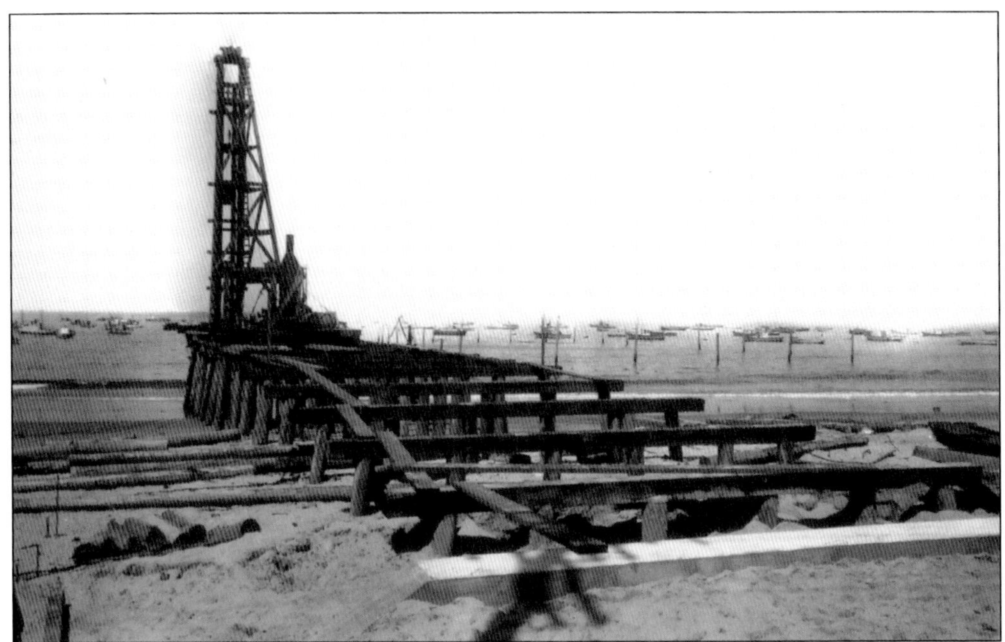

On April 25, 1926, the bulkhead of Wharf II was poured and construction of the new wharf was under way. The new wharf would become a commercial wharf for loading and offloading supplies. The small lampara boats are moored in the bay beyond the wharf. Below, freighters unload cargo at Wharf II three years after its construction. The ships' cargo booms hang over the wharf to load and unload cargo. The wharf has not changed much over the years; a few more buildings, parking spaces, and guardrails have appeared, and it also now serves as an entry point to the docking slips in the marina. (Both photographs by Anton Charles Heidrick, courtesy of Monterey Public Library's California Historic Room.)

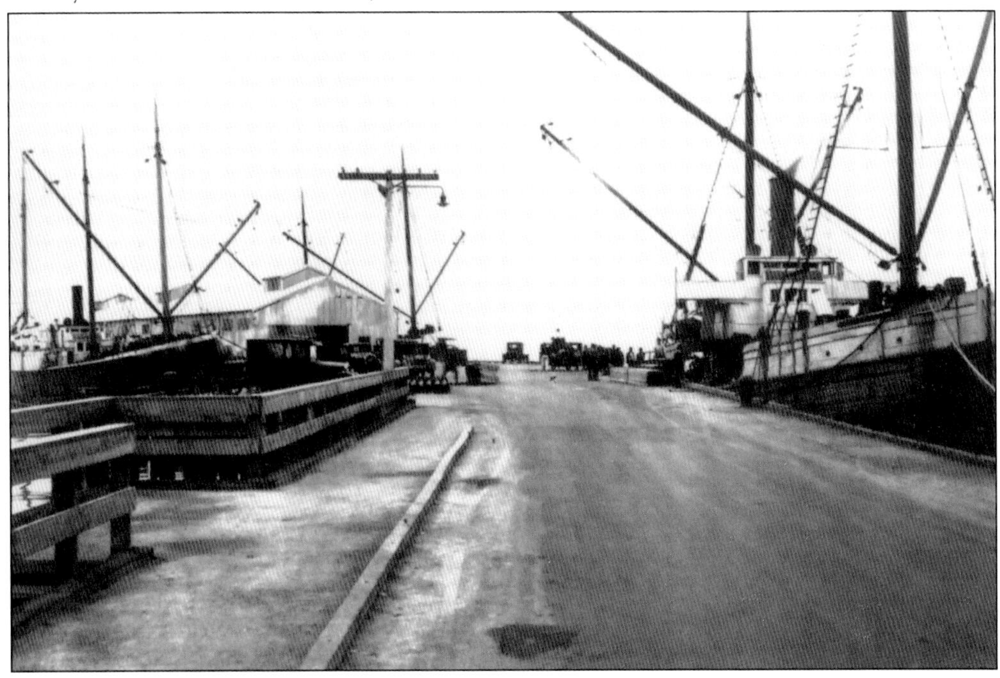

In 1947, female packers of the California Packing Company Inc. prepare tins for the cooker. These workers would stand on their feet for long hours canning fish before the implementation of a workers' bill of rights. Below, a woman is repacking sardines that have fallen out or have shifted in the oval tins at the cannery. Many of these women would work several jobs; if the whistle blew, they would leave and go to another cannery. (Both photographs by George Robinson, courtesy of Monterey Public Library's California Historic Room.)

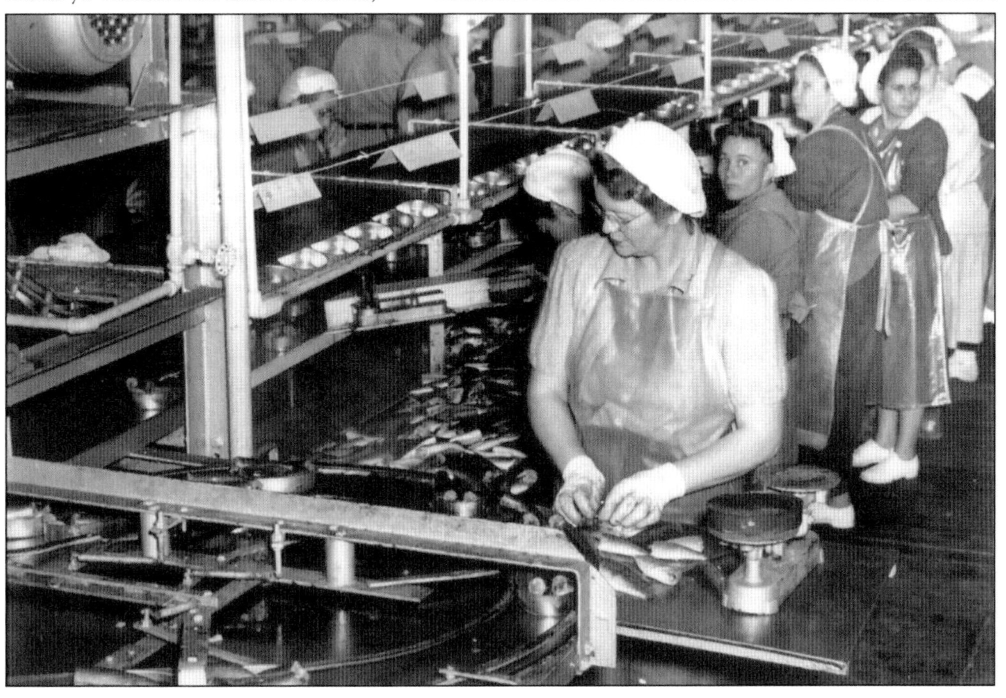

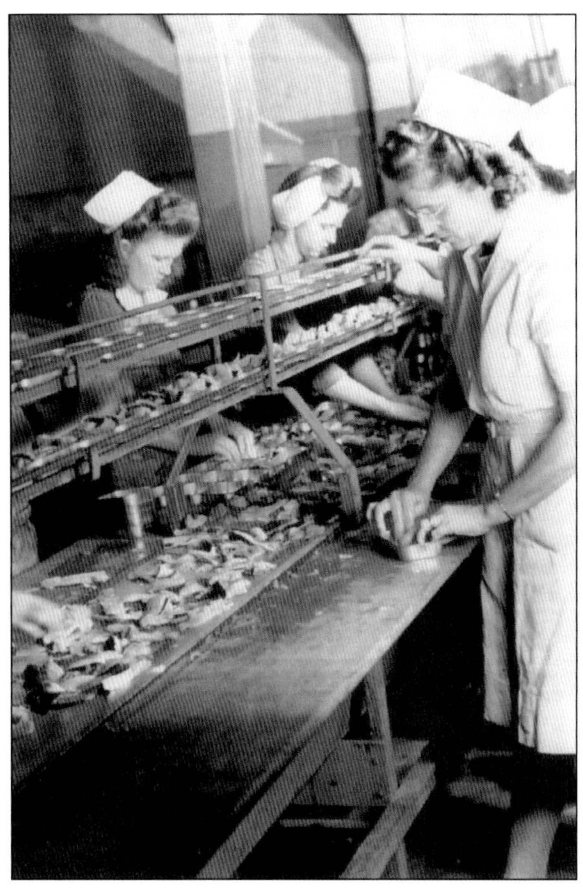

At left, a cannery worker diligently places sardines in the oval tins on an assembly line in 1943. One could only imagine how hard it must have been to remove the odor of fish after working with the oily sardines all day. Below, workers label sardine tins at Booth's Cannery. In 1918, a 15-year-old girl set a record by labeling 30 cases per hour, at two minutes per case. She earned $1.20 for her effort. When she left in 1919, her sister and another relative of hers were able to match her speed, according to the memoirs of Salvatore Ventimiglia, who owned California Frozen Fish Company in Monterey. Other labelers' speed was between 50 and 75 cases over eight hours for both young and older women. (Left, courtesy of Monterey Public Library's California Historic Room; below, courtesy of Pittsburg Historical Society.)

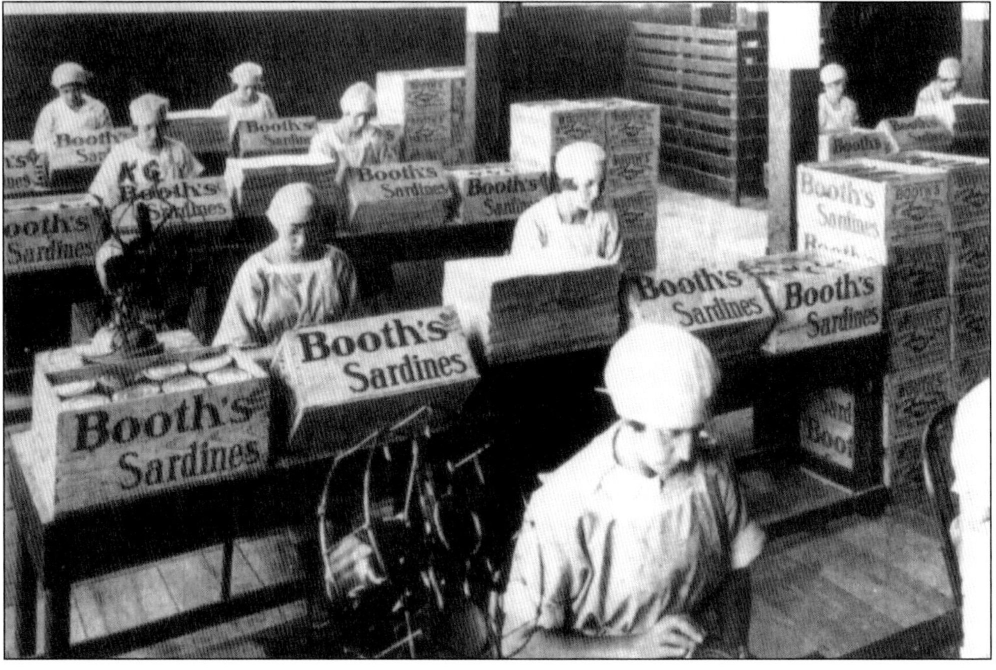

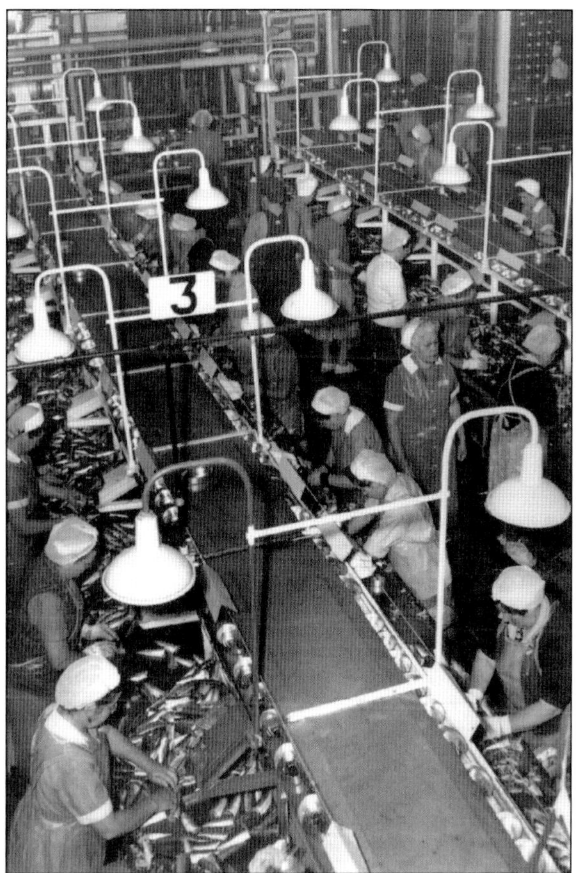


In 1949, a California Packing Corporation floor lady walks between the packers to ensure the production line kept moving. The sardine industry declined in the late 1940s through the 1950s, and canneries began to close down. Below, on September 1, 1948, sea lions rest on the fish hoppers behind canneries, waiting for the boat to fill the hoppers with fish. Fish were pumped from floating hoppers to the pump house, then lifted by conveyor belt to the weighing room and then to the holding tanks. (Right, photograph by George Robinson; below, photograph by William L. Morgan, courtesy of Monterey Public Library's California Historic Room.)

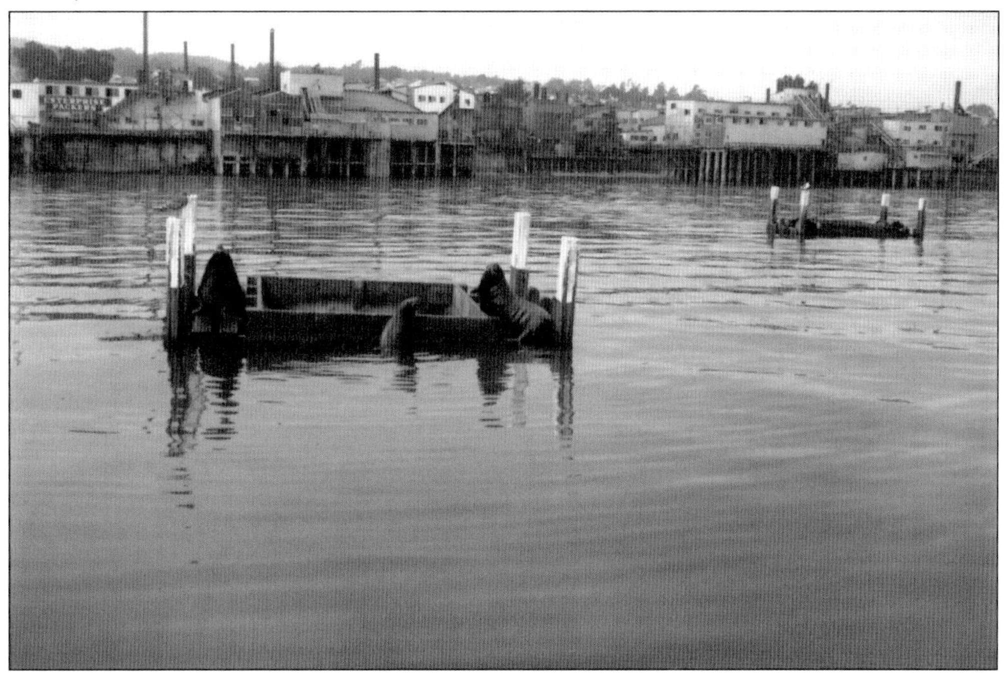

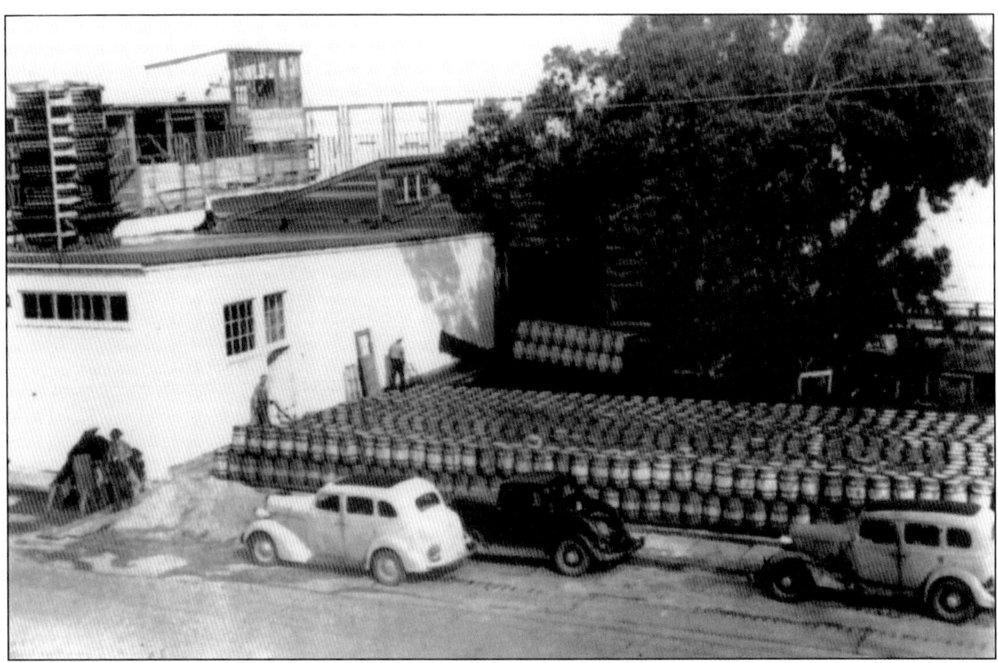

Barrels of sardines packed in salt sit in the storage yard of California Frozen Fish Company, located at 214 Wave Street in Monterey. California Frozen Fish Company had a contract with the US government to provide salted sardines to the military. The cannery was owned by Salvatore Ventimiglia, and canned sardines, squid, Pacific mackerel, and anchovies under the brand names New Hope and Mesa Del Rey. Pictured below are some of the businesses that lined Fisherman's Wharf in the 1950s. From left to right are A. D'Acquisto & Sons Marine Paints, Anastasia's Fish Market, General California Fish Company, and the Breakwater Fish Market. (Above, courtesy of Cathy Ventimiglia Gomez; below, photograph by Julius B. Phillips, courtesy of the Monterey Public Library's California Historic Room.)

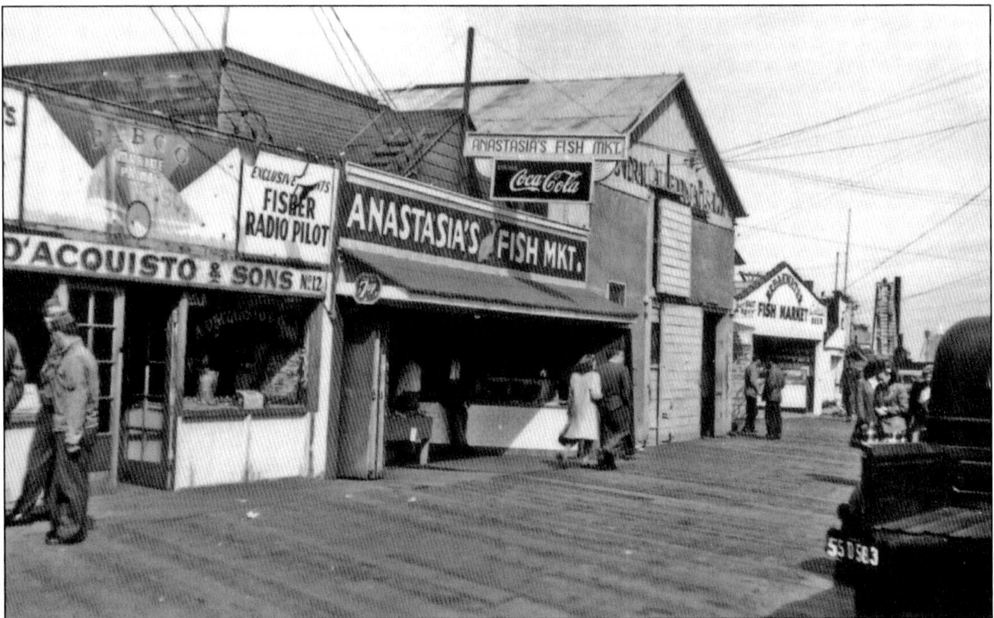

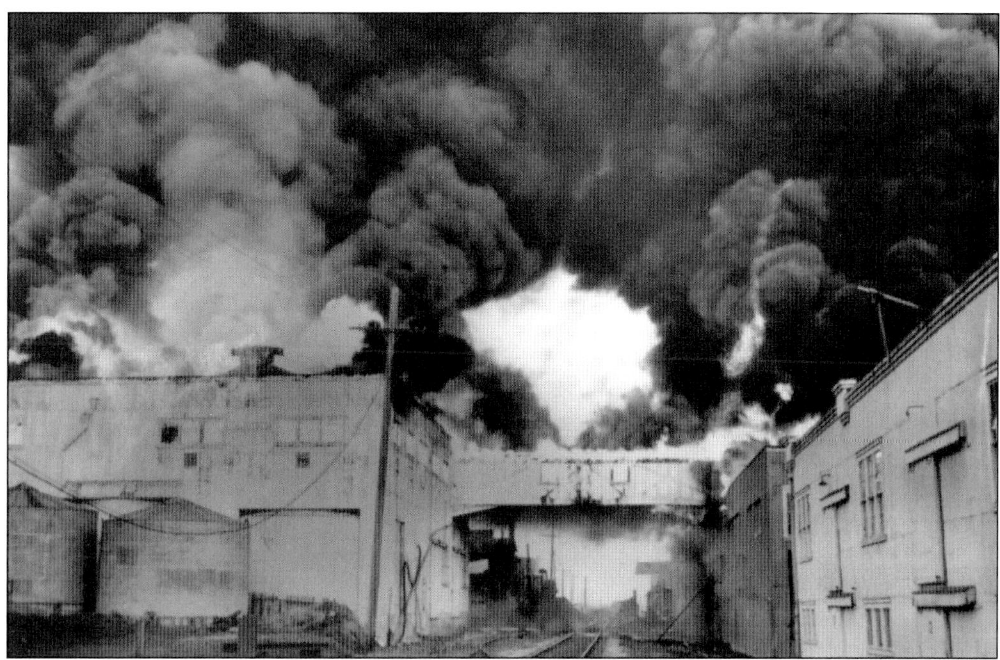

In 1951, the Westgate–Sun Harbor Cannery burned, but by this time the sardine industry was on the decline, as the sardines had left the bay. These canneries were made from wood and corrugated walls, with no fire safety features. The flooring was saturated with fish oil and byproducts from the reduction plants that were often part of the cannery. The buildings were engulfed as the fire traveled from the canning building to the warehouse through the overpass, igniting packing material. This cannery would be involved in three fires in 1950, 1951, and 1952, for a total loss of $3.8 million. Numerous other canneries would also be consumed by fire as Cannery Row began to change. (Both photographs by William L. Morgan, courtesy of Monterey Public Library's California Historic Room.)

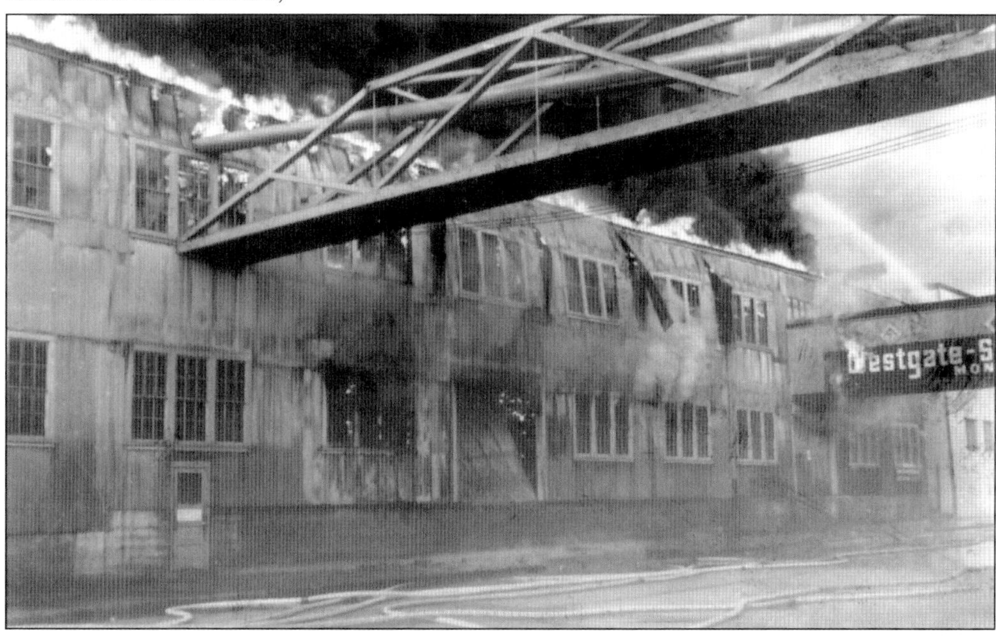

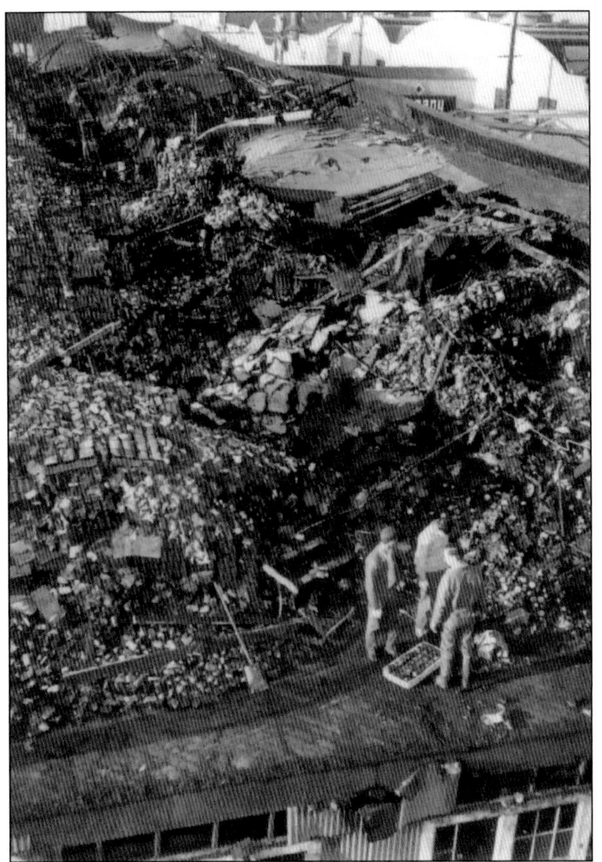

The three individuals in the photograph at left are salvaging canned fish for personal use after the fire. The Westgate–Sun Harbor warehouse was packed with fish ready for shipping. Warehouses were located on the opposite side of the street from the cannery, and once processed, the fish would be sent through the overpass to the warehouse for shipping. Pictured below on October 24, 1953, is the Sea Beach Canning and Custom House Packing Corporation conflagration. In the 20-year period between 1950 and 1970, several canneries burned; most of them were no longer processing fish and were either vacant or being used as storage warehouses. Often these dilapidated canneries were purposely set on fire by persons unknown. (Both photographs by William L. Morgan, courtesy of Monterey Public Library's California Historic Room.)

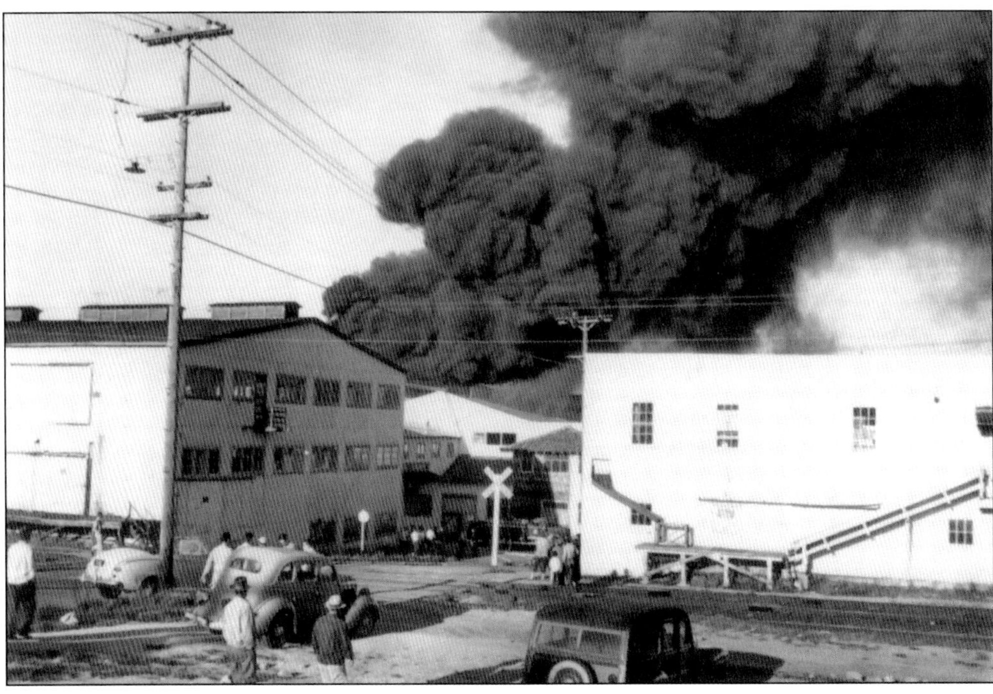

Pictured here is Cannery Row on June 11, 1953, at the end of the Silver Harvest. Fishing boats would have to fish the southern waters off Big Sur Coast for sardines. At lower right with the saw-tooth roofline is the National Automotive Fiber Company, which made laminated car panels and interior car parts. It is now the home of the American Tin Cannery, an outlet store. Train tracks can be seen running behind the canneries for shipping. Most of the canneries were closed, allowed to deteriorate, and succumbed to fire. Pictured below is the Outrigger restaurant on Cannery Row, purchased by Mark Thomas in 1965 after the demise of the fishing industry when tourism began to rise. The restaurant is now called the Fish Hopper. (Both, courtesy of the Monterey Public Library's California Historic Room.)

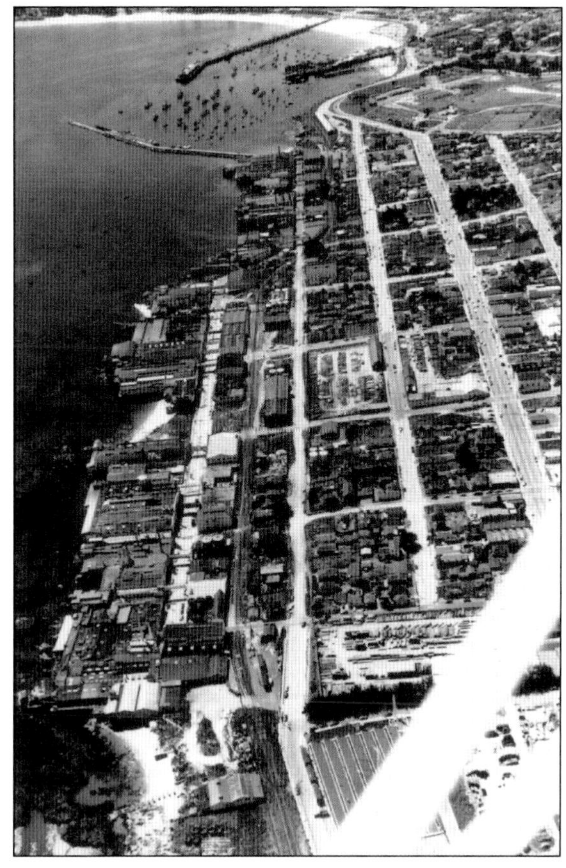

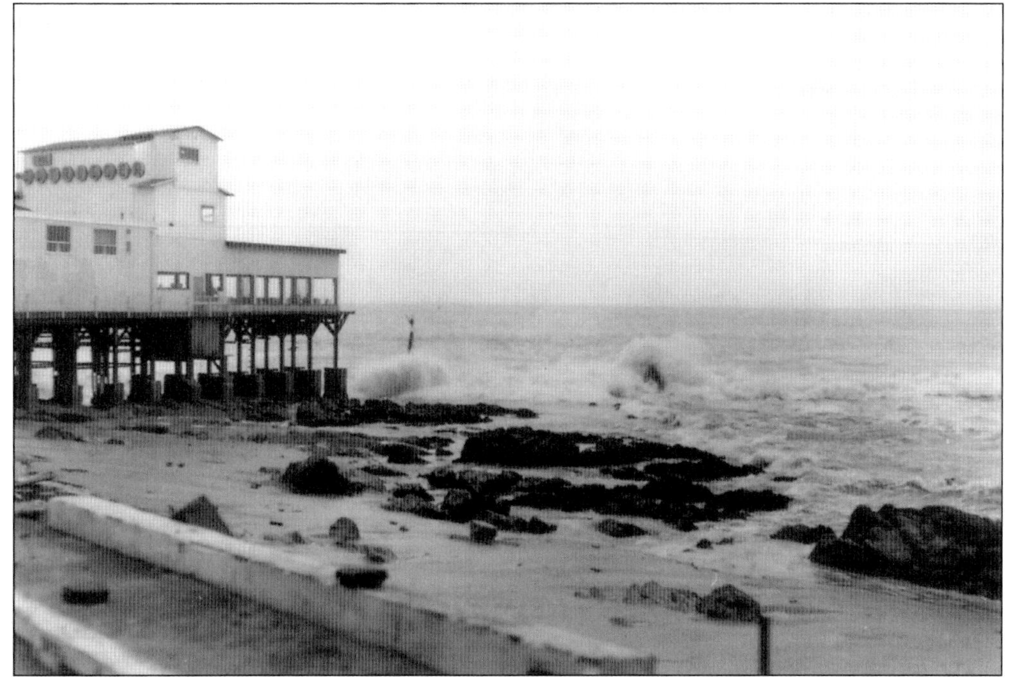

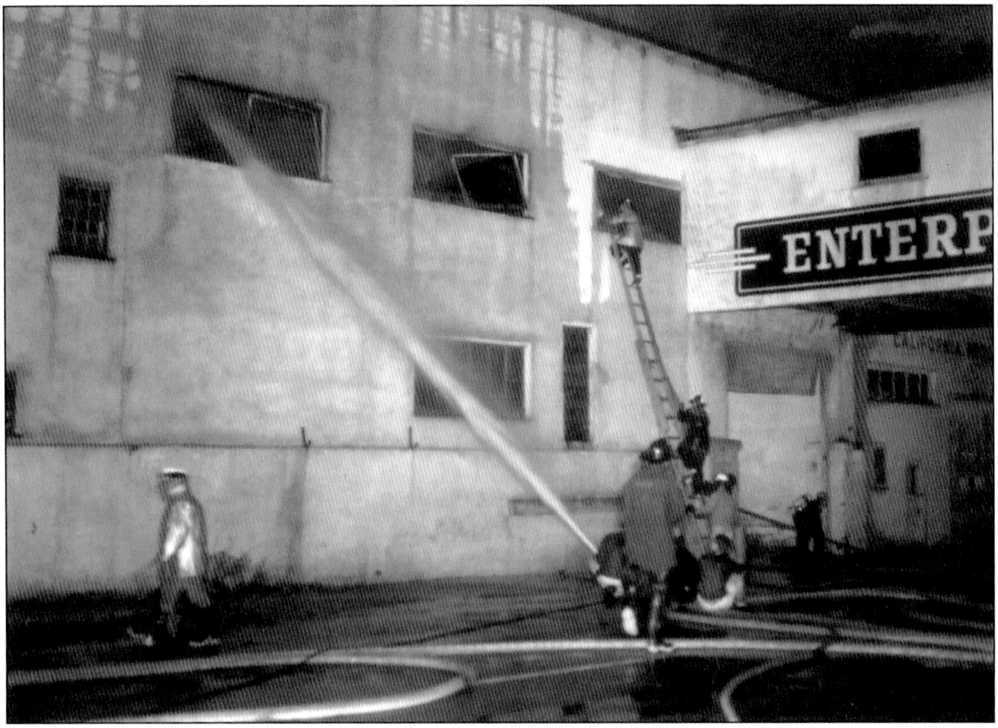

Enterprise Canning Company burned in 1967, injuring three firefighters when the overpass fell away from the cannery toward the warehouse. Over the following years, Cannery Row continued to develop a tourist-based economy as the vacant and dilapidated canneries continued to burn. Since most of the canneries were built over the water, it was too costly and impractical to tear them down. Fire became the primary means of removing the old buildings. As these canneries began to fail, owners sold off most of the canning and packing equipment to countries in South America, where the fishing industry was booming. Enterprise Canning Company packed its sardines under the label Captain Silver Sardines. (Above, photograph by William L. Morgan, courtesy of the Monterey Public Library's California Historic Room; below, author's collection.)

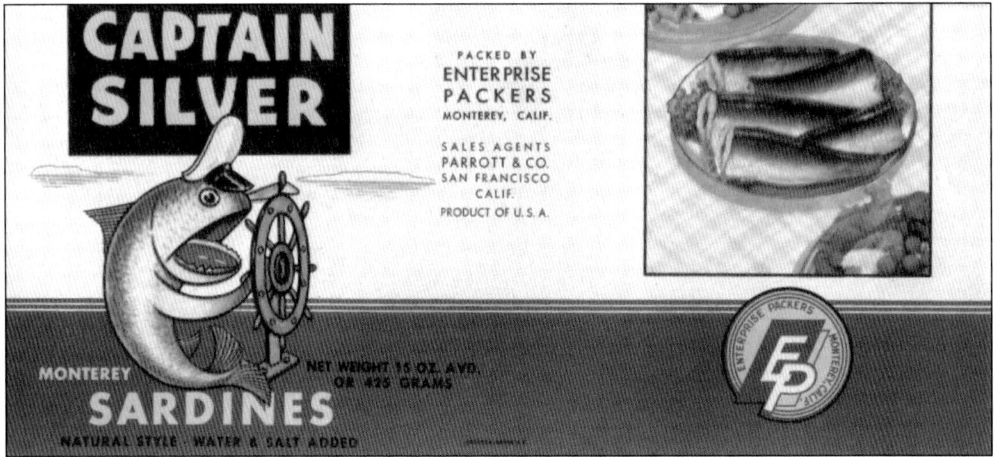

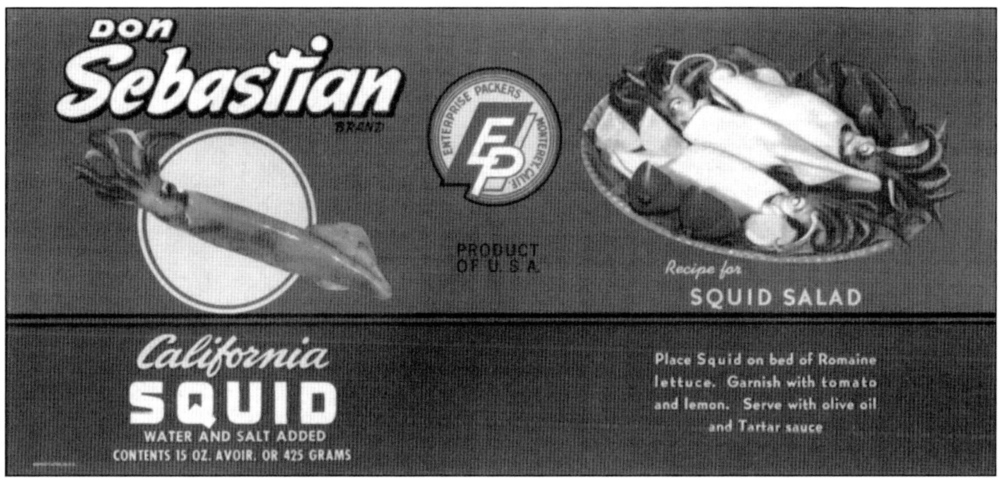


As the sardine population began to decline, canneries like the Enterprise Canning Company starting canning other fish products. Pictured above is one of its labels for squid. Below, on the evening of October 10, 1967, the San Xavier Cannery became another victim of a suspicious fire on Cannery Row. Three cannery fires would occur that year, making way for larger developments along Cannery Row. Later, local fire department personnel would be notified by the San Diego fire department that an individual calling himself the "Green Ranger" claimed to have started three cannery fires in Monterey. This was one of the last major cannery fires, bringing an end to a fishing industry that flourished for nearly five decades. (Above, author's collection; below, photograph by William L. Morgan, courtesy of Monterey Public Library's California Historic Room.)

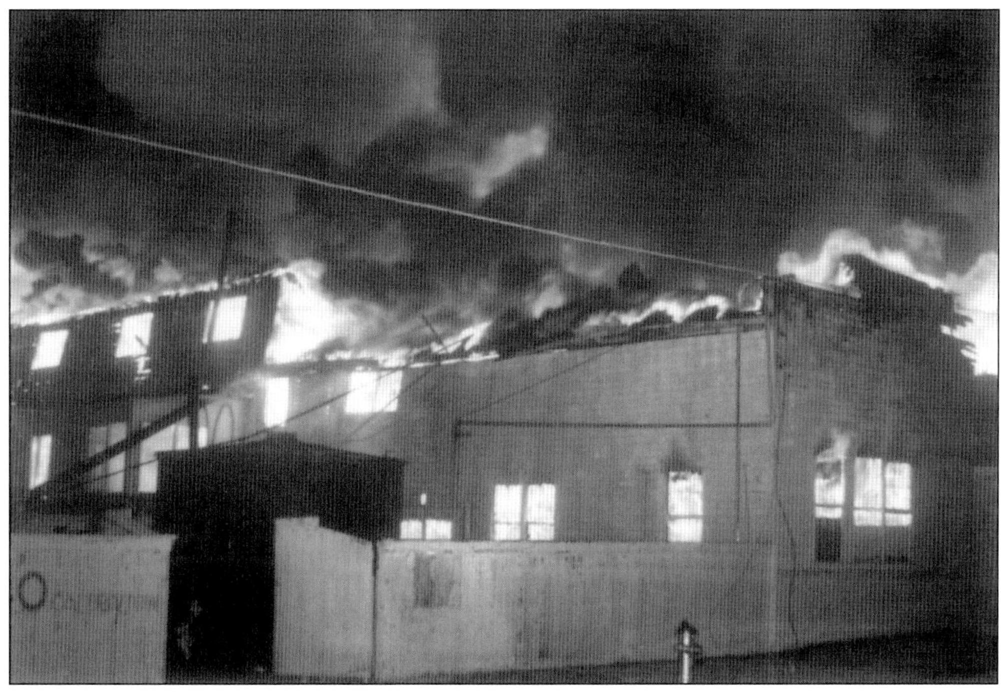

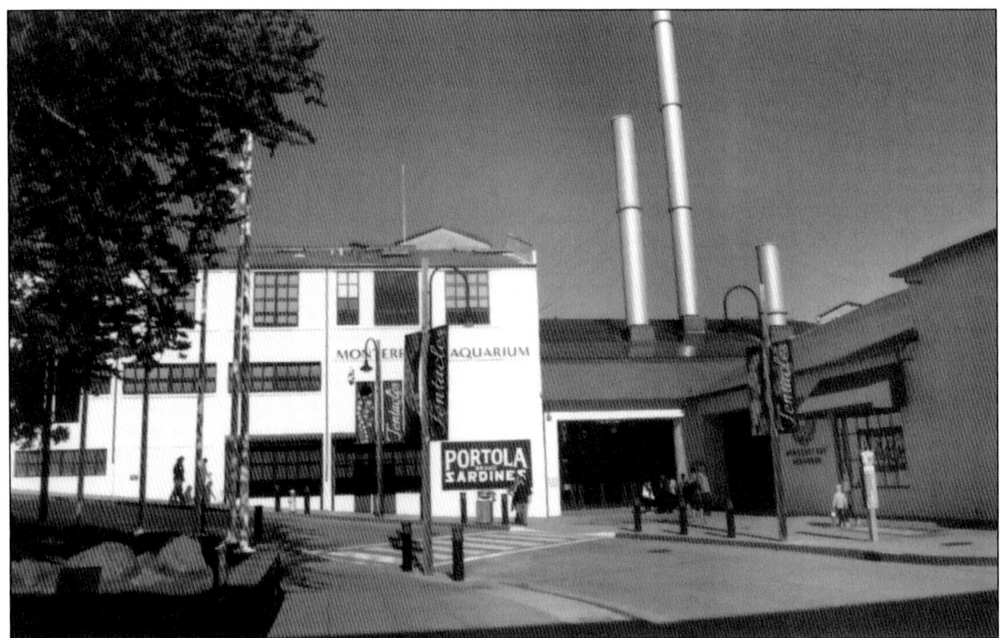


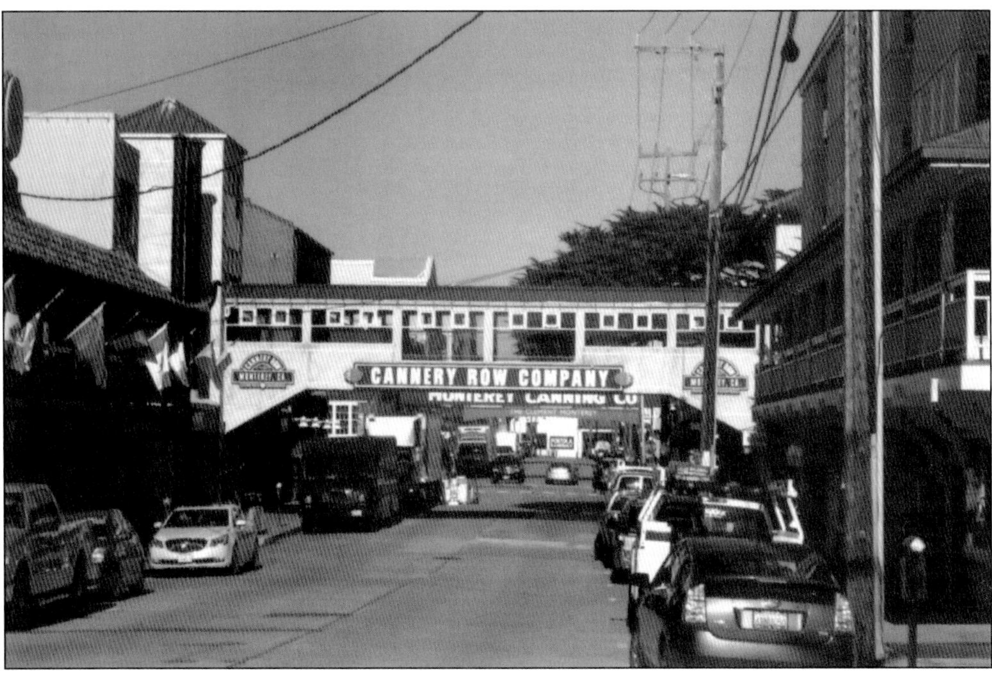


Since the demise of the canning industry, Cannery Row has capitalized on the tourist industry. It has become a mecca of first-class dining establishments and home of the Monterey Bay Aquarium. In 2014, the aquarium, on the former site of the Hovden Cannery, was rated one of the world's best aquariums. In the view of modern-day Cannery Row below looking back toward Monterey, the overpass is part of the Clement Intercontinental Hotel, one of several first-class hotels with breathtaking views of the ocean. Cannery Row, which was once laced with brothels and bars, is now filled with curio and souvenir shops luring tourists into restaurants and businesses. (Both, author's collection.)

# *Three*

# Fishing Boats and Nets

Salmon was the main resource in Monterey Bay, and sailboats or *felucca* were used to catch the flaky fish. Salmon were caught with gill nets, consisting of one or more panels of webbing fastened together. Gill nets are left free to drift with the current, usually near the surface or not far below it. The sailboats were approximately 16 to 20 feet in length and had a crew of five; the nets were hauled in by hand.

Sailboats gave way to lampara boats around 1915, named after the lampara net that replaced the gill net. These boats were powered by a small gas engine and towed a skiff called a lighter, which could carry five to seven tons of sardines back to the canneries. The outbreak of World War I in 1917 brought about improvements in the lampara boat. The boats were made larger, and the lighters were also made larger so that they could carry 20 to 25 tons of sardines. The boats were approximately 30 feet in length and were powered by larger gas engines. About 25 lampara boats operated out of Monterey during this time.

Between 1925 and 1929, the boats continued to get larger. In time, the lampara net was phased out and the half-ring net was introduced, leading to the half-ring boats. The half-ring net was capable of trapping large amounts of sardines in one set, using a hydraulic winch to close the net. Older lampara boats had winches installed and were converted into half-ring boats.

The purse seiner was introduced between 1929 and 1932. These boats received their name from the type of net they used. The boat would set the net, anchoring one end, and a skiff at the other end would encircle the fish. The two boats would come together, and the bottom of the net would be closed, capturing the fish. A large purse seiner, approximately 80 feet in length, had a hold in the hull that could accommodate 70 to 140 tons of fish.

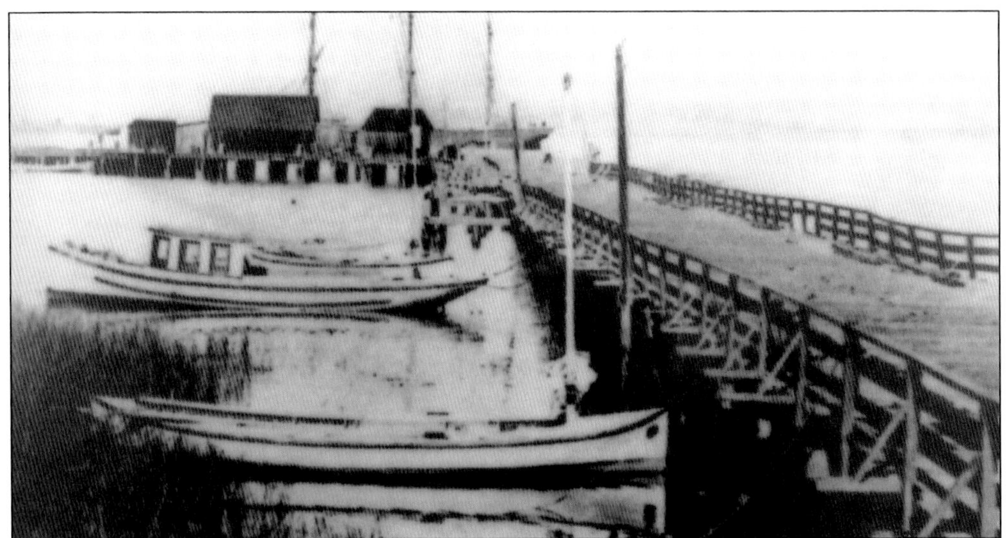

Granger's Wharf, located in Martinez, California, was about half a mile below Richardson Street in Old Town Martinez. This section of town was predominately Sicilian; they lived within walking distance of the wharf, where their fishing boats were located. A close bond between these cities and Monterey still exists today. Monterey fishermen would travel to Alaska in their off season to fish for salmon. Sailboats were used there to fish for salmon with gill nets, and the boats had a two-man crew. The Alaskan sailboats pictured below in 1929 are tied together and are being towed by a monkey boat with a motor after a day of fishing for salmon. (Above, courtesy of Contra Costa Historical Society; below, courtesy of Monterey Public Library's California Historic Room.)

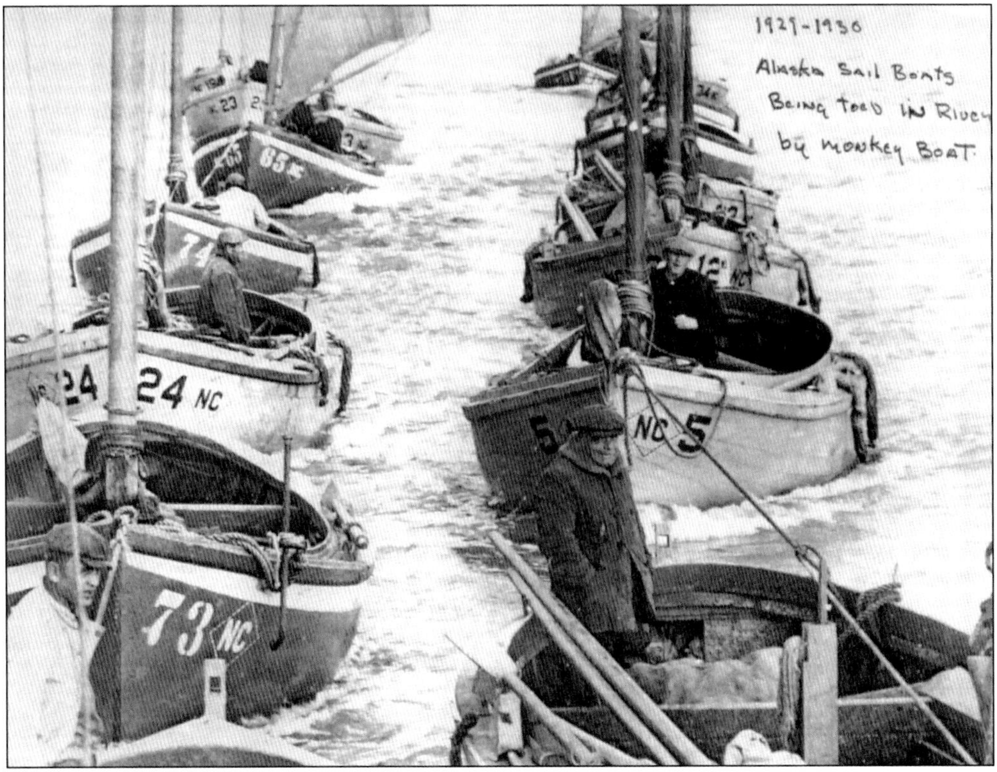

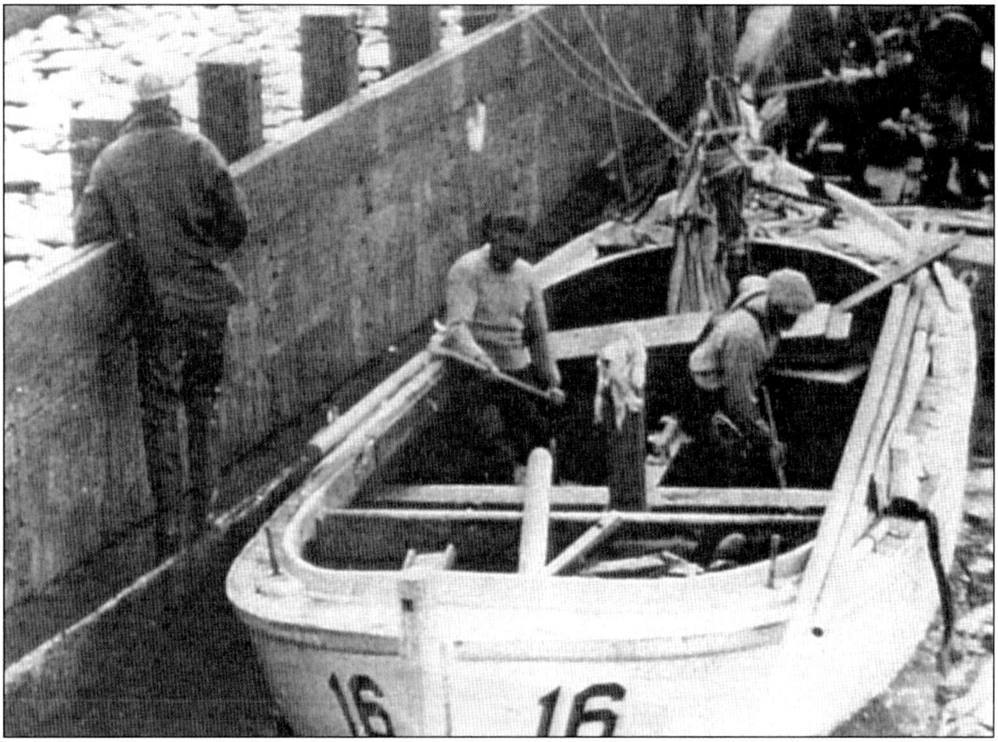

Above, a double-ender cannery boat identified with a large number 16 unloads its catch of salmon onto a barge in Alaska. The fishermen toss the fish into the barge as a man on the barge counts the fish for the cannery. A price of 4¢ to 5¢ each was paid for each fish, but today's price is paid by the pound. Below, sailboats make their way to the holding barge to begin unloading their salmon catch to the canneries. In 2012, the price that Alaskan canneries were paying fishermen for salmon ranged from $1 to $1.50 per pound. (Both, courtesy of Monterey Public Library's California Historic Room.)

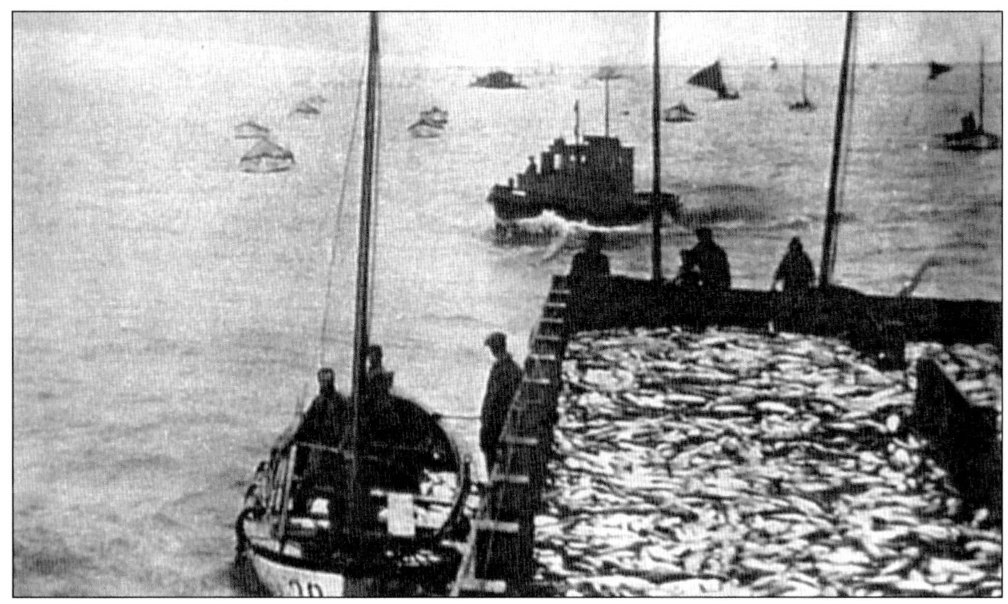

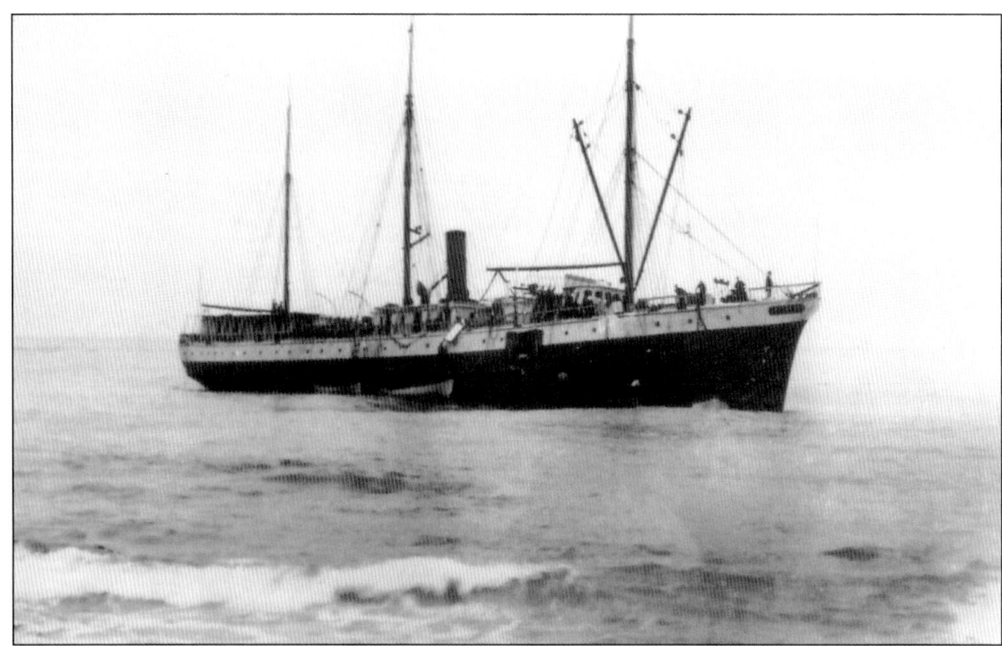

A freighter carrying supplies into Monterey goes aground on the beach east of Wharf II. Freighters were a main source of transportation, carrying supplies into Monterey from San Francisco and other ports. Associated Oil Company brought petroleum products into Monterey for fuel to operate the canneries and the fishing fleet. Pictured below is a double-ender boat, which was widely used and replaced the sailboat. The building at the end of Wharf II in the photograph is Pacific Coast Steam Ship Company's freight and ticket office. Freighters and steamships would dock, load, and unload freight and passengers from ports like San Francisco. (Above, courtesy of the Amici Club Monterey; below, courtesy of Monterey Public Library's California Historic Room.)

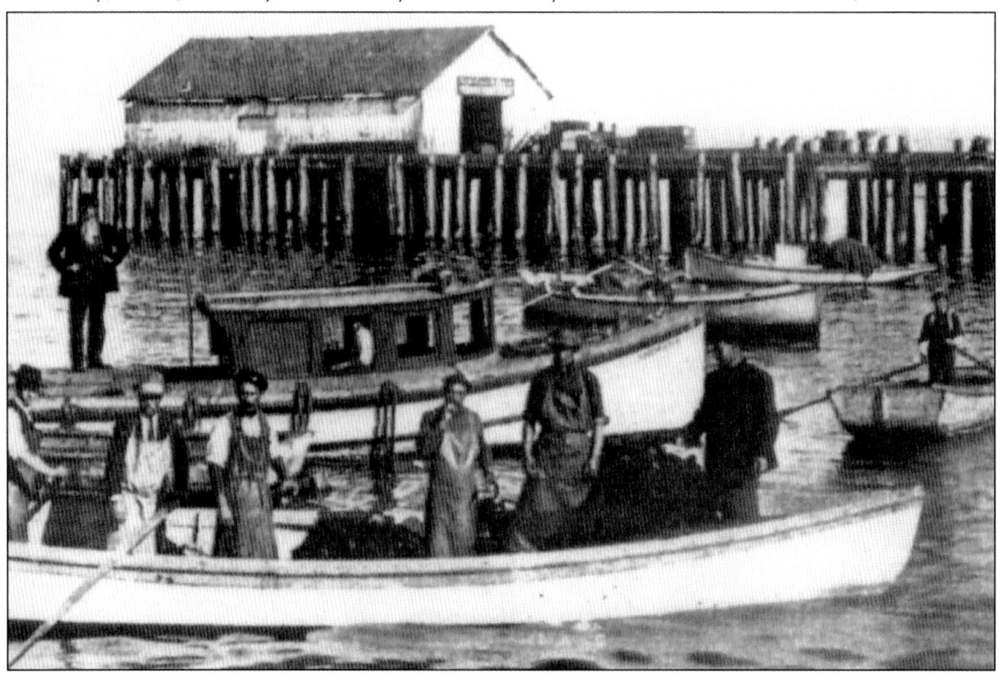

Monterey Fishermen's Protective Union organized November 27, 1925, and the original labor union banner is part of a display at the Stanton Museum in Monterey. The display of early fishing and canning equipment pays tribute to the Sicilian fishermen who fished in Monterey. Pictured below is the 1927 lampara fishing fleet moored in Monterey Harbor, with Municipal Wharf II in the background. The Associated Oil tank farm can be seen on the sand dunes in the background. The tank farm was relocated from Presidio Curve after the 1924 Associated Oil tank fire, as the city would not allow Associated Oil to rebuild at the same location. (Right, author's collection; below, photograph by Anton Charles Heidrick, courtesy of Monterey Public Library's California Historic Room.)

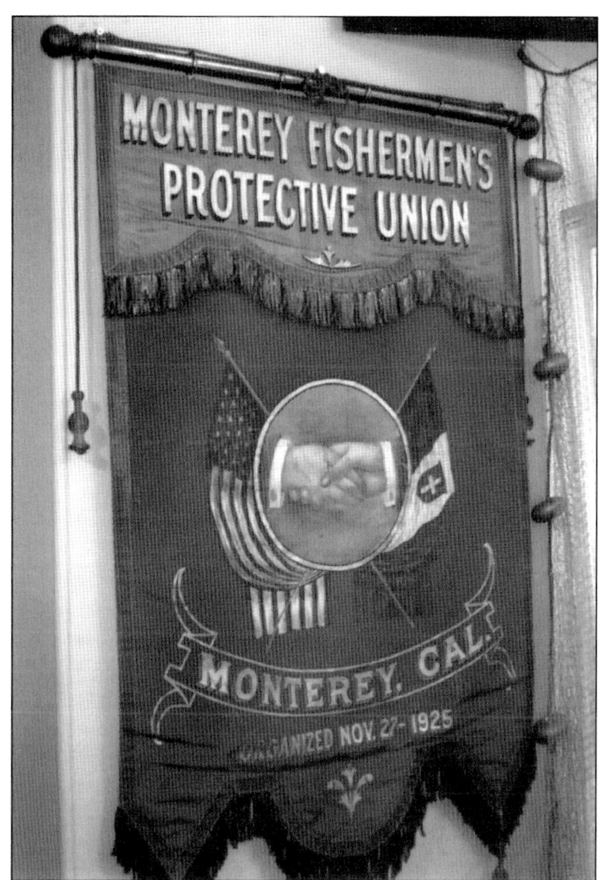


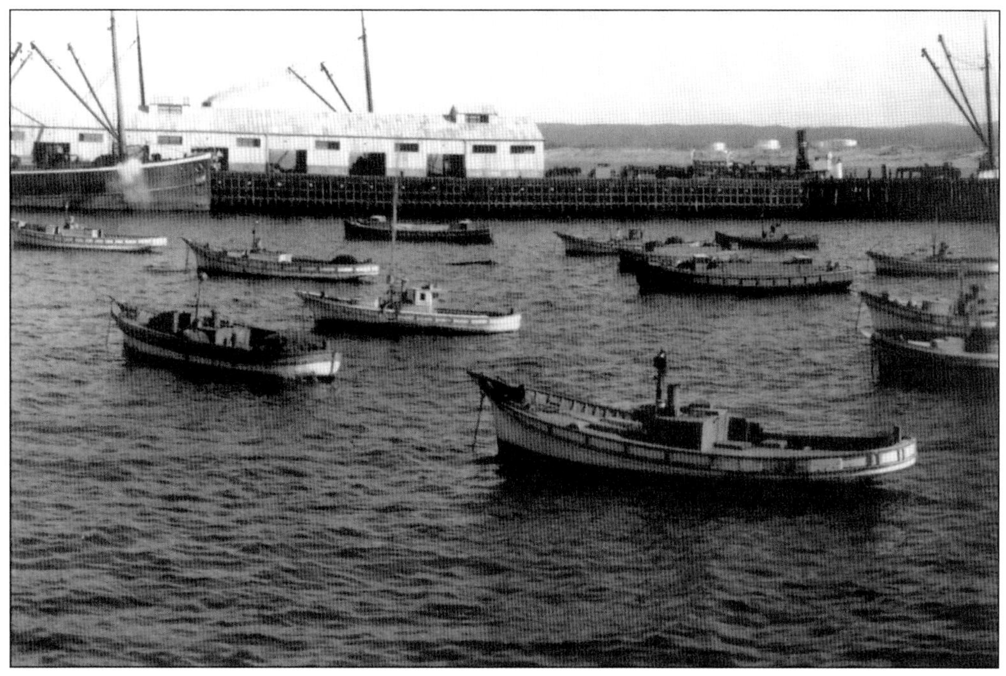

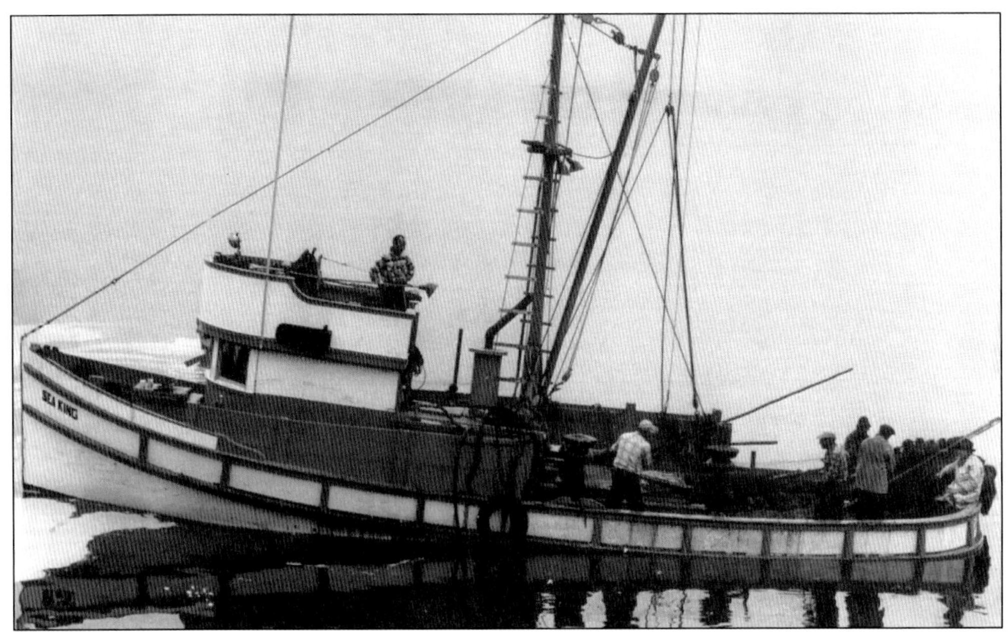

The *Sea King*'s owner, Mariano Torrente, built a winch and boom to operate a half-ring net. The half-ring net was an improvement over the older lampara net, with which all work was done by hand and which pulled evenly at the stern of the boat so as not to lose the fish. Older lampara boats were converted by their owners to take advantage of a winch and transitioned from the lampara net to the half-ring net. Pictured below is the *Eneas*. Orazio Enea was listed as the boat's owner in the 1939–1940 fishing season, and he fished for San Carlos Canning Company, ranking 19th in 1937–1938 fishing season at 2,070 tons of fish. (Above, courtesy of Peter Torrente; below, photograph by William L. Morgan, courtesy of the Monterey Public Library's California Historic Room.)

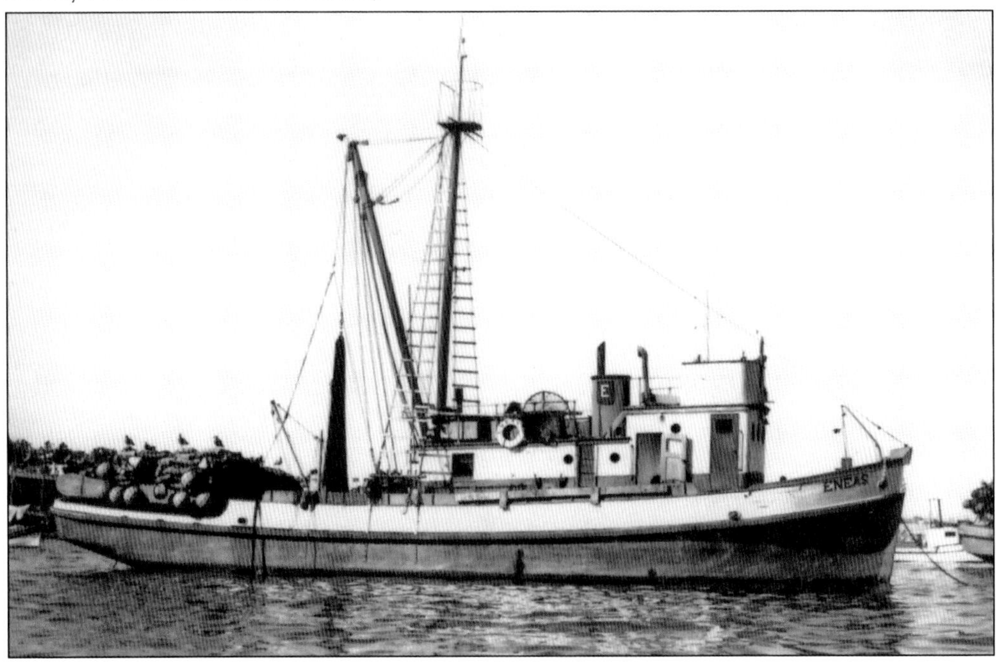

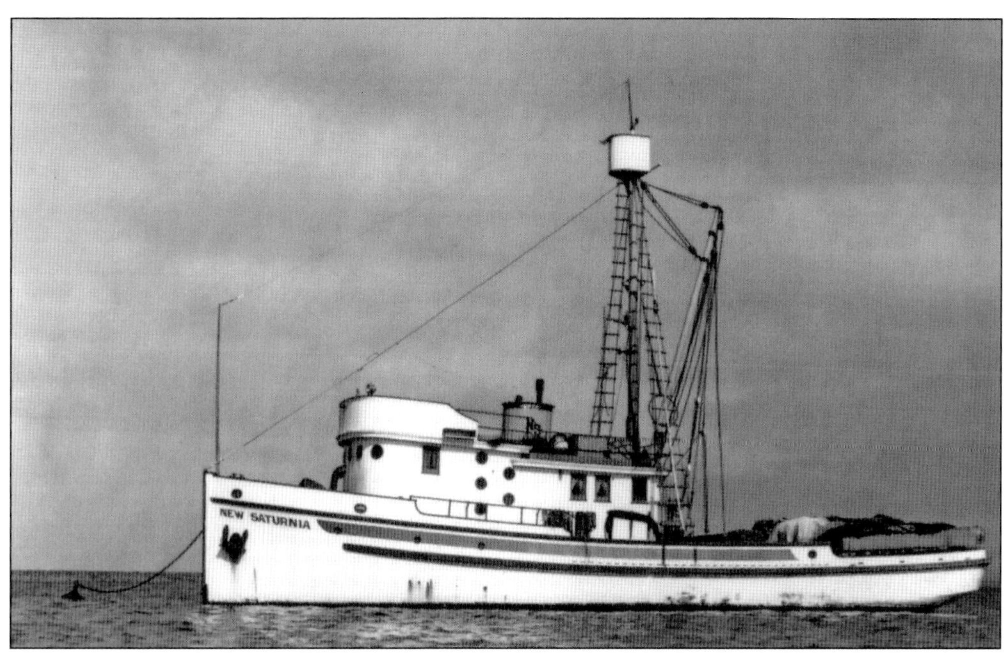


Frank Tardio was listed as the owner of *New Saturnia*, pictured above, during the 1939–1940 fishing season, and he fished for Hovden Food Products Corporation, ranking 38th in the 1937–1938 fishing season at 1,132 tons. The 1940 census shows Tardio lived with his family at 439 Jackson Street in Monterey, and they owned their own home, which cost about $2,000. Pictured below on the *California Star*, the purse seine net on the deck in the stern of the boat is prepared for setting in 1937. These nets were made of a cotton fiber and subject to mildew, so they would be dipped into tanning tanks to preserve them. (Both photographs by William L. Morgan, courtesy of the Monterey Public Library's California Historic Room.)

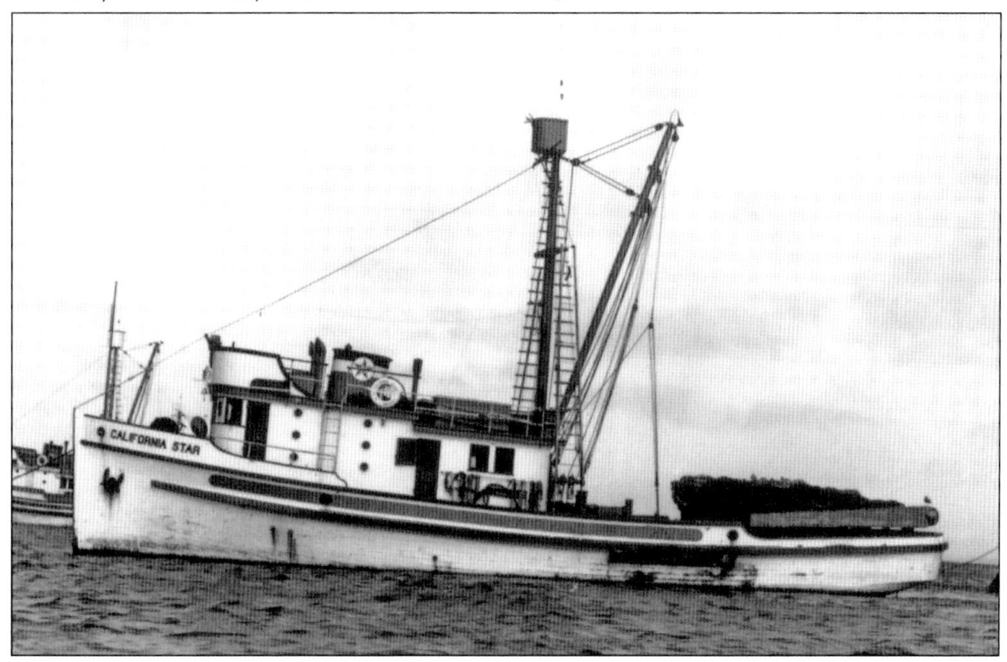

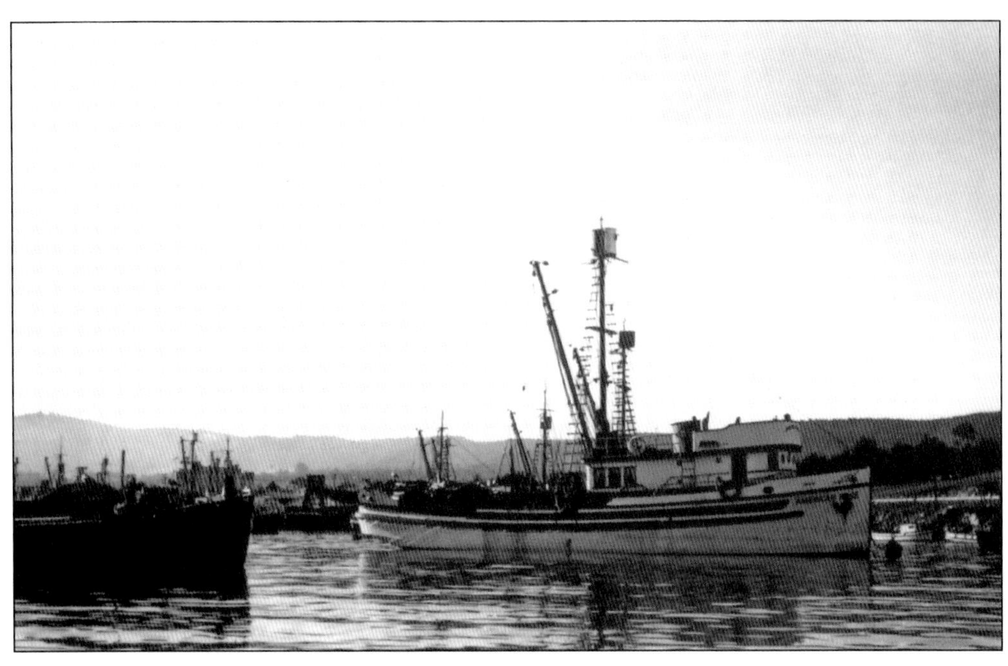

The *American Rose*, pictured here on December 24, 1937, is equipped with a crows' nest to spot schools of fish, like most all purse seiners. The boat is moored off Presidio Curve, and in the background, work is being done on the new US Coast Guard breakwater pier. Pictured below in 1937 is an old style half-ring boat, the *E.S. Lucido*. The older, smaller half-ring boats were not equipped with a crows' nest, nor could they carry much fish in the hold, and would need to tow a lighter or barge in which to place the sardines. (Both photographs by William L. Morgan, courtesy of the Monterey Public Library's California Historic Room.)

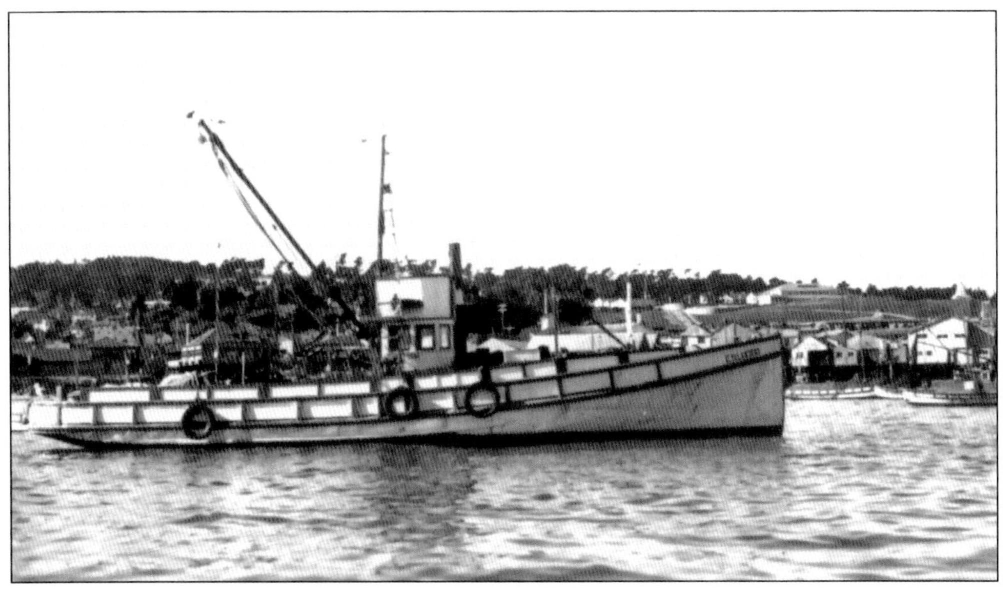

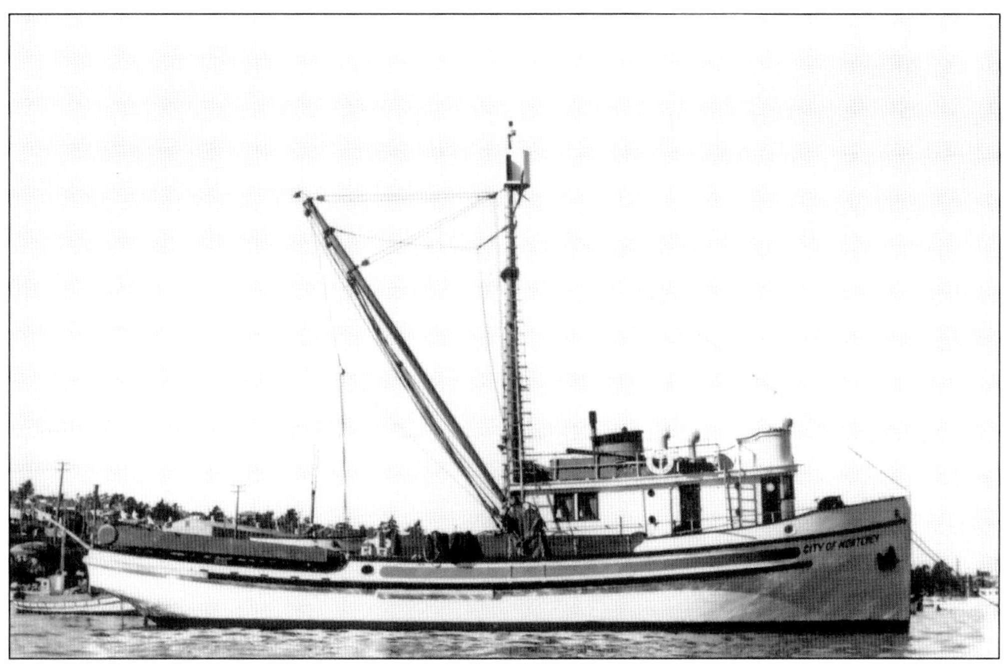


The purse seine *City of Monterey* is shown above on December 24, 1937. In the period between 1930 and 1940, there was a dramatic rise in the fishing fleet out of Monterey. The larger purse seiner boats dominated the local waters, and boats would travel from as far away as Washington to the north and San Diego to the south to fish in Monterey. Below, also in 1937, the purse seiner *Cesare Augusto* sits high in the water, and the net is missing from the back of the boat, probably being repaired or in the tanning tank for preservation. (Both photographs by William L. Morgan, courtesy of the Monterey Public Library's California Historic Room.)

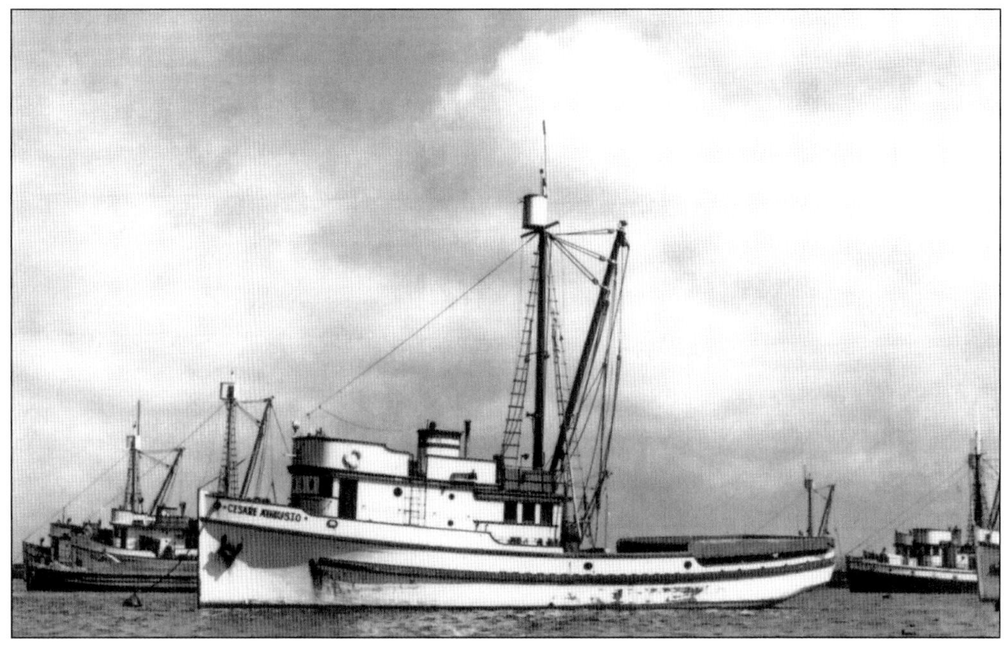

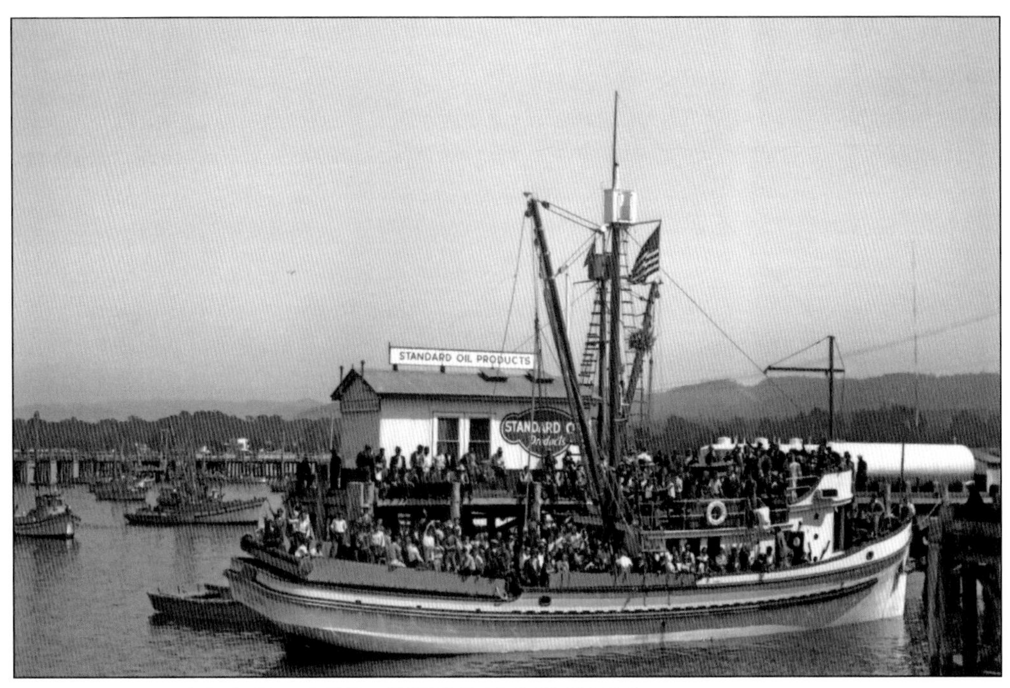


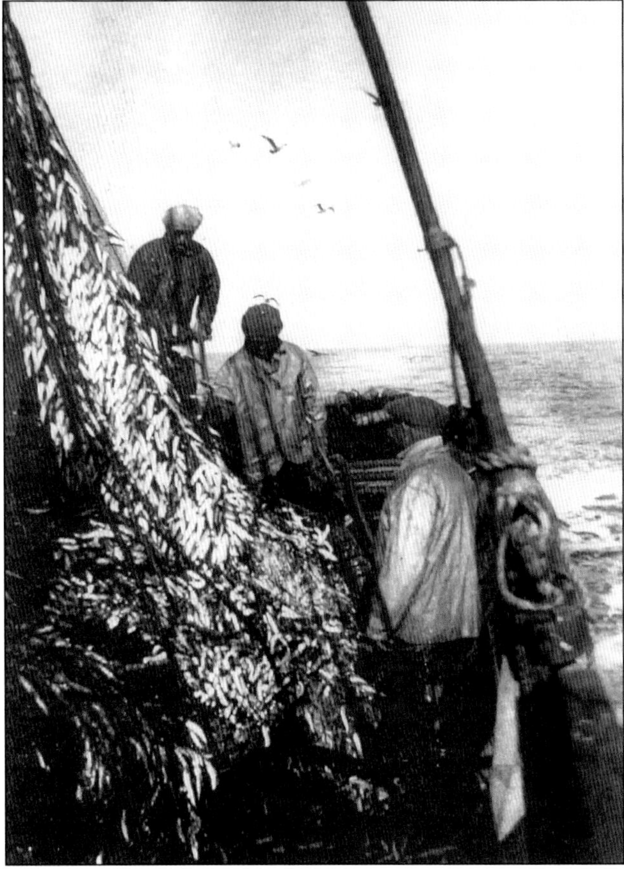

Pictured above on August 12, 1939, is the christening of the *San Giovanni*. Ben Compagno was listed as owner in the 1939–1940 fishing season, and he fished for San Carlos Canning Company. The new purse seiner has aboard family and friends as it enters Fisherman's Wharf after its christening cruise. Pictured below in 1939, the *New Rex* crew makes a common mistake and sets its nets into a school of anchovies, which appear much like a group of sardines with their silver shimmer. This put an end to the night's fishing, as the net had to be dipped into tanning tanks to remove the anchovies. (Above, photograph by William L. Morgan, courtesy of the Monterey Public Library's California Historic Room; left, courtesy of Peter Torrente.)

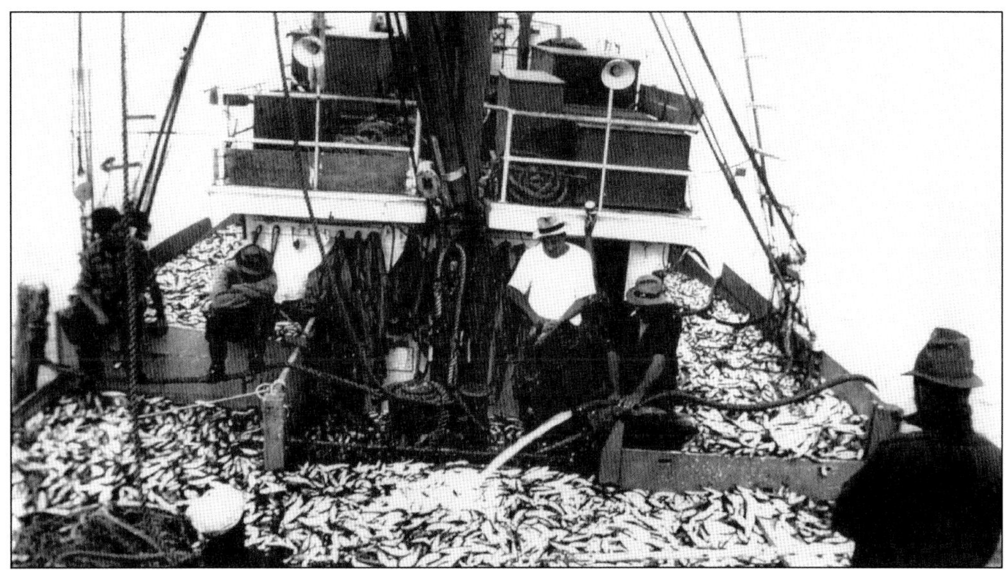

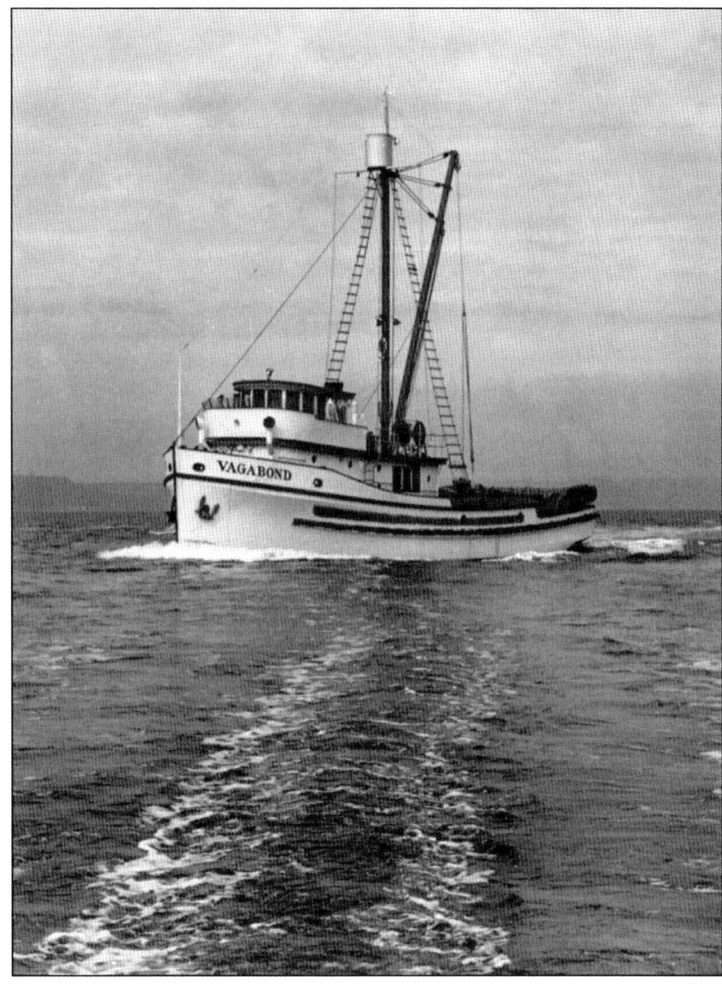


Pictured above in the 1939 fishing season, the *New Rex*, owned by Mariano Torrente, has a hold filled with sardines, with the remainder spread over the deck. It was estimated that the catch for the day was 144 tons of sardines. The crew working the boat was totally exhausted from the catch but still had to unload at the cannery hopper. At right, *Vagabond*, also owned by Mariano Torrente, was one of the early purse seiners providing beds and cooking equipment for the crew. The *Vagabond* would be replaced by the *Vagabond II*, a bigger and more modern purse seiner. (Both, courtesy of Peter Torrente.)

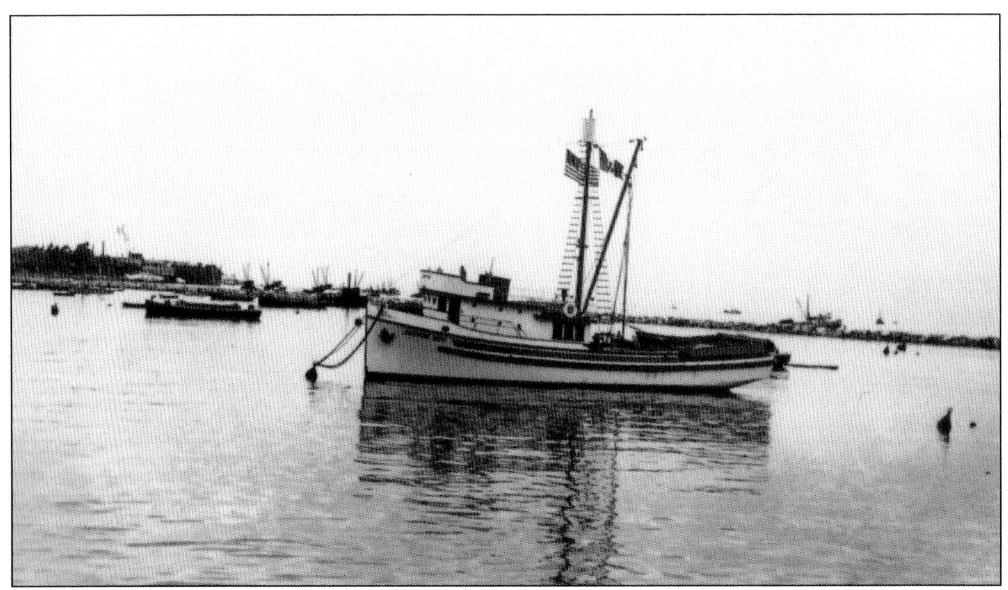

Giuseppe Aliotti owned *Jackie Boy* (pictured above), and during the 1937–1938 fishing season, he was ranked 26th with 1,725 tons for the Monterey Canning Company. Below, *Santa Rosalie* leaves the shipyard in Sausalito, California. Standing on the bridge is the unidentified boat builder (left) and Paul Cutino, the boat owner. The boat was approximately 38 feet in length and could carry 16 tons of fish in the hold and four tons on deck. The larger purse seiners were between 80 and 90 feet in length and could carry approximately 100 tons in the hold. (Above, photograph by William L. Morgan, courtesy of the Monterey Public Library's California Historic Room; below, courtesy of the Bert Cutino family.)

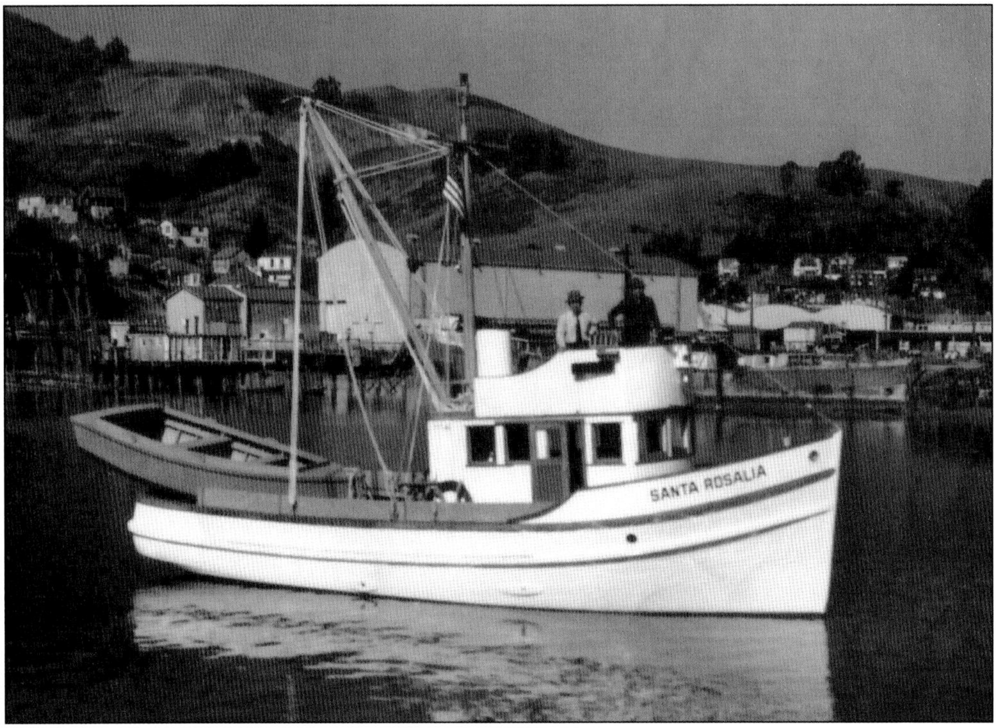

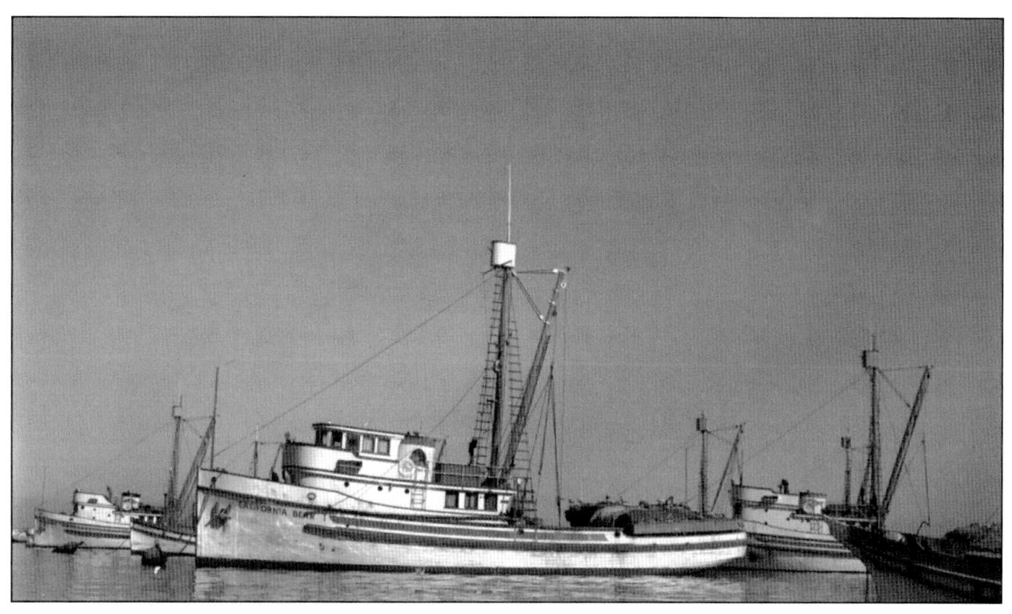

The *California Bear*, owned by Salvatore Balesteri in 1939–1940, was what was called a switch boat and fished for various canneries. Most boats were under contract to a particular cannery and would deliver their catch to that cannery alone. The *Santa Rita*, pictured below, was owned by John Compagno, who fished for San Carlos Canning Company, one of the largest on Cannery Row. In 1939, California Packing Corporation was located 507 Ocean View Avenue, but the street name would later be changed to Cannery Row. (Both photographs by William L. Morgan, courtesy of the Monterey Public Library's California Historic Room.)

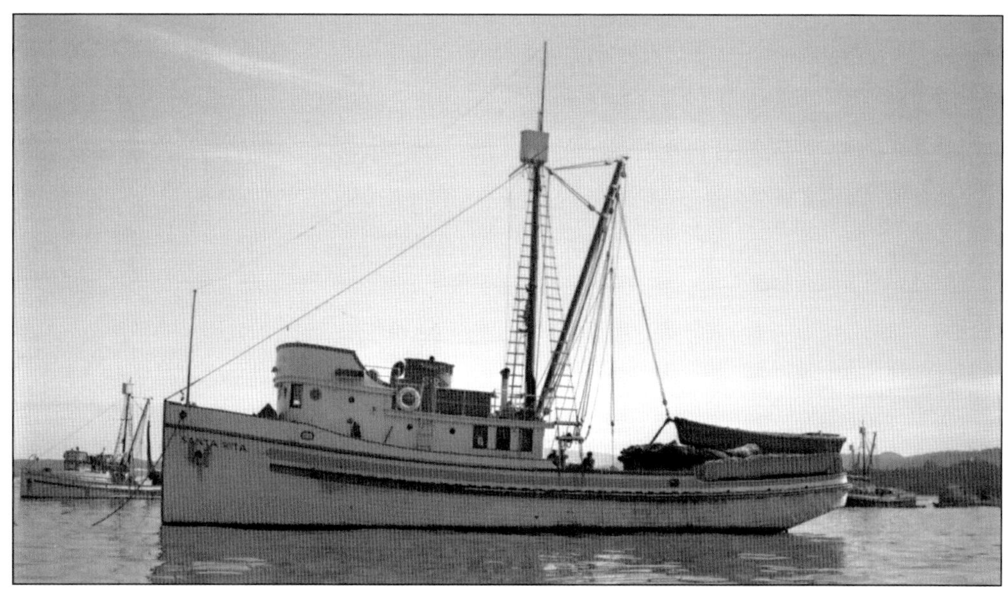

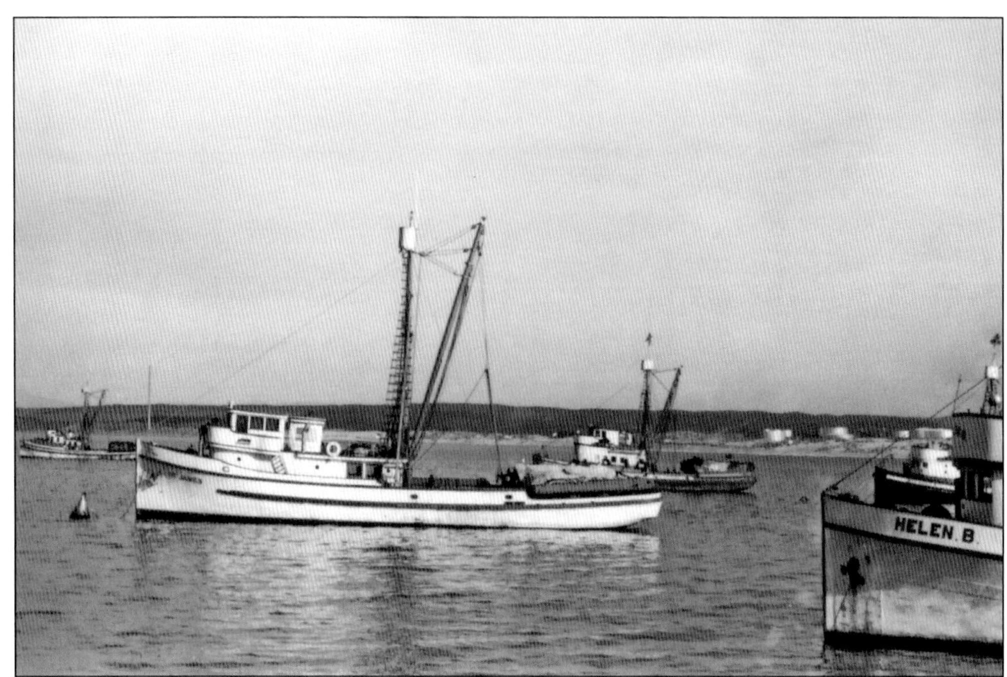


James A. Davi was listed as the owner of the *St. James* (above) in the 1939–1940 fishing season, and he fished for the San Carlos Canning Company. Below, in 1940, a storm in the bay slams boats moored in the inner harbor together. Crewmembers are manning *Saint Anthony*, *San Giovanni*, and the *Little Flower* in case the boats break away from their moorings. The crews are ready to pilot the boats away from the wharves and beaches and take them out into the bay to keep them from being damaged or washing up on the shore. (Both photographs by William L. Morgan, courtesy of the Monterey Public Library's California Historic Room.)

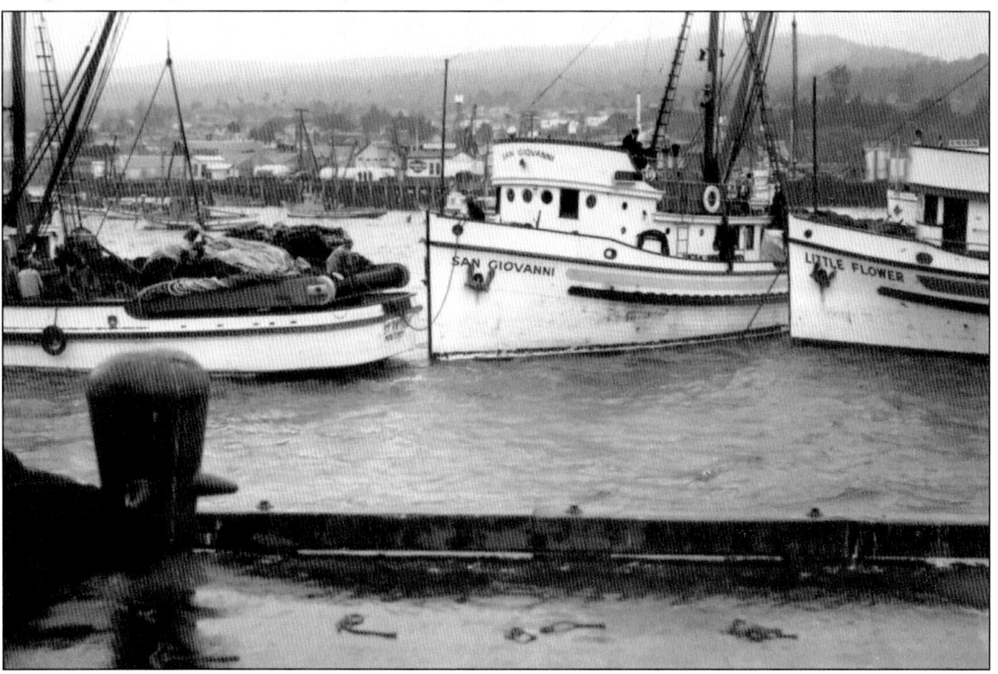

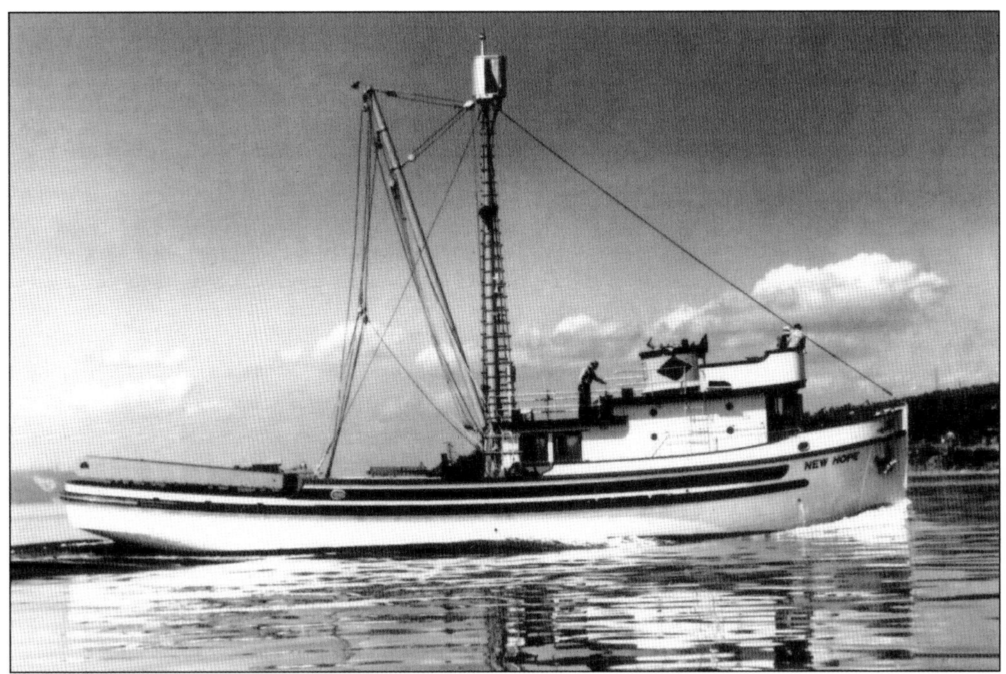


Salvatore Ventimiglia was listed as the owner of *New Hope* (above) in the 1939–1940 fishing season, and he fished for Custom House Packing Company in the boat named after his daughter. A purse seiner boat, it was able to carry 150 or more tons of fish. The *New Hope* was used by the US Navy during World War II along the central coast. Salvatore Ventimiglia received a letter of commendation from the Department of the Navy. Pictured below, *Two Sisters* washes up on the beach east of Wharf II after a storm; in the background is the old Sea Scout Hall, which is now the home of Monterey Beach Party. (Above, courtesy of Cathy Ventimiglia Gomez; below, courtesy of the Amici Club Monterey.)

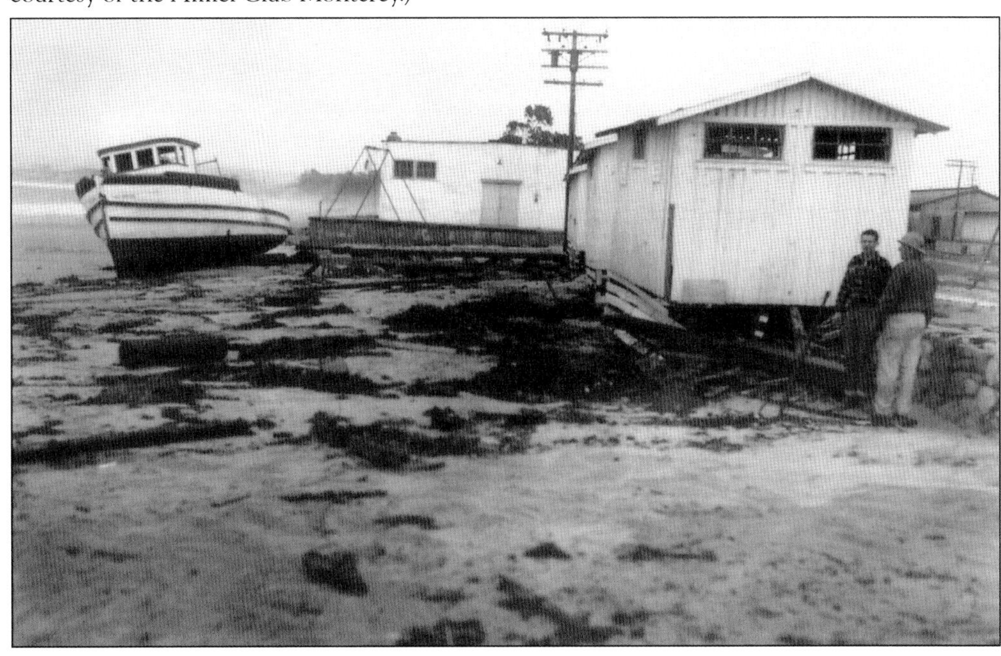

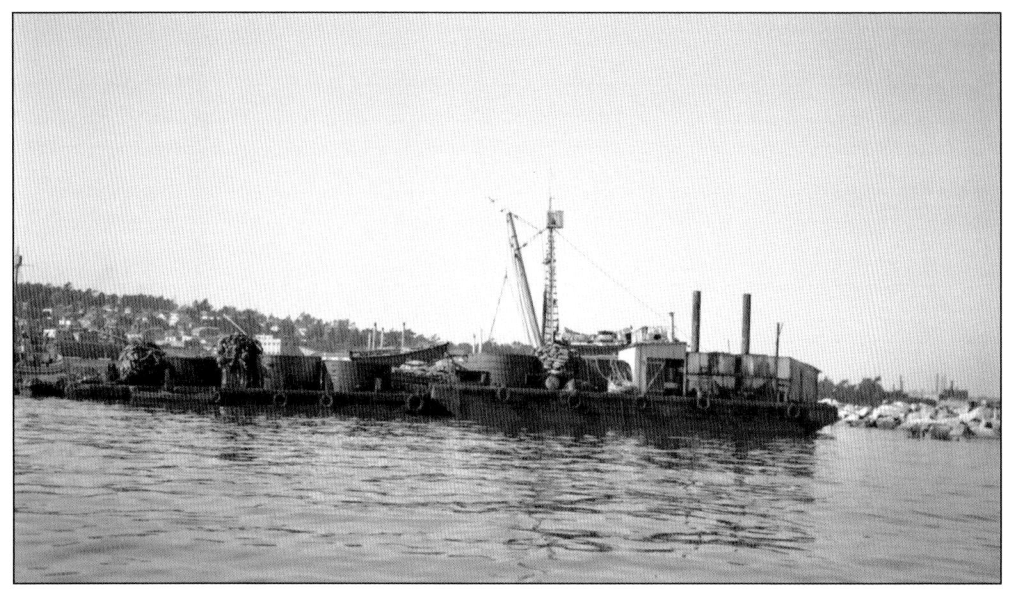

Tanning barges are pictured above in the inner harbor. There were two methods of preservation: cold tanning tanks and hot tanning tanks. The objective was to preserve the expensive cotton fishing nets. The nets would be dipped into the tanks to remove bacteria, make the net insoluble, and protect the fibers from oxidation. Pictured below in 1947, the *Lina V-II*, owned by Frank Mineo, was a purse seiner that carried 120 tons of fish in the hold and 40 tons on the deck. (Above, photograph by William L. Morgan, courtesy of the Monterey Public Library's California Historic Room; below, courtesy of Vito Spadaro.)

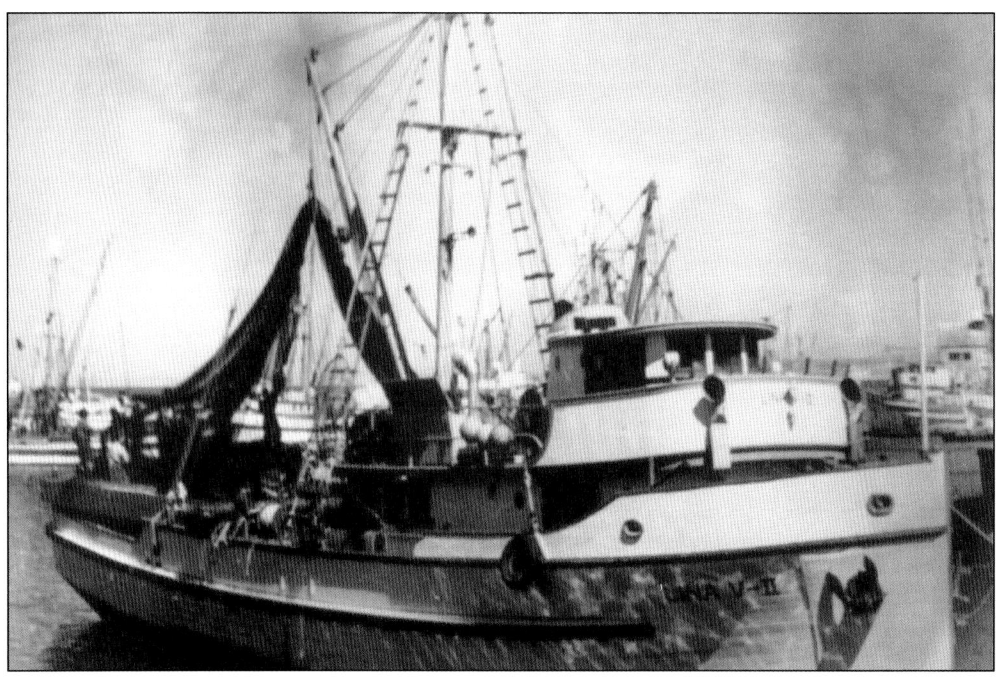

A fishing boat makes it way to the cannery with unidentified fishermen. The deck is overflowing with Pilchard sardines. Often the catch was so great that the towed lighter boat could not contain all the sardines, and the fishermen would dump the excess fish onto the deck of the boat. This was precarious, as the boat would ride low in the water, leaving only about one foot to the water line. Pictured below is the *Mineo Brothers*; Frank Mineo was listed as the owner in the 1930–1940 fishing season, and he fished for Hovden Food Products Corporation. (Right, courtesy of the Amici Club Monterey; below, photograph by William L. Morgan, courtesy of the Monterey Public Library's California Historic Room.)

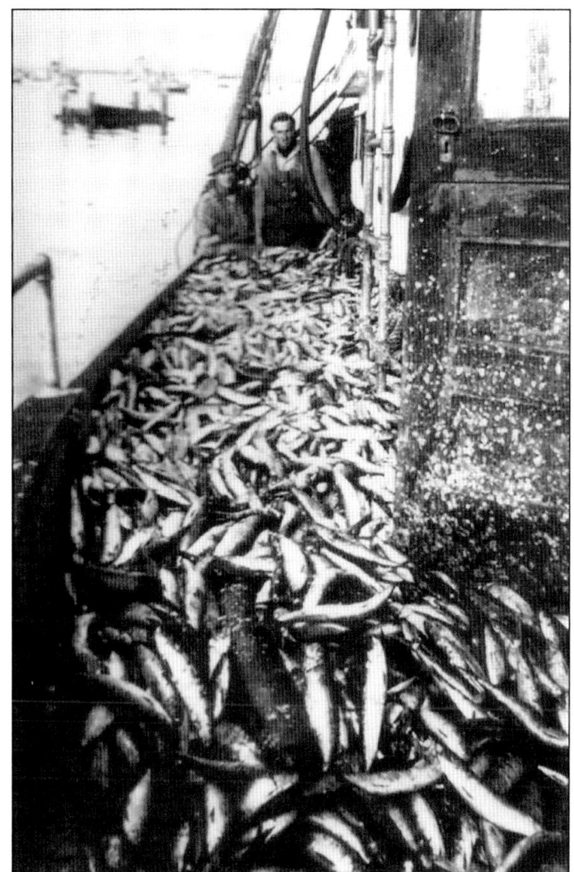

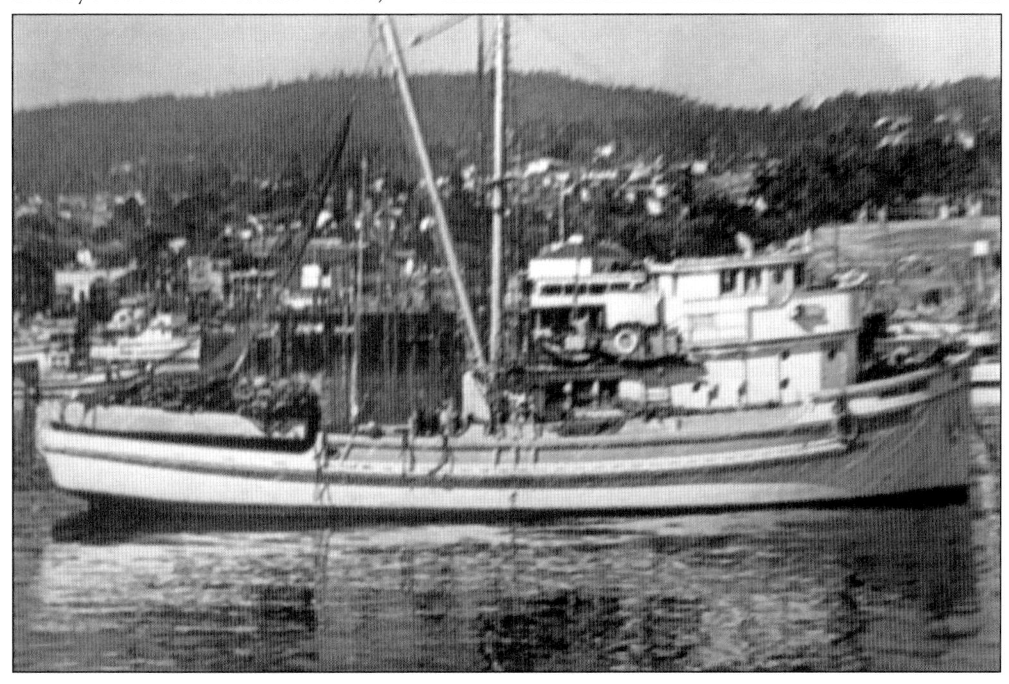

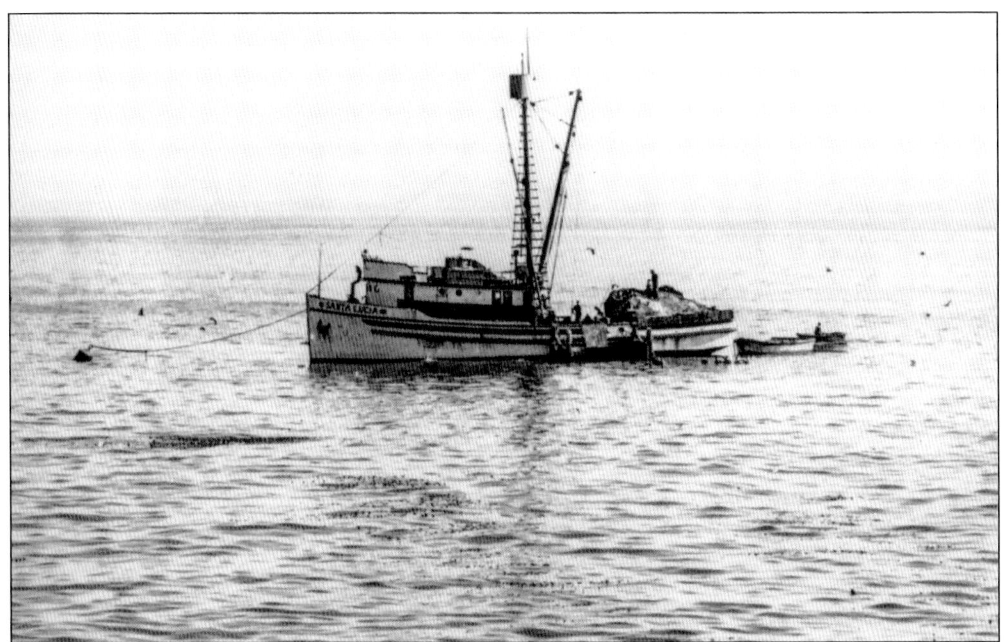

Above, in 1949, the *Santa Lucia* is unloading sardines from her hold into one of the floating hoppers operated by the cannery. The purse seiner's nets are on the stern. Below, the purse seiner *New Hope*, owned by Salvatore Ventimiglia, washes up on shore after a violent storm on February 23, 1954. The boats broke their mooring lines and washed up on the beach with several other boats. In the background is Del Monte Avenue, with some old buildings that still remain today. On the far right are the old hotel San Carlos and the Professional Building, but the San Carlos was razed to make way for the Marriot. (Both photographs by William L. Morgan, courtesy of Monterey Public Library's California Historic Room.)

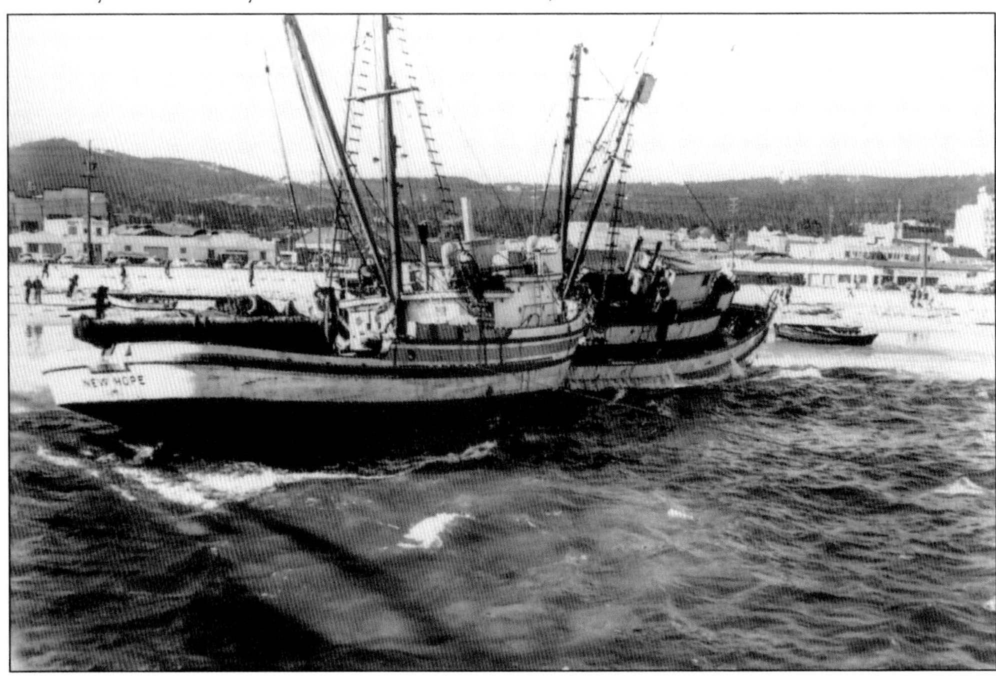

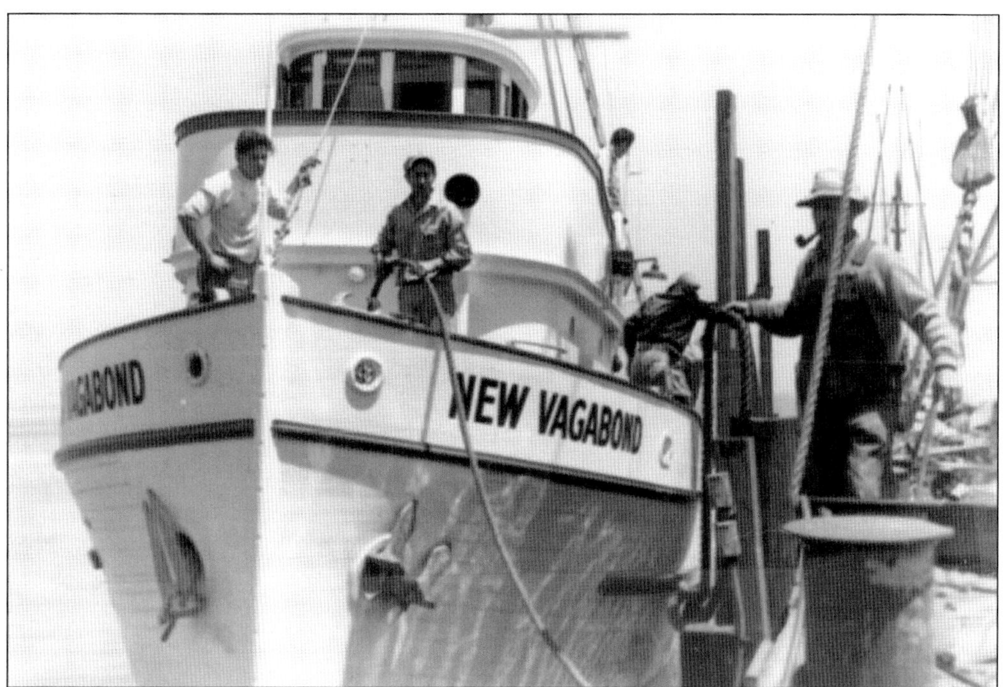


The purse seiner *New Vagabond*, built in 1947, was owned by Mariano Torrente. From left to right are Peter Torrente, Mike Ventimiglia, and other unidentified seamen. The boat took the place of the older *Vagabond* and provided lager holding capacities and improved cooking facilities and crew quarters. Below, Mariano Torrente (left) and crewmember Salvatore "Dan" Ventimiglia are on the bow of the *New Rex*. The larger purse seiners like the *New Rex* allowed the crew to fish farther out, travel up and down the coast, and stay out for days at a time. The crew would share cooking and night watch responsibilities. (Both, courtesy of Peter Torrente.)

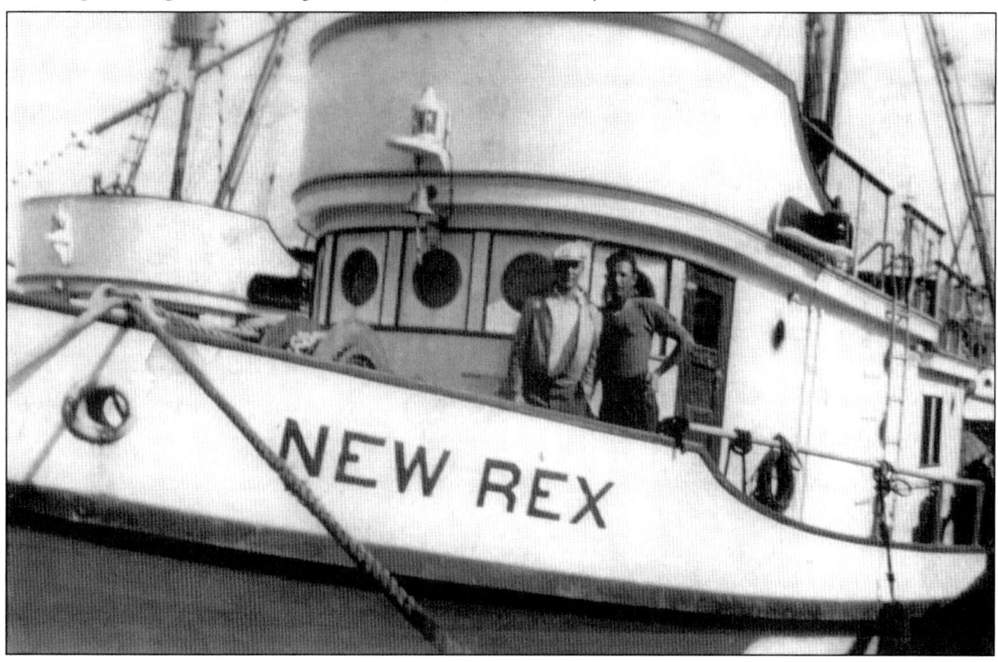

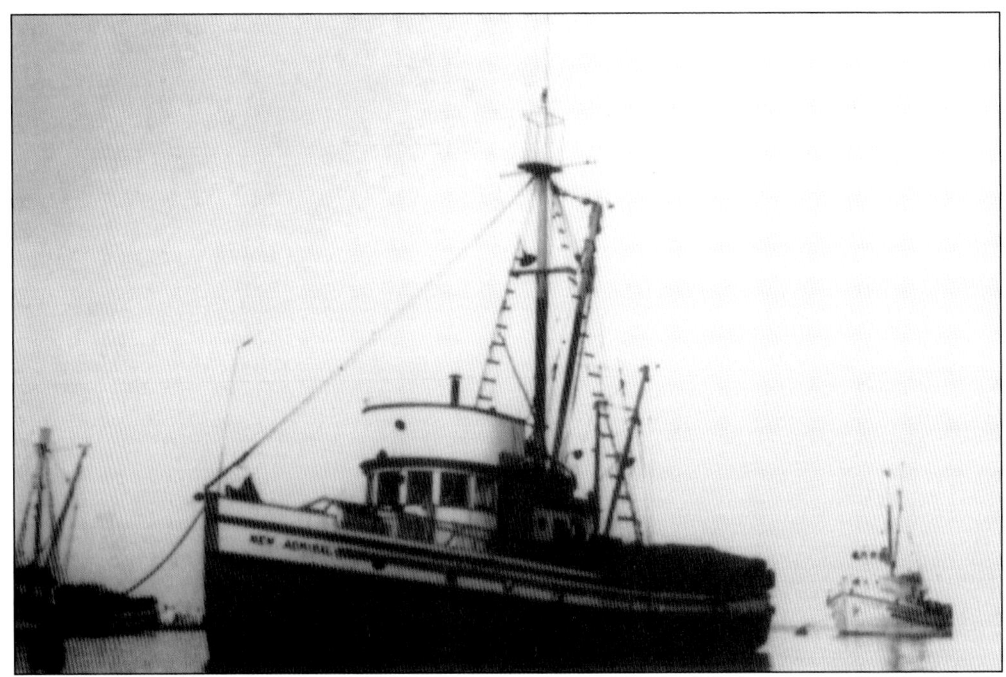

The 85-foot purse seiner *New Admiral* was purchased by Vincenzo Ferrante in the mid-1930s from John Gradis. Based in Monterey, they fished from Oregon to the Sea of Cortez for sardines, salmon, albacore tuna, and squid. In 1942, the vessel was requisitioned by the US government for service in World War II. It was affiliated with Monterey Fish Products Company between the 1930–1940 fishing seasons. John Steinbeck, the famous author, accompanied the crew on a fishing trip to the Sea of Cortez. Pictured below is Salvatore Arancio's purse seiner *Vivian A*, which fished for the Monterey Canning Company. (Above, courtesy of Vince Ferrante; below, photograph by William L. Morgan, courtesy of the Monterey Public Library's California Historic Room.)

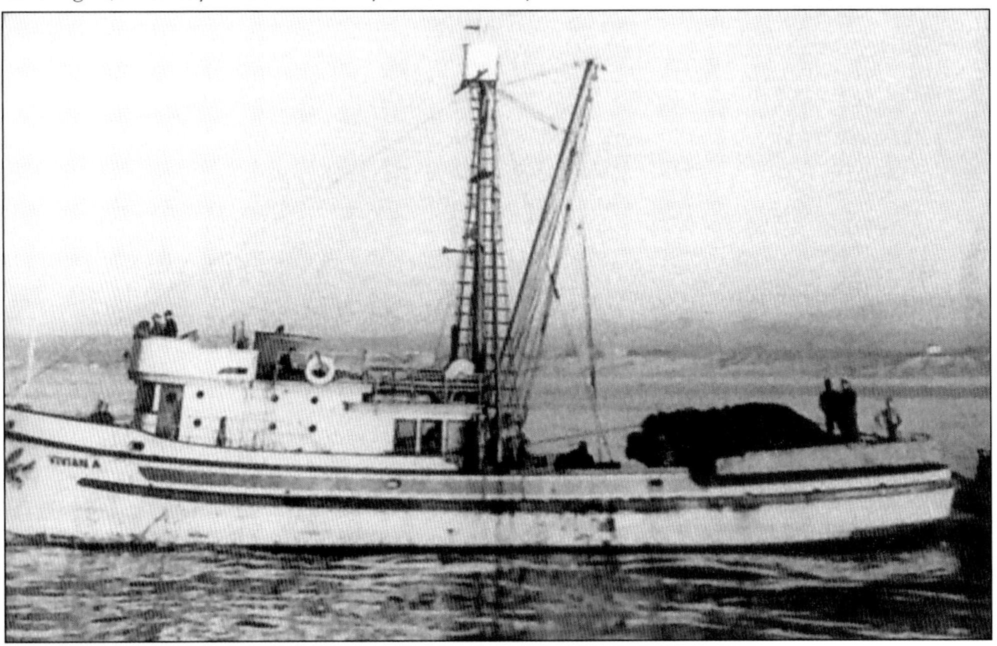

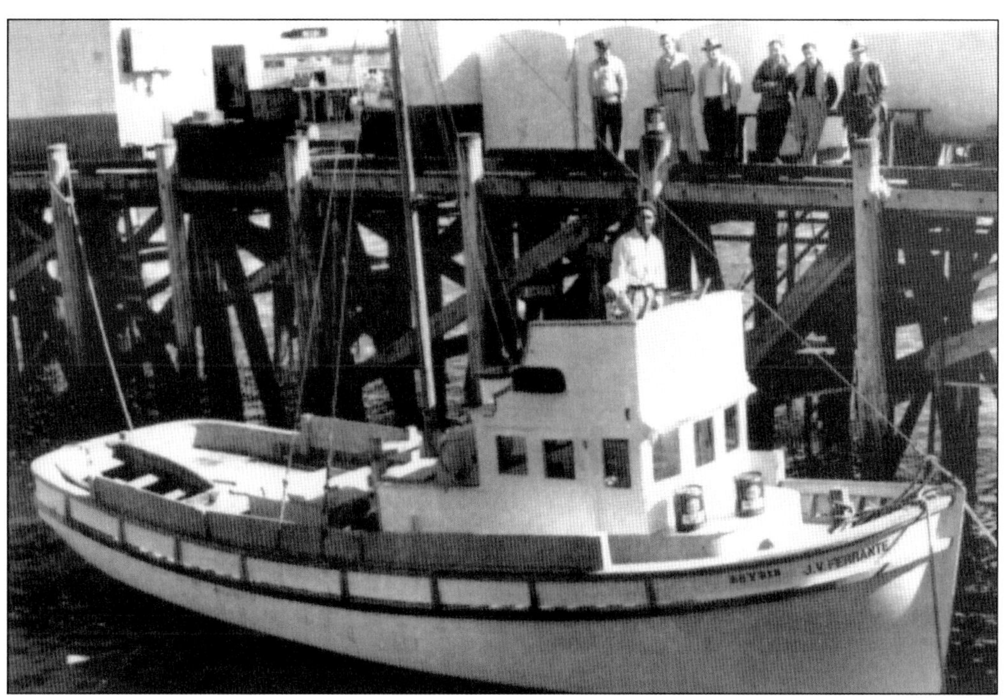

Above, the *J.V. Ferrante* pulls into the Wharf II fuel station in Monterey. The boat was built in 1947 by Frank Pasquinucci at Sausalito Boat Works and christened by Vince Ferrante. At the helm is Antonio "Tony" Ferrante, who owned the boat with his brothers Oratzio "Horace" Ferrante and Giuseppe "Joe" Ferrante. From left to right standing on the dock are Archy Sanchez, Ted Melicia, Raoul Bruno, Joe Ferrante, Frank Pomilia, and Salvatore "Shirk" Russo. At right, the purse seiner *New Crivello* runs aground on the rocks of Point Pinos in Pacific Grove, near the entrance to Monterey Bay, on September 20, 1936. (Above, courtesy of Vince Ferrante; right, courtesy of Marie R. McCrary Shade of Monterey, Monterey Public Library's California Historic Room.)

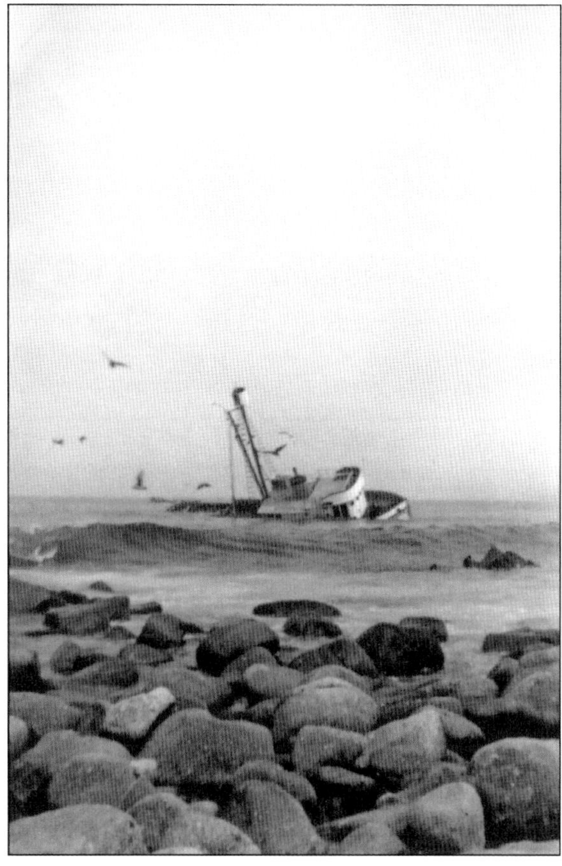

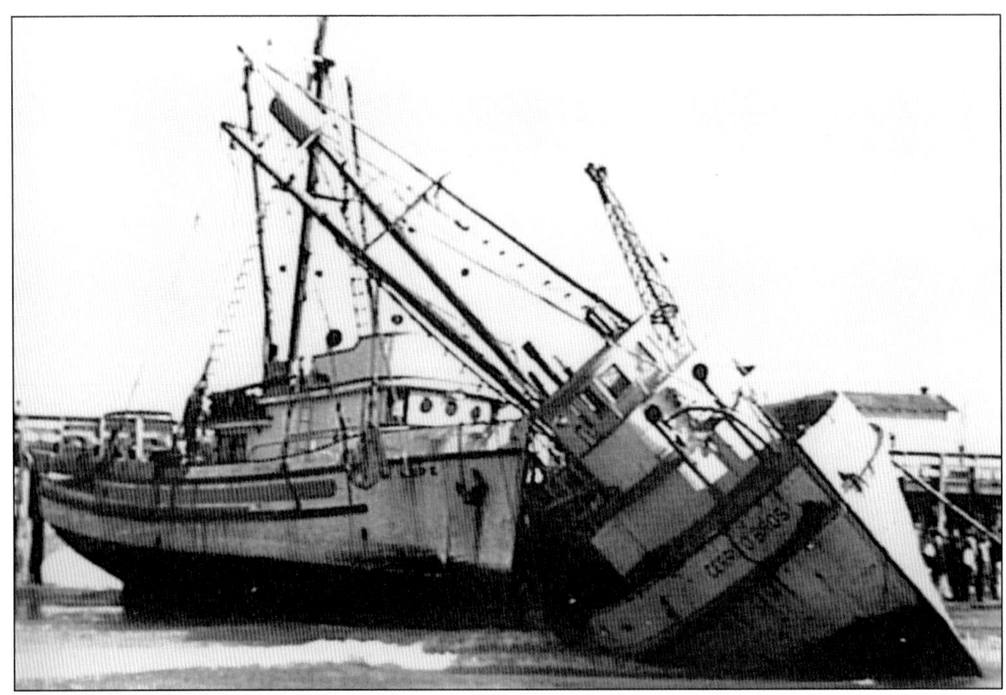

*New Hope* and *Cerrito Brothers* purse seiners are pictured above washed up on shore after a storm hit Monterey Bay on February 23, 1953, off of Wharf II. Below, Anthony Castaldo is working on his boat *Lucky Star* at the Siino Boat Works, which is located on Ocean View Avenue in Pacific Grove. Angelo Siino was a master boatwright, fabricating sailboats and double-enders. The Siino Boat Works was originally located on Wave Street in Monterey about 1923, and was expanded in 1937. (Above, photograph by William L. Morgan, courtesy of the Monterey Public Library's California Historic Room; below, courtesy of Anne Castaldo Jay.)

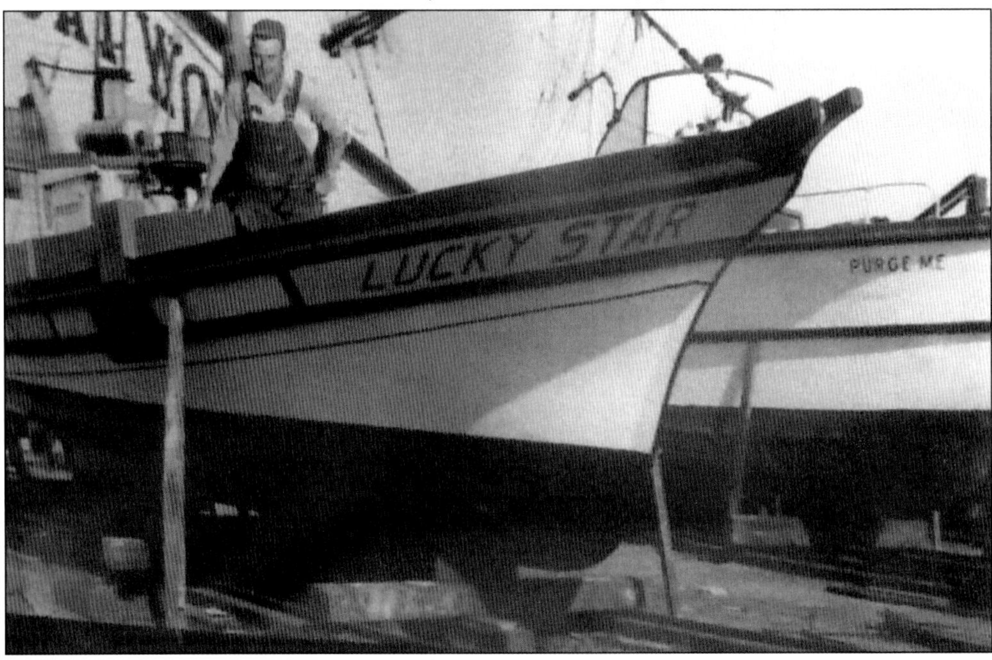

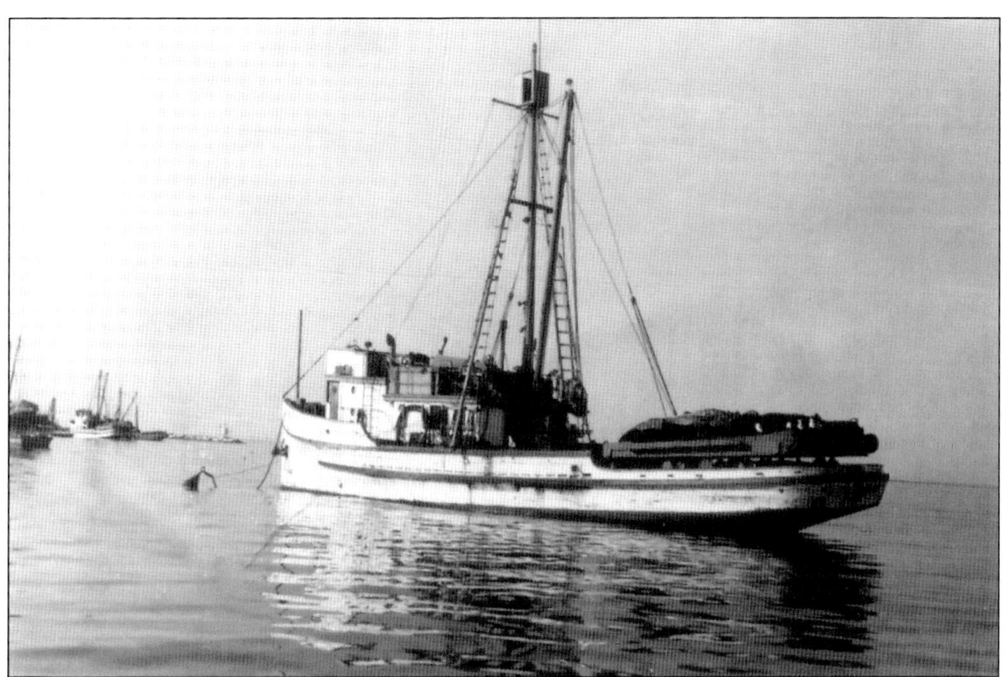

The *Star of Monterey* was owned by three partners, John Russo (captain), Raoul Bruno, and Tom DiMaggio, and they fished for the Del Mar Canning Company as the number one boat in the 1937–1938 fishing season, bringing in 3,944 tons of fish. This boat, along with so many others, was secured by the government and used to patrol the coastline during World War II. The boat was sold in 1965, and the new owners planned to fish for king crab off the coast of Alaska. Below, fishing boats wash up on shore east of Wharf II after a severe storm in November 1943. (Above, courtesy of Mary D'Agui Wells; below, photograph by George Esaki, courtesy of Jean Esaki Shades of Monterey, Monterey Public Library's California Historic Room.)

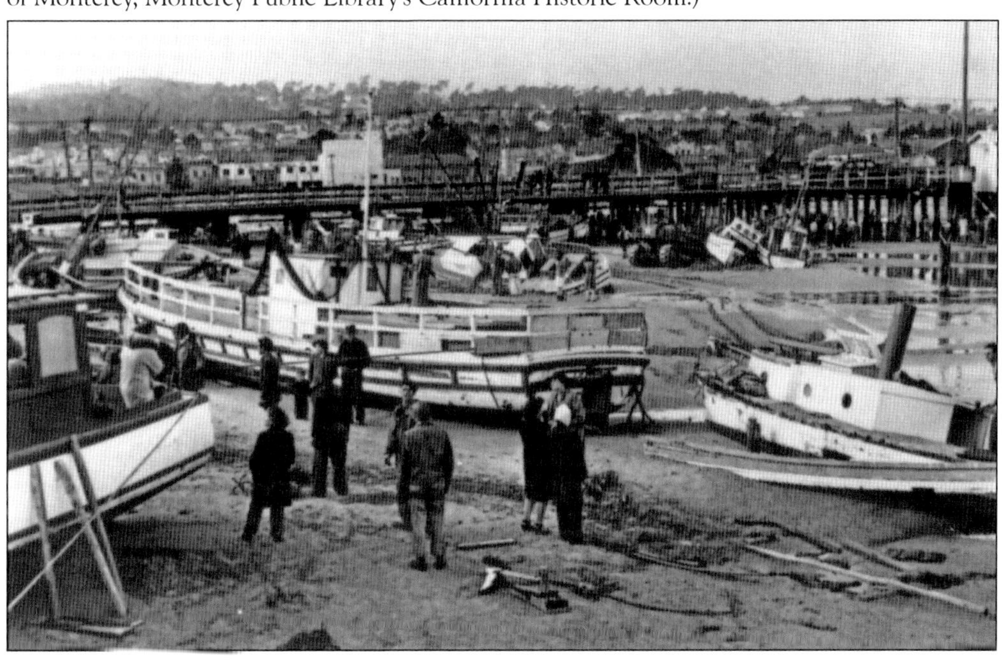

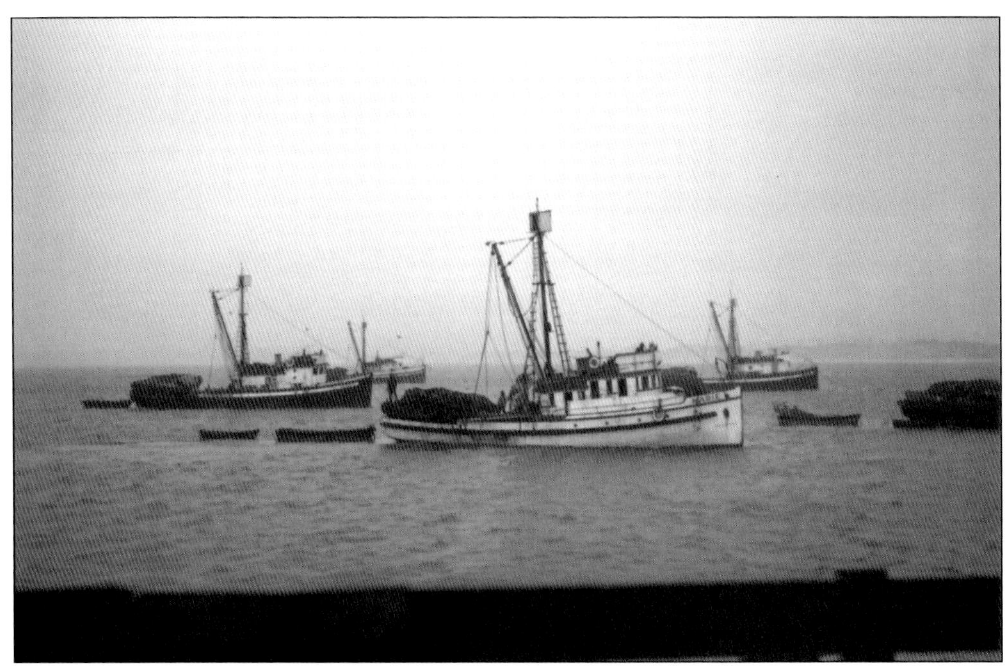

Above, a storm hits Monterey Bay's inner harbor, and crewmembers remain aboard the *Marie* in case the boat breaks away from its mooring so they can pilot the boat away from the wharves and beaches. Below, the evolution of the fishing boat is caught in one image: the smaller boats are lampara boats, the boats with the booms are half-ringers, and the larger boats with boom and crow's nest are the purse seiners. In the background are a submarine and a warship paying a visit to Monterey in 1940. (Both photographs by William L. Morgan, courtesy of Monterey Public Library's California Historic Room.)

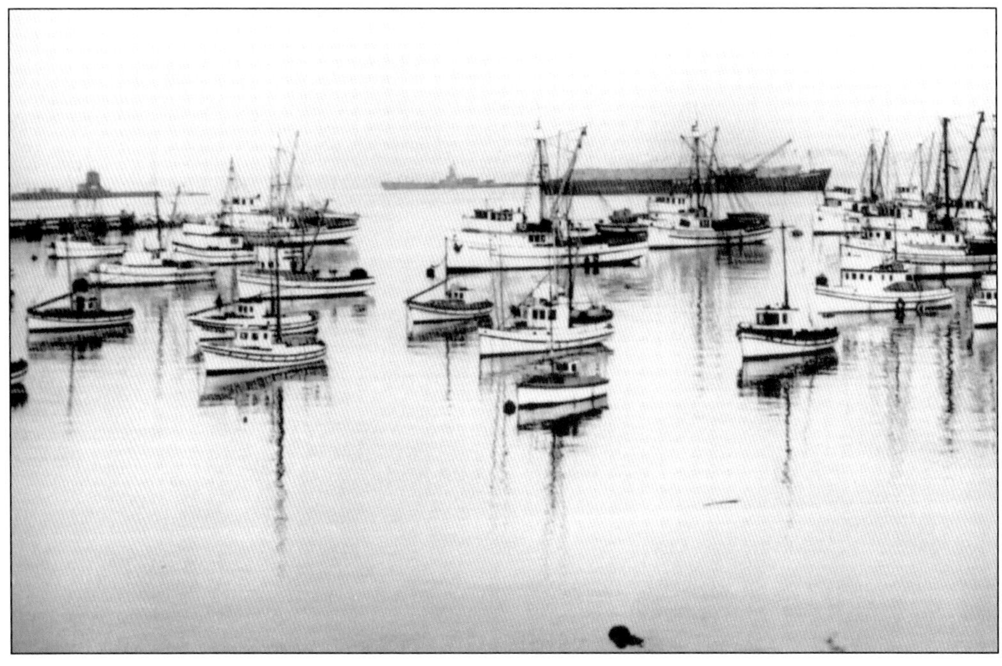

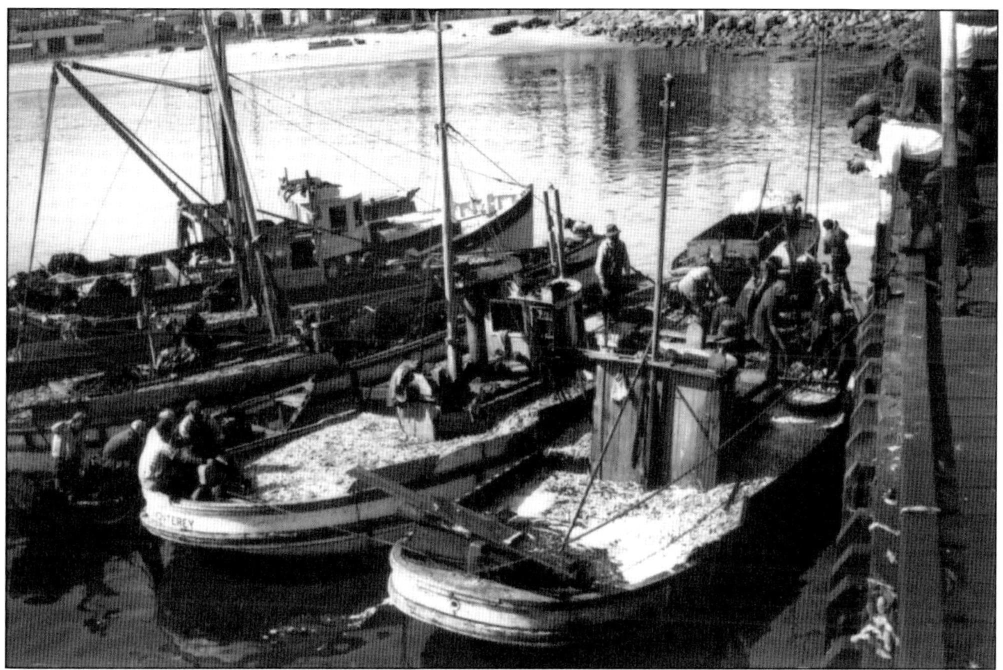

Pictured above on May 12, 1930, lampara boat decks are loaded with squid. The boat next to the dock is not equipped with a winch. The boats to the left have been converted by adding a winch to aid hauling in the net. Pictured below at Wharf II on May 2, 1941, crewmembers tend to the fishing nets, inspecting and loading the large purse seine net on the stern of the boat. (Above, photograph by Julius B. Phillips; below, photograph by William L. Morgan, both courtesy of the Monterey Public Library's California Historic Room.)

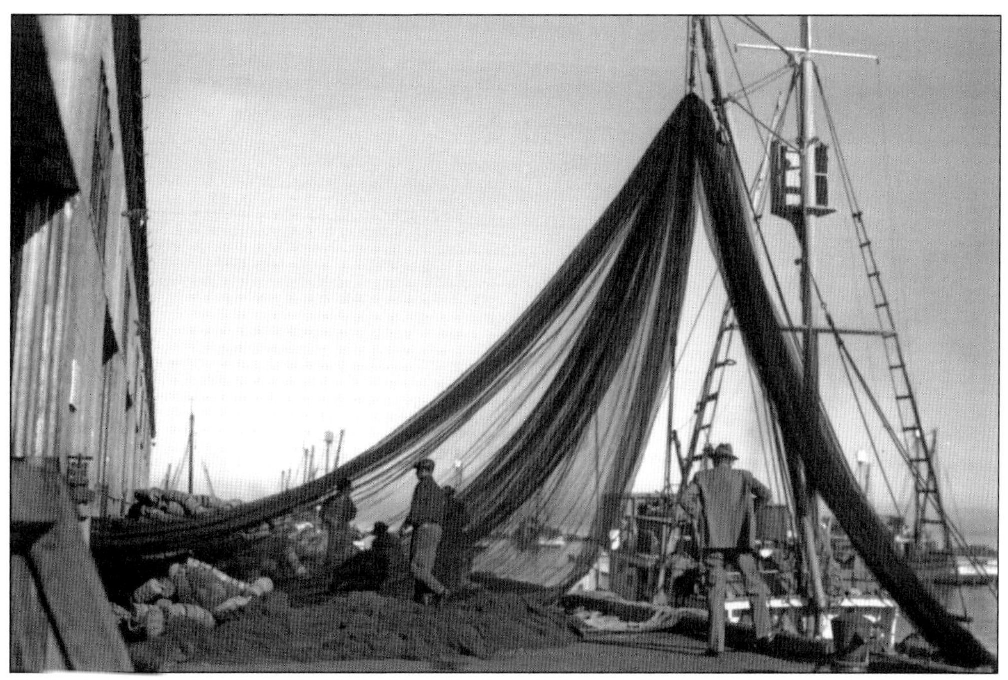

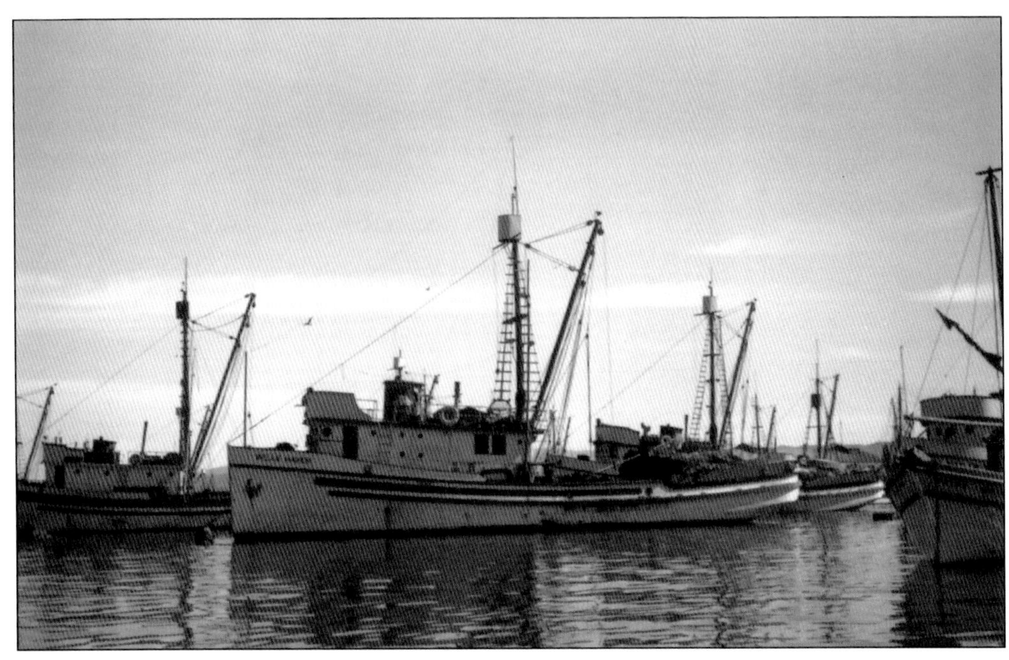

Salvatore Ruccello owned *Belle Haven* (above) and fished for the E.B. Gross Canning Company during the 1939–1940 season. Below is a view northwest from what is now Randy's Fishing Trips, where Union Oil was located at one time. Tied to the dock at Wharf I are four large purse seiners; from left to right are *Western Maid* captained by Joe Giamona, *Marettimo* captained by Joe Spadaro, *New Rex* captained by Mariano Torrente, *St. Anthony* captained by James A. Davi, and the *Star of Monterey* captained by John Russo. (Above, photograph by William L. Morgan; below, courtesy of John Napoli, shades of Monterey, Monterey Public Library's California Historic Room.)

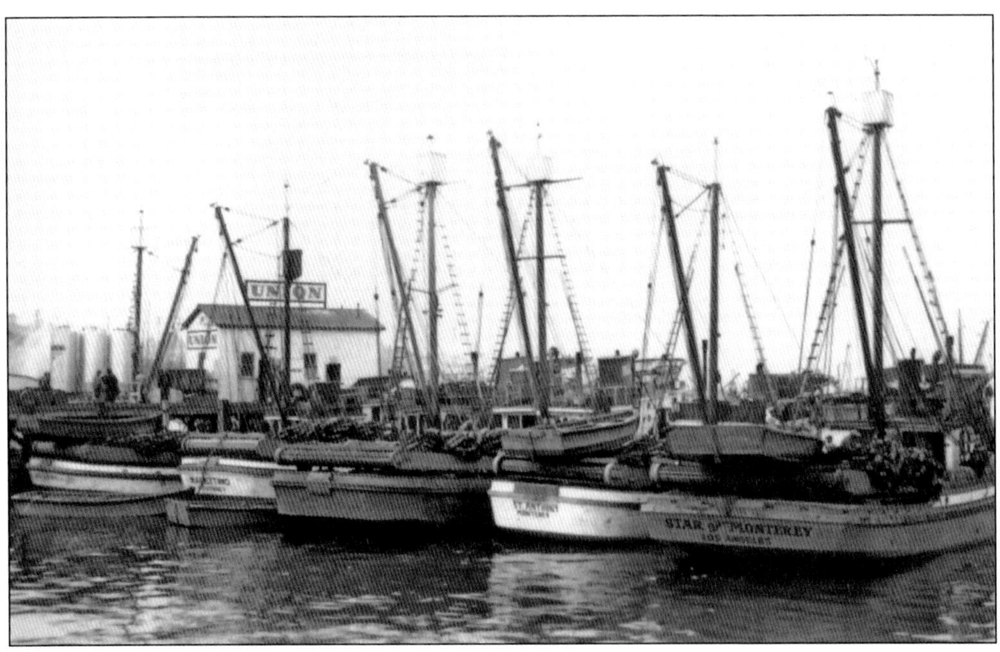

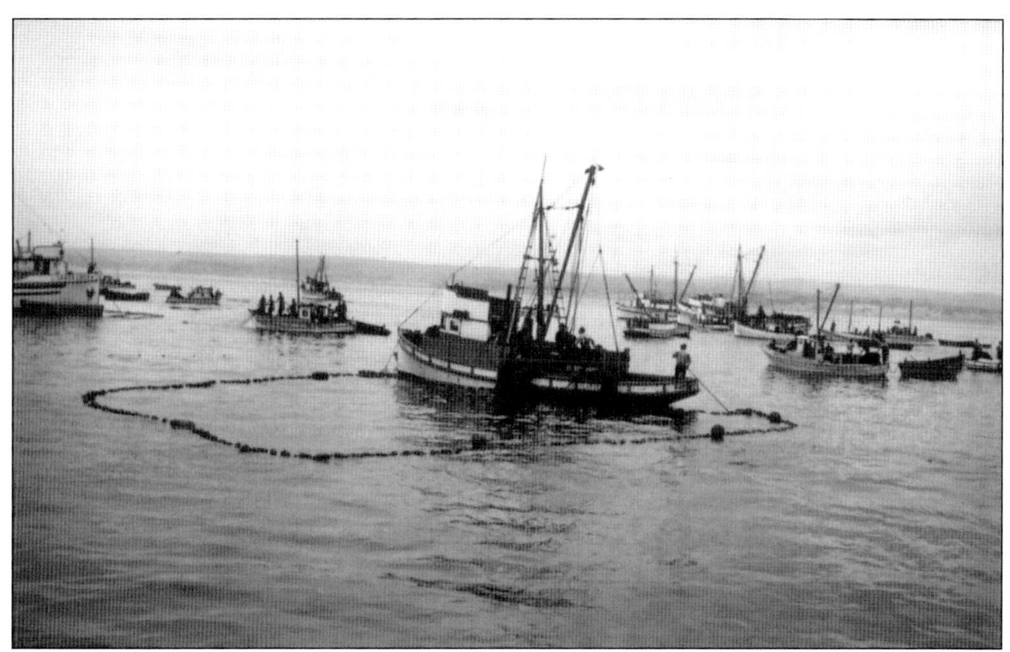

Above, on May 14, 1946, a half-ringer boat sets a net in Monterey Bay. As the sardine population was diminished, fishermen concentrated on other fish like squid, anchovies, mackerel, and rockfish. Below, a purse seiner sets its net and utilizes a skiff anchored at one end, while the purse seiner encircles the school of fish, letting the net pay out the stern. The purse seiner would meet up with the skiff and close the net. The two methods of setting the nets were unique to each type of boat, and the purse seine net was much more efficient and yielded larger catches. (Above, photograph by Julius B. Phillips; both courtesy of Monterey Public Library's California Historic Room.)

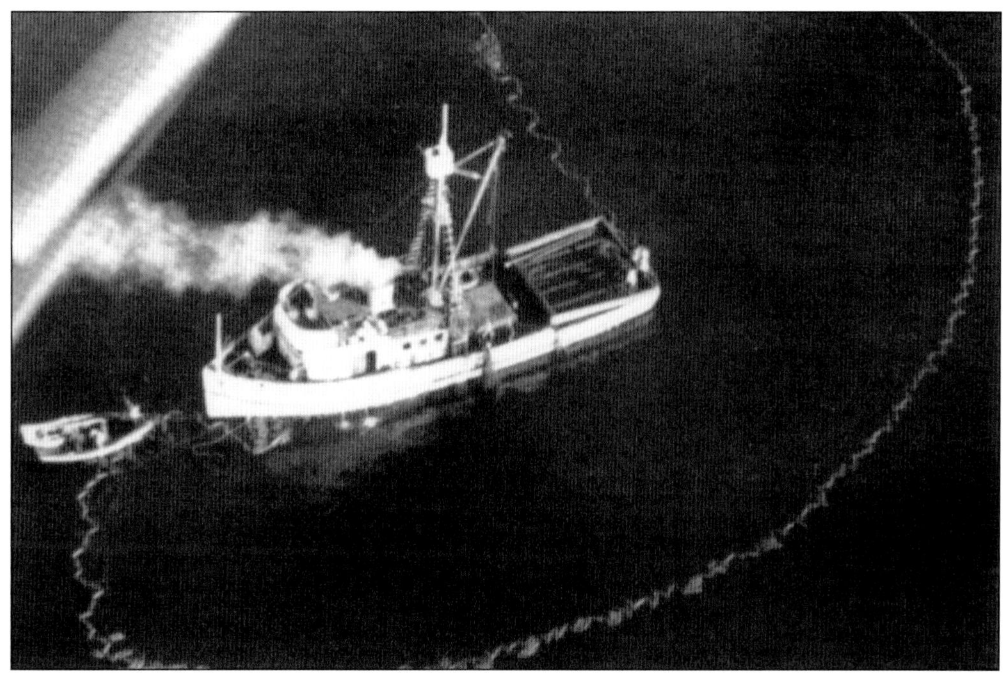

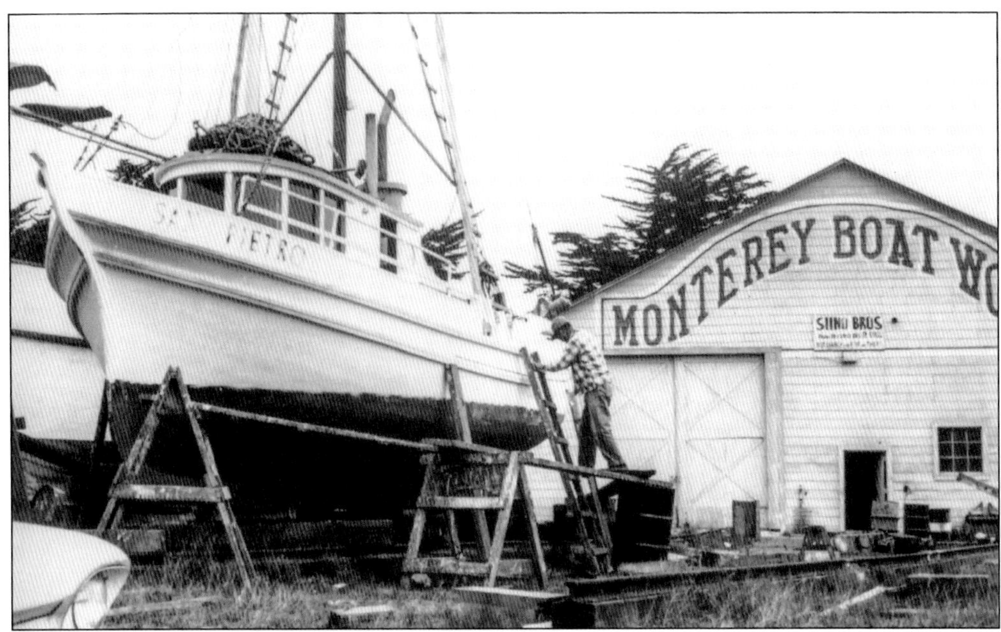


Pictured above on March 17, 1949, is Siino Boat Works (later known as Monterey Boat Works), owned by Angelo Siino, a master boatwright who fabricated feluccas and double-enders. An unidentified fisherman works on the *San Pietro*. Pictured below is Frank Sardina in 1964, piloting his small commercial fishing boat *Bessi* out to sea. After the sardines left Monterey, many of the fishermen continued to fish with smaller fishing boats and provided a variety of fish like halibut, rockfish, and flounder to the local markets, which provided fresh fish to the restaurants and private customers. (Above, photograph by Nick LeFevre, courtesy of Monterey Public Library's California Historic Room; below, courtesy of the Sardina family.)

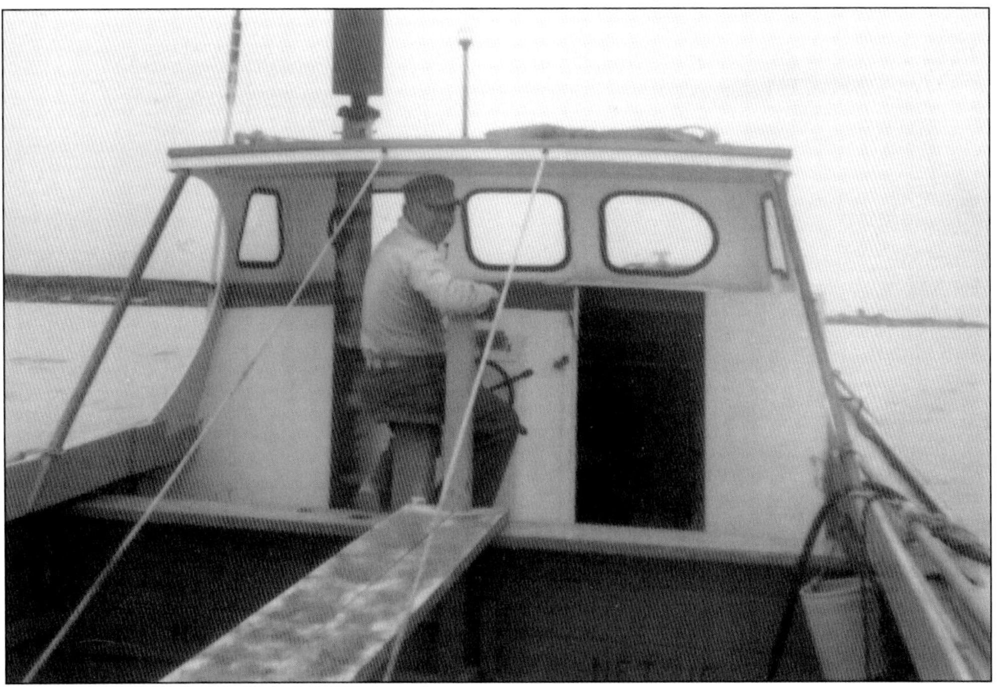

## *Four*

# Santa Rosalia Festival Blessing of the Fleet

Festivals have always been part of Italian culture. Whether celebrating the annual Columbus Day Parade or the Santa Rosalia Festival, these are times to come together and celebrate with family and friends. The Santa Rosalia Festival is a traditional, colorful festival that was brought to Monterey by the Sicilians.

Rosalia was the daughter of Count Sinibaldo della Quisquina, who lived in Palermo, Sicily, from 1130 to 1166. She loved the Lord so much, she left the family and lived in a cave on top of Monte Pellegrino, situated at the west end of the harbor, and devoted herself to prayer. She eventually died, but no one knew, and her bones lay in the cave. Some 450 years after her death, the Black Plague hit the city of Palermo, killing thousands of its residents. A young soap maker whose wife died in the plague went to the top of Monte Pellegrino to pray to God that he could also die, missing his wife. While he was praying, a beautiful young woman stood before him—it was Rosalia. She told the young man that she had not had a Christian burial, and if her bones would be carried though the streets of Palermo, the plague would be ended. Her bones were carried through the streets of Palermo, and the plague ceased.

Every year, a festival is held in the city of Palermo to honor Saint Rosalia, who became the patron saint of the mariner. In 1935, the Santa Rosalia Festival was renewed due to the efforts of four women: Rosa Ferrante, Giovanna Balbo, Domenica Enea, and Francesca Giamona. The Italian community gathers together, and the statue of Santa Rosalia is carried through the streets of Monterey to the wharf for the blessing of the fleet and to honor those fishermen who have died. Wreaths are dropped upon the water to float out to sea in their memory.

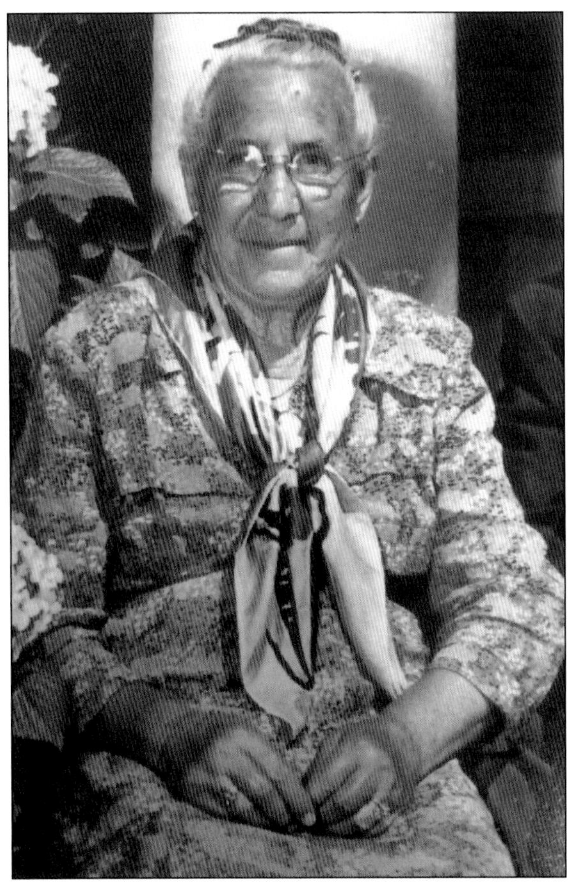

Rosa Enea Ferrante, wife of Pietro Ferrante, along with Francesca Ferrante Giamona, Giovanna Balbo, and Domenica Enea, restored the Santa Rosalia Festival in 1935. Through the efforts of Francesca Ferrante Giamona, the Santa Rosalia Festival was established in Monterey. The festival, along with the blessing of the fleet, was held in Pittsburg. Pictured below is the 1937 Santa Rosalia Festival and blessing of the fleeting at the end of Wharf II. The purse seiner tied to the wharf is the *New Rex*, owned by Mariano Torrente. (Left, courtesy of Vince Ferrante; below, photograph by William L. Morgan, courtesy of the Monterey Public Library's California Historic Room.)

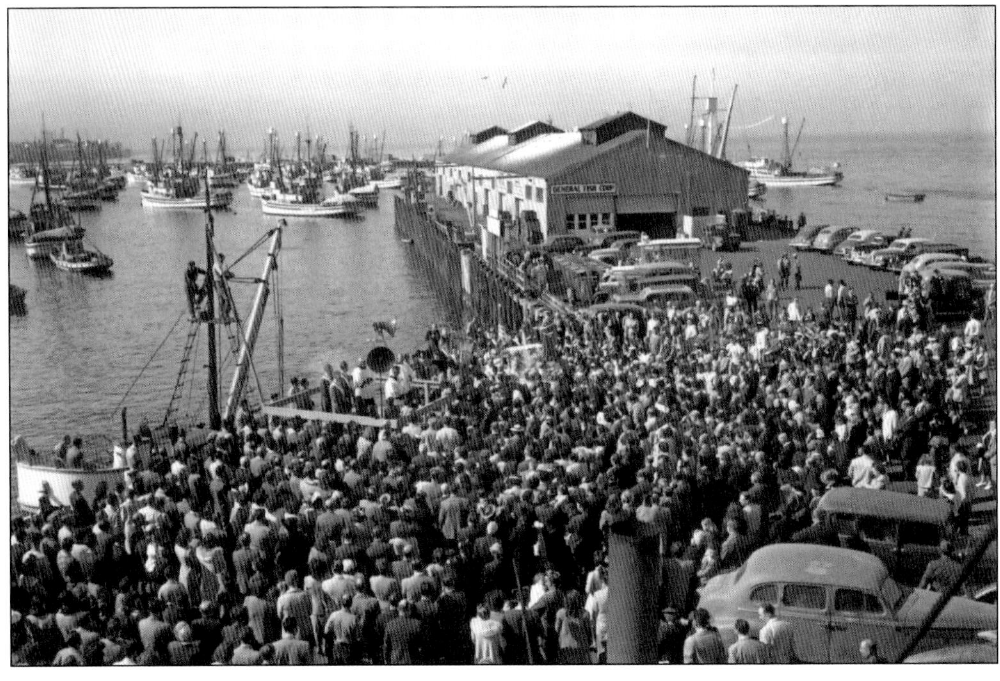

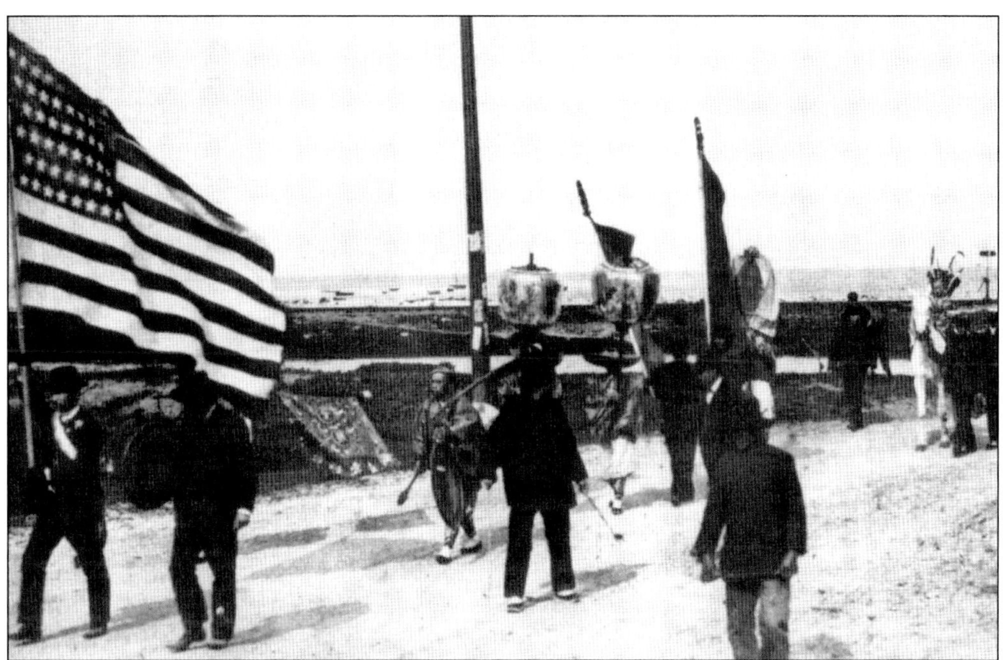

Above, in the 1946 Santa Rosalia Parade, a Chinese contingent shares in the festival as early participants in the fishing history of Monterey. Sicilians and Italians who migrated into the area had a working relationship with Chinese fishermen, but sardine fishing and deployment of the lampara net were skills mostly dominated by the Sicilian fishermen. Pictured below in September 1941, a fishermen's barbeque takes place at Wharf II during the Santa Rosalia Festival. (Below, photograph by Rey Ruppel, both courtesy of Monterey Public Library's California Historic Room.)

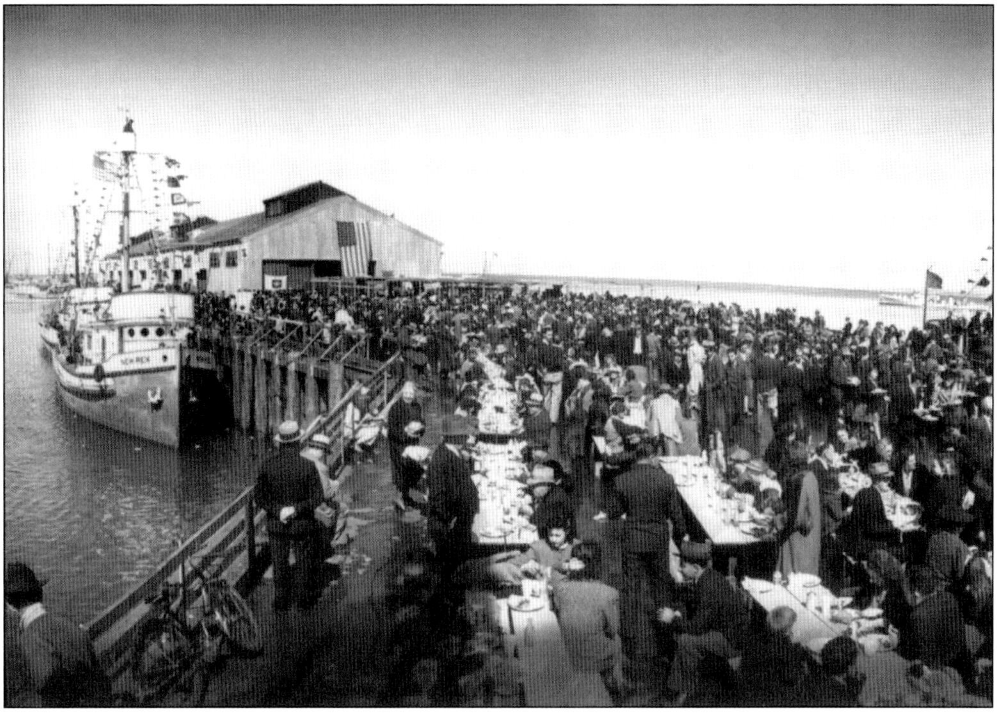

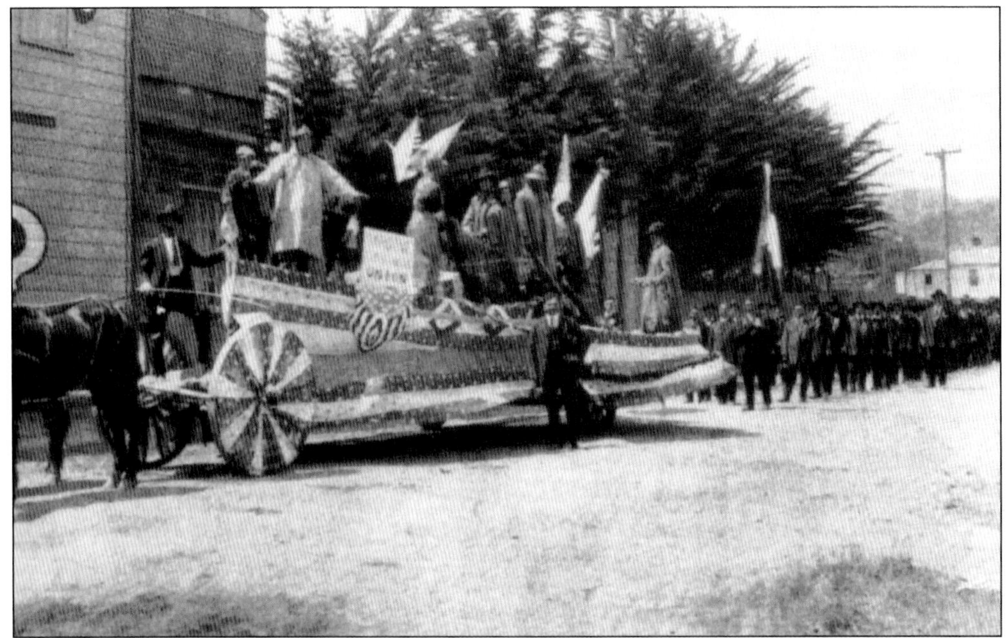

Aboard the fishermen's float (above) in the 1946 Santa Rosalia Parade are members of the fishermen's union dressed in foul weather gear. Following the float are more members of the union. Below, the Santa Rosalia Festival procession makes its way down Municipal Wharf II carrying the statue of the patron saint Rosalia. The ceremony begins with high mass at the San Carlos Church with a sermon in Italian and breakfast at the Casa Munras, and continues with a night of festivities at the San Carlos Parish Hall. (Both, courtesy of Monterey Public Library's California Historic Room.)

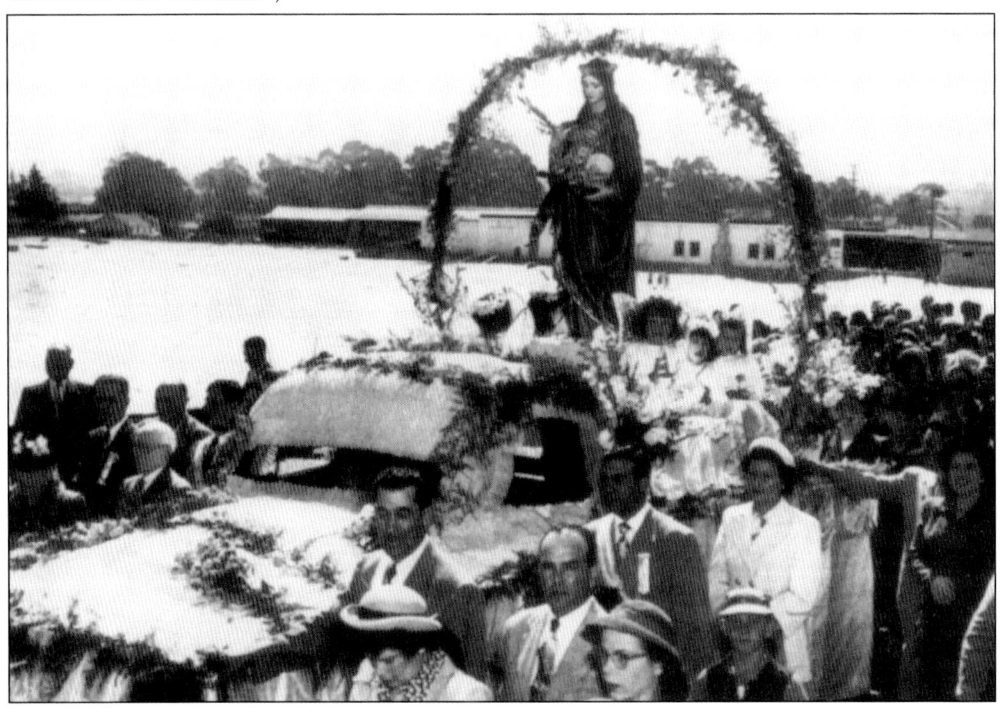

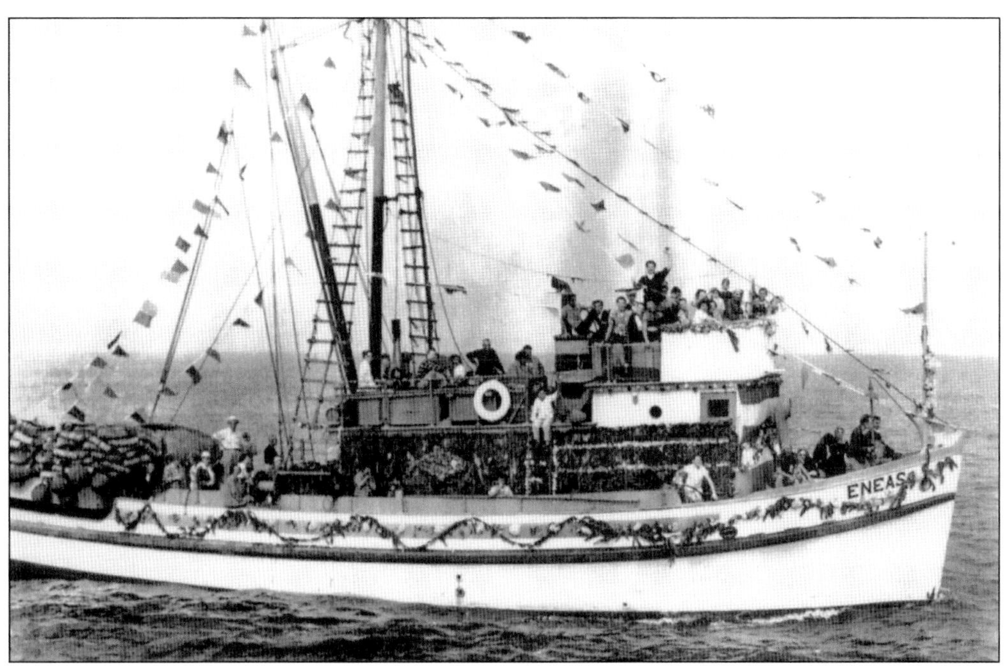


Pictured above on September 1, 1945, the purse seiner *Eneas* was built in 1935. Boat owner Orazio Enea takes his family and friends out on his boat, which is decorated for the Santa Rosalia Festival. The Santa Rosalia Parade starts from the San Carlos Mission (below) after mass and makes its way to Wharf II for the blessing of the fleet. The cathedral is the oldest continuously operating parish and the oldest stone building in California. It was built in 1794, making it the oldest (and smallest) serving cathedral along with St. Louis Cathedral in New Orleans. (Both, courtesy of the Monterey Public Library's California Historic Room.)

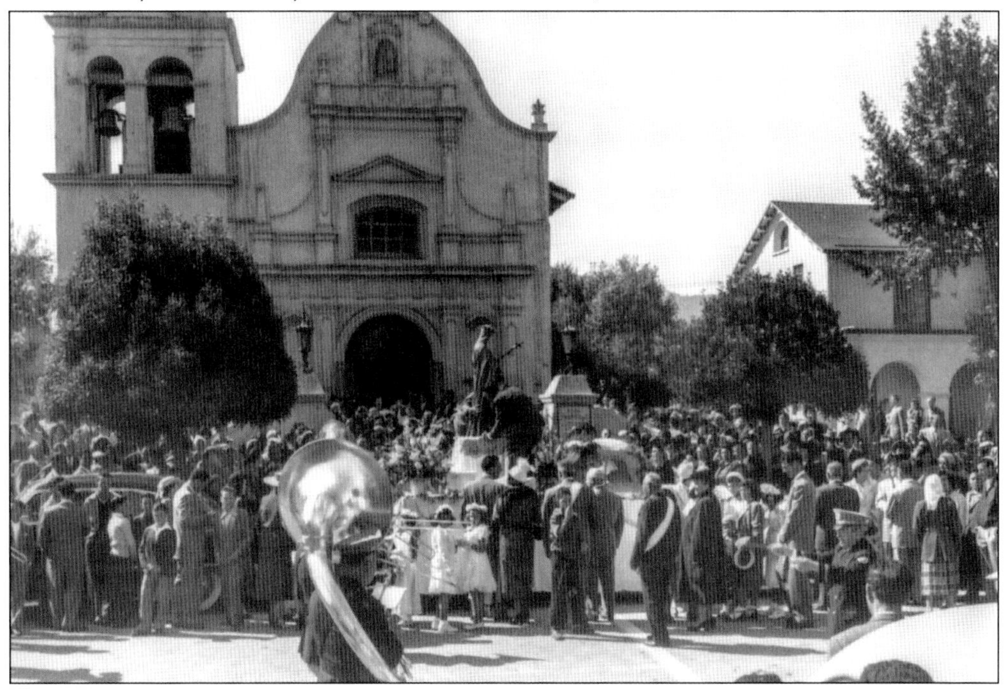

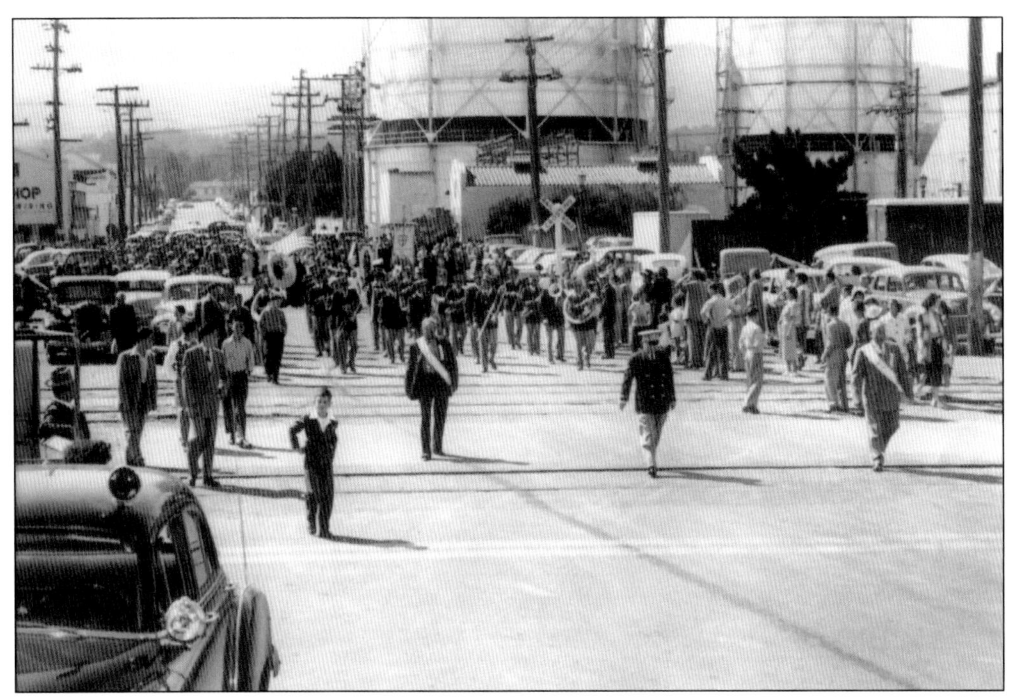


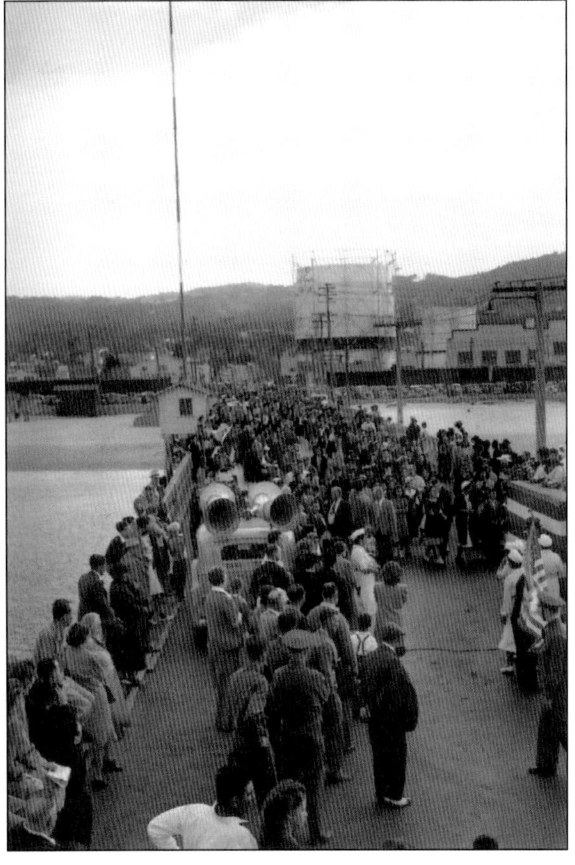

On September 24, 1950, the Santa Rosalia Festival parade makes its way down Figueroa Street to Wharf II for the blessing of the fleet. The old natural gas manufacturing plant and storage tanks are in the background. Monterey Credit Union is across the street, and Jack's Ball Park is to the rear on Franklin Street. At left, the Santa Rosalia Festival parade makes its way from San Carlos Mission to Wharf II, where the blessing of the fishing fleet will take place. (Both, courtesy of the Monterey Public Library's California Historic Room.)

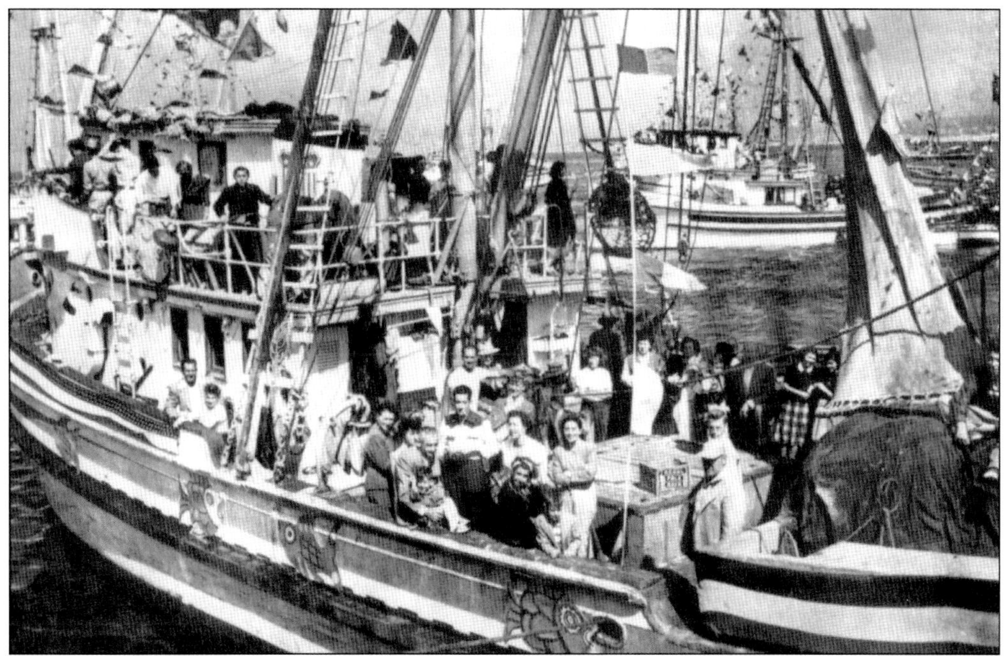

Above, at the Santa Rosalia Festival parade of boats on April 17, 1959, the public was invited aboard to get a firsthand view of the fishing boats. Several of the large purse seiners were decorated for this event. This would normally end with a ride around the harbor during the festival. Pictured below on September 8, 1946, is the Santa Rosalia Festival blessing of the fleet on Wharf II. Hundreds of Italians gather around the statute of Santa Rosalia. (Above, courtesy of the Amici Club Monterey; below, photograph by William L. Morgan, courtesy of the Monterey Public Library's California Historic Room.)

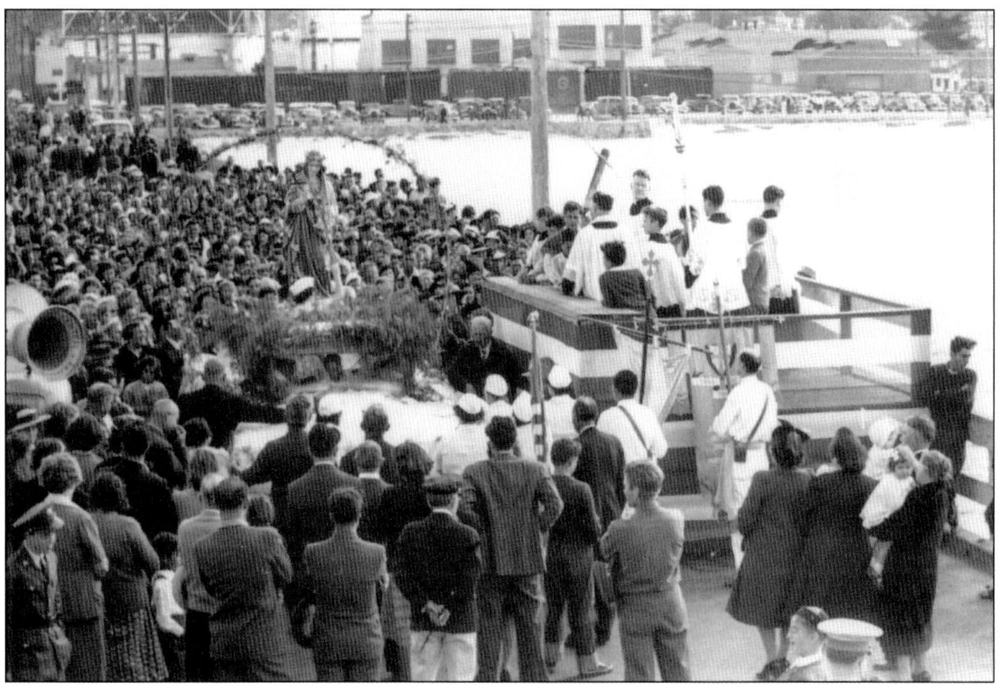

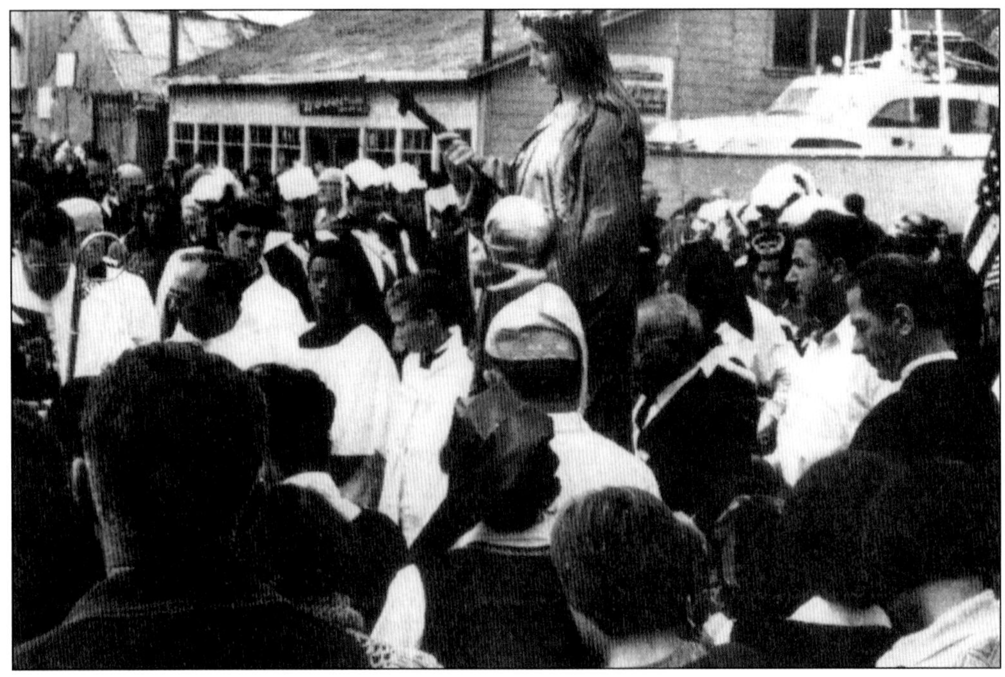

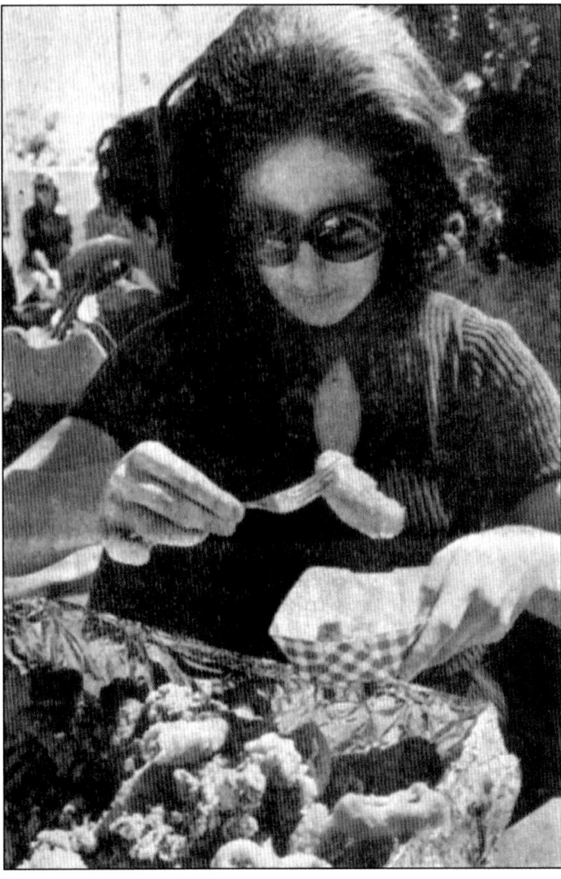

Above, on September 15, 1974, the Santa Rosalia Festival parade stops at the end of Wharf I to bless the fleet, in front of what is now Abalonetti's Bar and Grill. This ritual was an important part of the parade, honoring those fishermen who over the last year died at sea. At left, Ursula Torrente Arancio, wife of Peter Arancio, enjoys some home-cooked Italian food at the Santa Rosalia Festival. (Both, courtesy of Monterey Public Library's California Historic Room.)

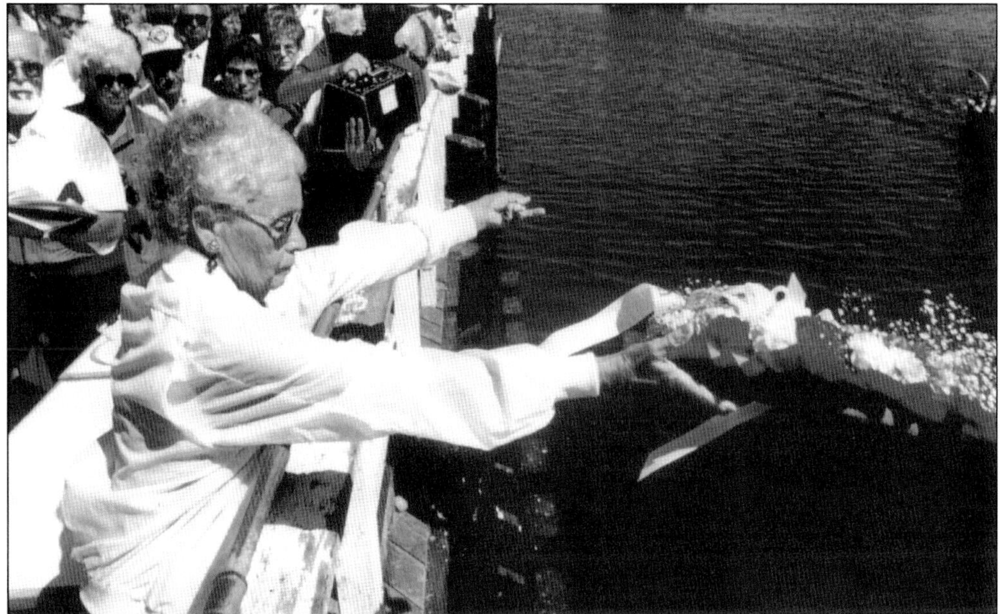

Above, Florence Iannotta Ventimiglia pays tribute to her late husband, Mike, who died in 1997. Mike Ventimiglia was born into a fishing family and fished the waters of Monterey, San Francisco, and Alaska for over two decades. He was honored by the members of the Santa Rosalia Festival and remembered in the Sicilian tradition by tossing a wreath into the sea to commemorate his years as a fisherman. Below, the Monterey Council No. 1465 of the Knights of Columbus was formed on February 6, 1910, and is among the oldest councils in California. Members of the Knights of Columbus provide an escort for the statue of Santa Rosalia during the parade. (Above, author's collection; below, courtesy of the Festa Italia–Santa Rosalia Festival.)

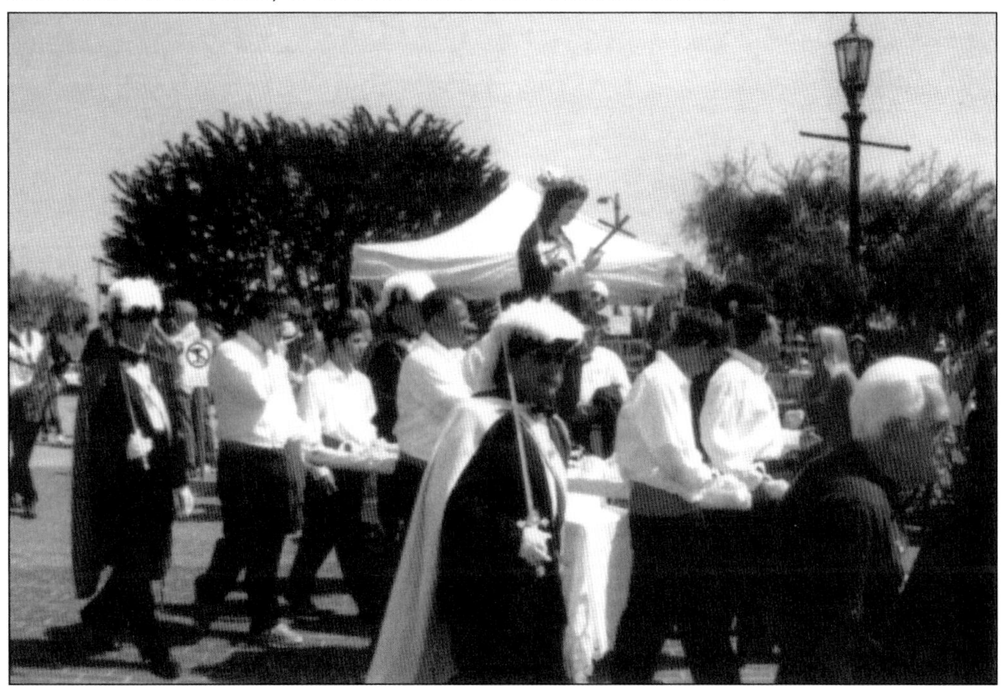

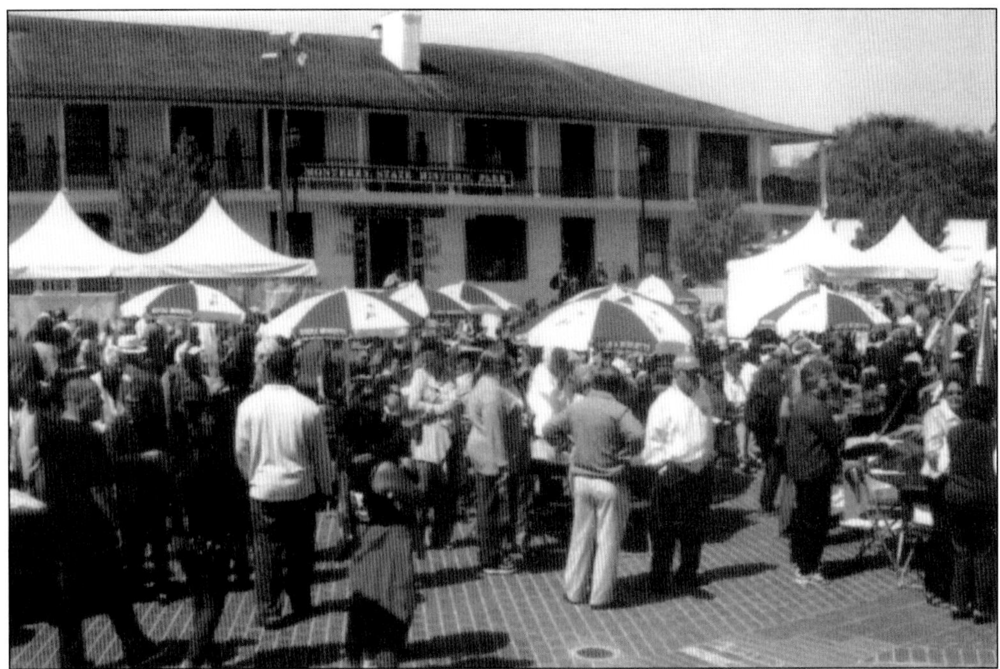

Crowds line up at Custom House Plaza for the 2012 Festa Italia–Santa Rosalia Festival, which is a three day event beginning on Friday providing Italian food, wine, music, vendor booths, a bocce ball tournament, dancing, and the blessing of the fishing fleet. Bocce ball clubs were organized in Italy and flourish in the United States. During its beginnings in the United States, there were many versions of the game. Shown below are the champions of the 2012 bocce ball tournament; from left to right are Giovanni Napoli, Ben Nicosia, Erasmo Aiello, David Clanclini, and Tony Randazzo. (Both, courtesy of the Festa Italia–Santa Rosalia Festival.)

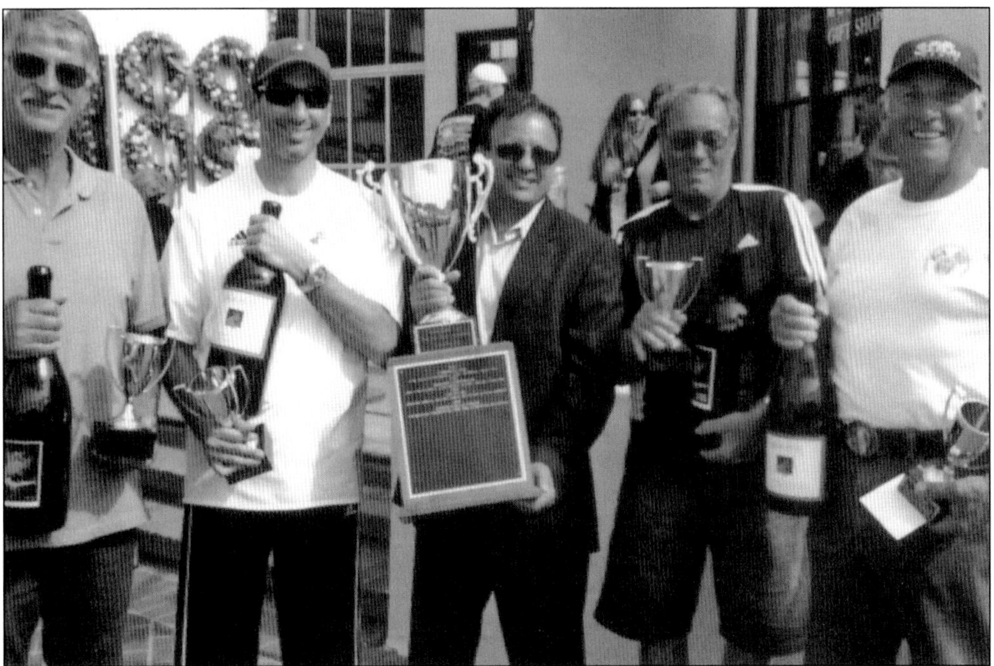

# *Five*

# Families and Traditions

The families that worked on the fishing boats and in the canneries were the fabric of the canning and fishing industry and made the businesses successful. This chapter gives tribute to the unsung families who worked and lived in Monterey and bonded as a community. They celebrated at weddings, religious ceremonies, and festivals. They learned how to enjoy the simpler things in life, like family, friends, and good food. The families were driven by a strong work ethic, and strived to improve their lifestyle over what they had in Sicily and Italy, as most could not afford property.

The tradition of naming sons after their father or grandfather would at times cause a family to have three generations under the same roof sharing the same name. Sicilian fishermen were quick to give nicknames to eliminate confusion as to who they were talking about. Names like Sloan, Ike, Trixie, Duggie, Matches, Legs, Spats, and others were used to identify specific individuals. There was usually some idiosyncrasy that caused a particular nickname to become attached to a person.

Families enjoyed coming together, as there was very limited entertainment available, perhaps a show or a dance at the Moose lodge on Saturday night or lying on the living room floor listening to fishermen talk over the shortwave radio. Weddings were a high point; nothing was spared, and the receptions were filled with ancestral food, wine, and homemade Italian cookies.

The Festa Italia in Monterey is a three-day cultural event incorporated with the Santa Rosalia Parade and blessing of the fleet. Monies generated from the Festa Italia go toward scholarships, the Monterey High School band, San Carlos School, and San Carlos Church. Over 20,000 people experience Italian culture, food, wine, singing, and dancing.

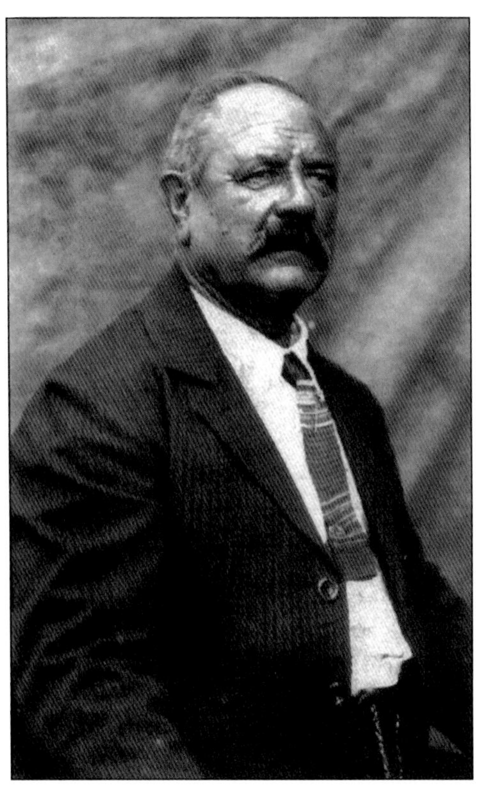

Pietro Cutino (left) came to America and fished the San Joaquin and Sacramento Rivers for salmon in Pittsburg and Martinez. He became upset about fishing regulations that would prevent him from fishing with the closing of seasons and returned home to Sicily. He married Rosa Siino Cutino, who died giving birth to her son, Paul. Pictured below, Speranza Bruno Ventimiglia was born in Isola delle Femmine in 1859, married Salvatore Costanzo Ventimiglia on February 12, 1878, and died in Isola delle Femmine in 1908. Salvatore continued to fish in Martinez, California, with his sons, leaving two daughters in Sicily. He died on March 1, 1915, on his boat in Martinez, California. (Left, courtesy of the Bert Cutino family; below, courtesy of Maria Ferrante Favalora.)

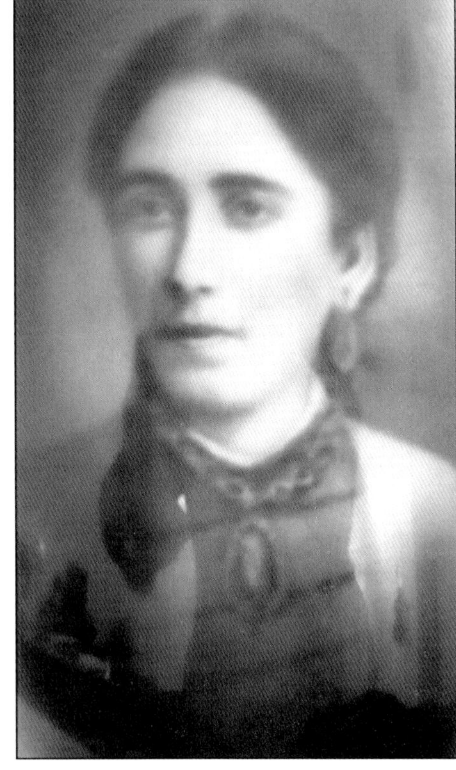

Giuseppe Iannotta (right), born in Curti, Naples, Italy, was the father of Florence Ventimiglia, the wife of Mike Ventimiglia. Giuseppe was killed by a car in a hit-and-run accident while the family was crossing the street after seeing a movie in Oakland, California. The Italian women endured so much hardship in the old country, and showed remarkable strength during hard times and continued moving forward. Pictured below is Giuseppe "Joe" Belleci in 1899, dressed in an Italian navy uniform. Joe never made it to America, but his family migrated here and started a new life. The story of the separation of families is told over and over again in the Sicilian Italian migration to America. (Right, author's collection; below, courtesy of Cathy Ventimiglia Gomez.)

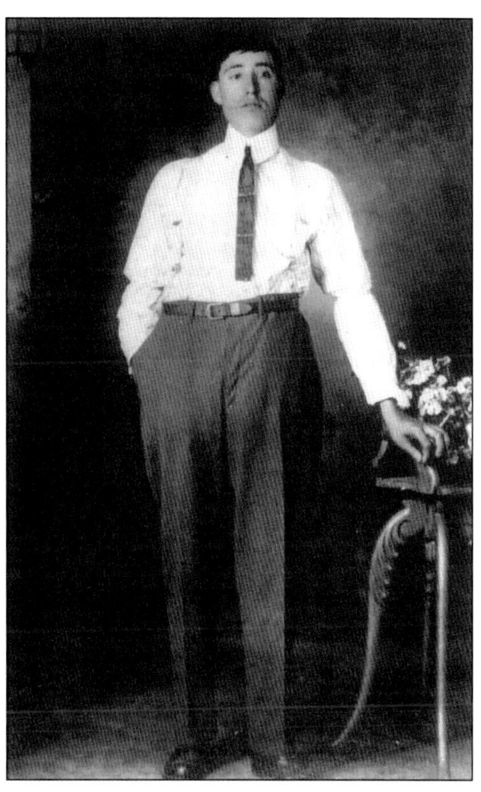

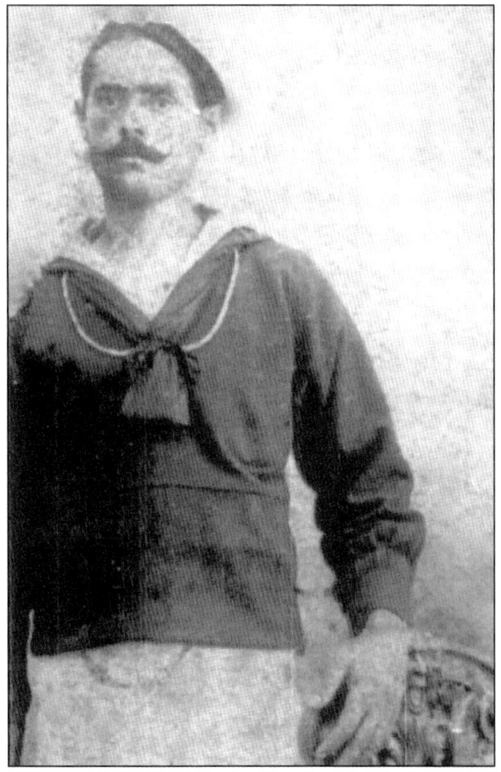

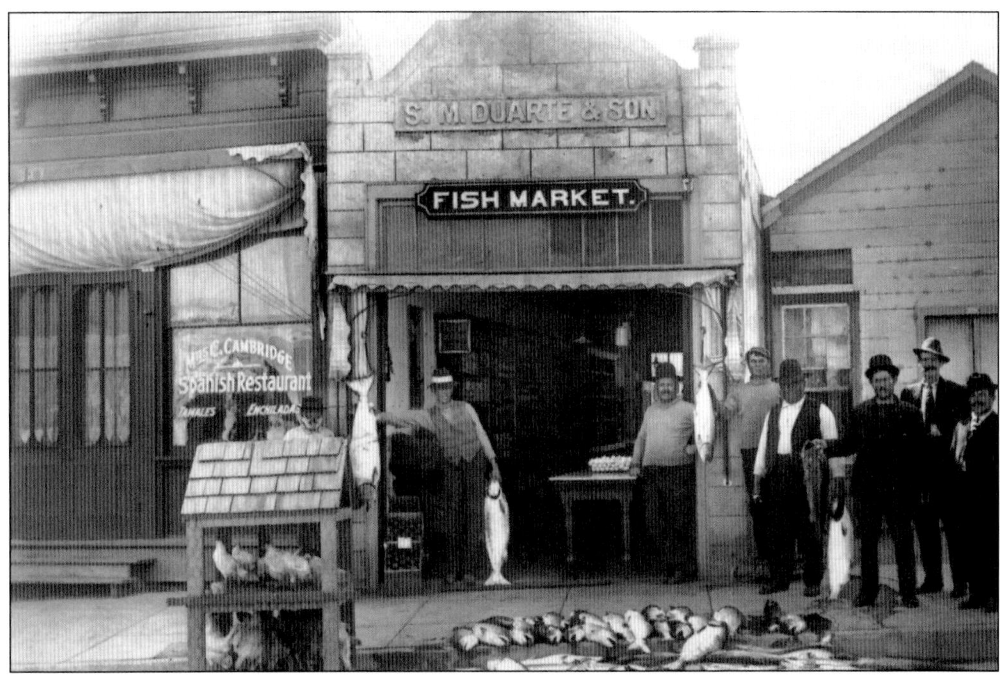


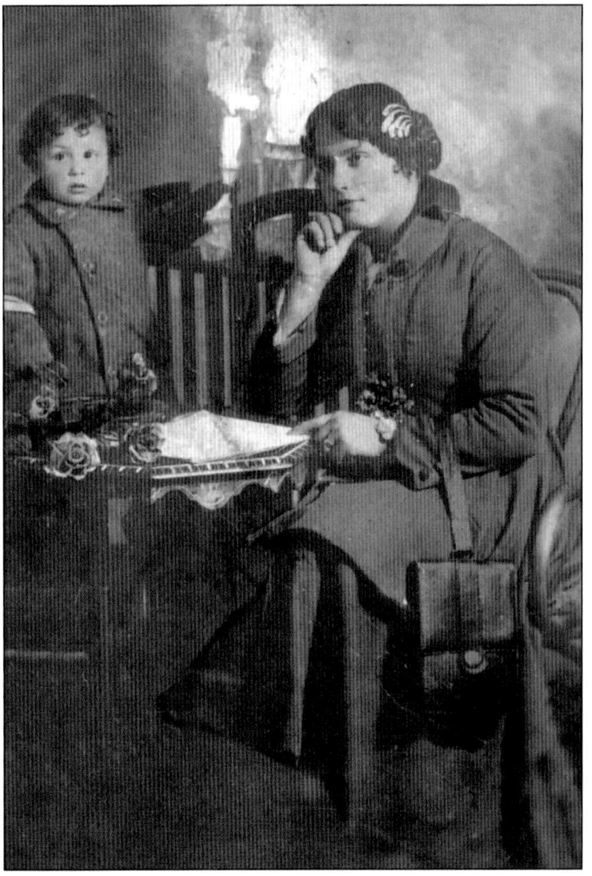

S.M. Duarte & Son (above) was owned by Santa Maria Duarte, whose father was of Mexican descent and, according to the 1910 census, lived at 503 Van Buren Street in Monterey. Duarte and his wife, Pauline, had three children, James, Leona, and Eddie. Duarte operated a popular fish market next to Mrs. C. Cambridge's Spanish Restaurant at Alvarado and Decatur Streets near Wharf I. At left, Mary Marotta DiMaria poses with her son Angelo DiMaria in the 1910s. Mary was a tailor who made all her own clothes. (Above, courtesy of Monterey Public Library's California Historic Room; left, courtesy of Laurie Hambaro, Shades of Monterey.)

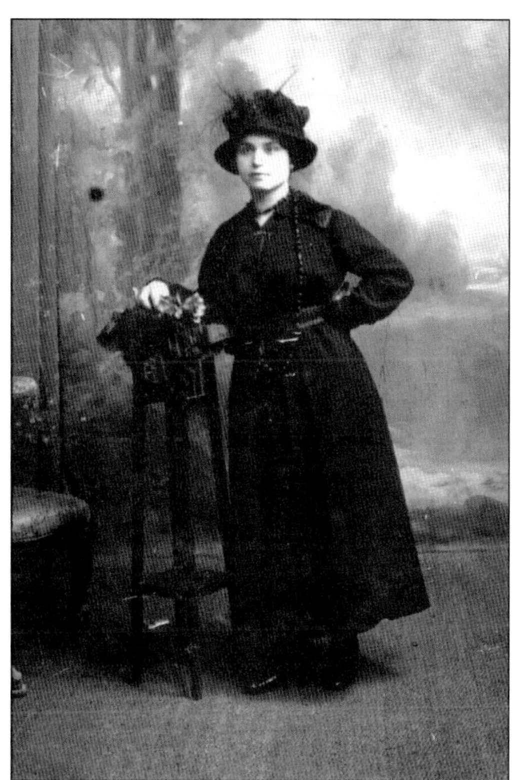

Mary Marotta DiMaria (right) was widowed in 1918, and the old Catholic rules from Europe dictated one year of heavy mourning for a widow, followed by six months of half mourning and six months of light mourning, for a total of two years. Pictured below from left to right are Tony Calabro, Ann Calabro, and Mary Calabro Roncarati. Mary would later marry Chinto "Charles" Roncarati, and they had a son, Eugene "Geno" Roncarati, who owned Calamari Specialties in Monterey. The 1940 census shows that Mary worked in the canneries as a fish packer, and the family lived at 275-A Alvarado Street in Monterey. (Right, courtesy of Laurie Hambaro, Shades of Monterey, Monterey Public Library's California Historic Room; below, courtesy of Dr. Pamela Brown.)

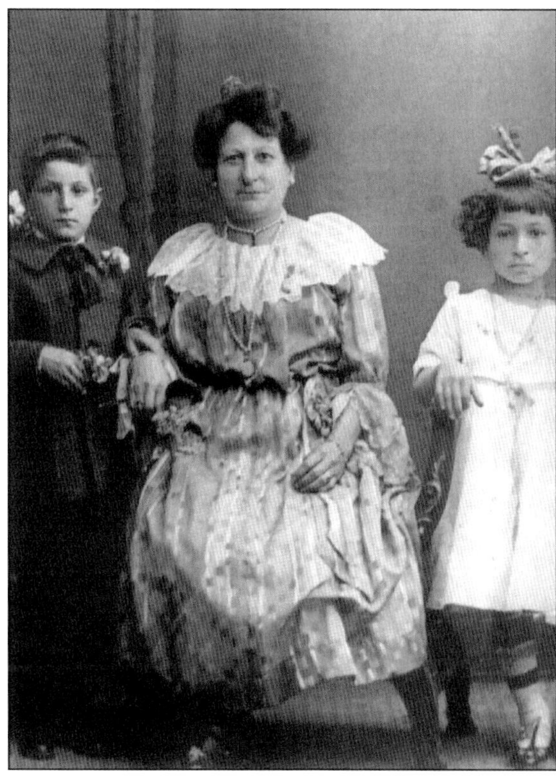

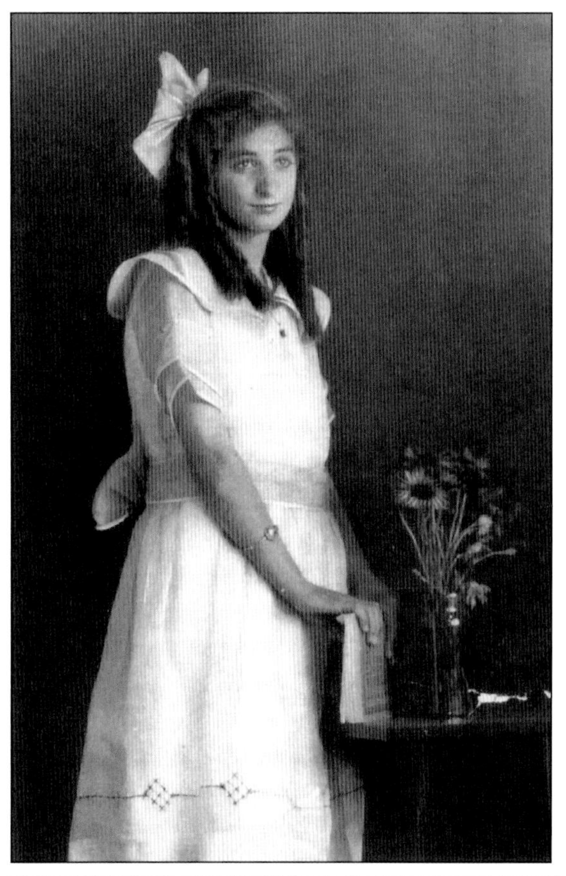

At left, Girolama Ventimiglia Torrente is shown in her confirmation gown after receiving the sacrament of confirmation from the Catholic Church at the age of 12, around 1921. She would later marry Mariano Torrente, a successful fisherman and boat owner. Pictured below in 1926, a group of Italian men gather together for a pickup game of baseball. They often played at Jack's Baseball Park in downtown Monterey, a few short blocks from Wharf II. In the first row at center is Mike Ventimiglia, age 15, holding the bat. Mike's younger brother Joseph would die in 1931 from being hit in the head with a baseball at Jack's Park. They would always have a gallon jug of homemade wine and pass it around, making the game a little more interesting. (Left, courtesy of Peter Torrente; below, author's collection.)

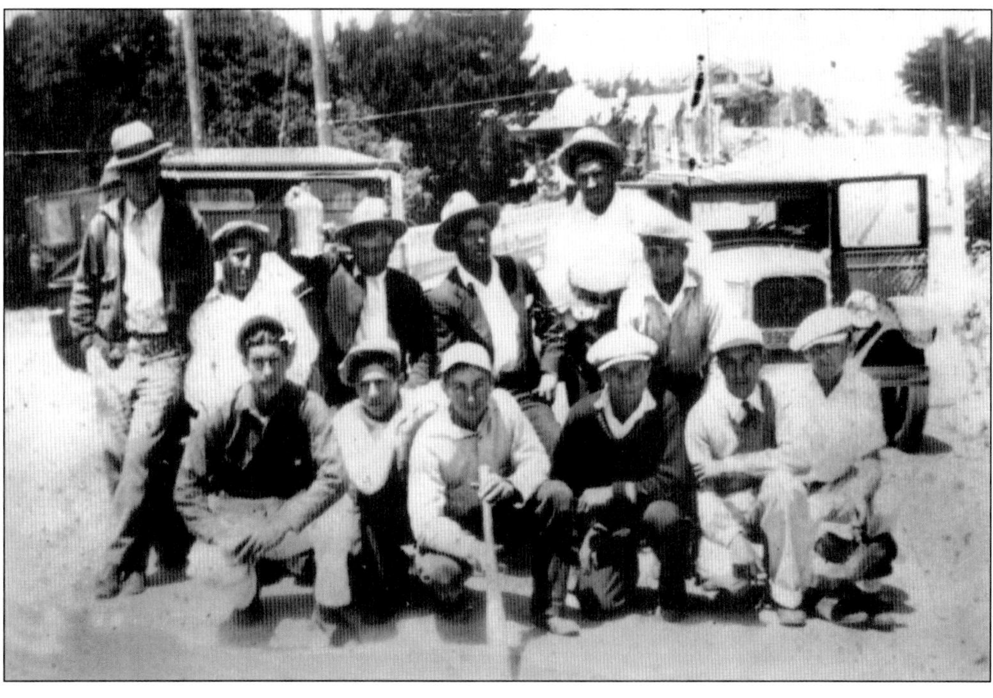

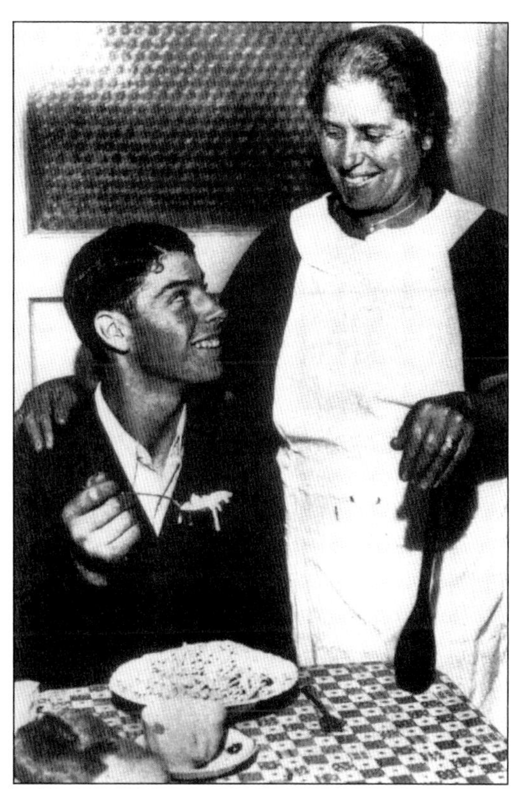

Joseph Paul "Joe" DiMaggio is pictured at right with his mother, Rosalie Mercurio DiMaggio. Joe was born in Martinez, California, on November 25, 1914, and moved to San Francisco at the age of six. He often visited the Monterey Peninsula, as he had many relatives both in Monterey and Pittsburg. Joe went on to play professional baseball for the New York Yankees, earning the nickname the "Yankee Clipper." Joe's mother's sister was Mary Grace Mercurio Ventimiglia, married to Orazio Ventimiglia. Pictured below is Maria Ventimiglia Ferrante and her son Vito Ferrante; when Vito when older, he left Sicily to come to Monterey to fish for sardines for his uncle. (Right, author's collection; below, courtesy of Maria Ferrante Favalora.)

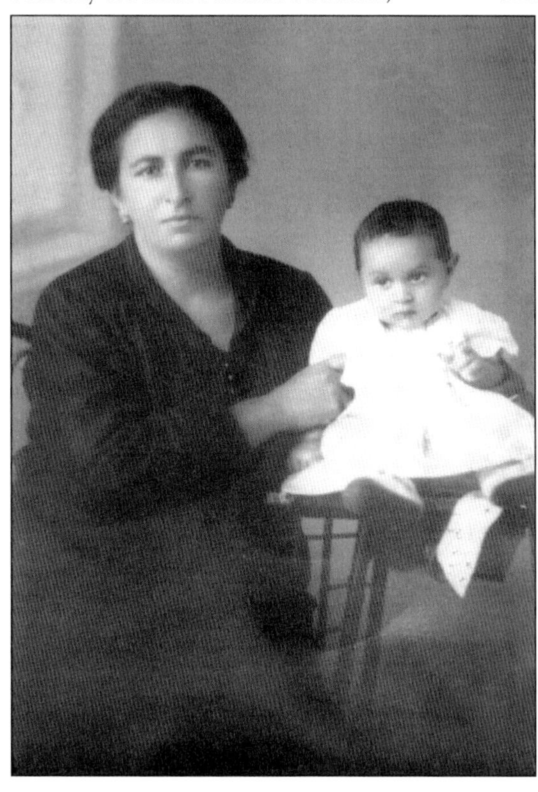

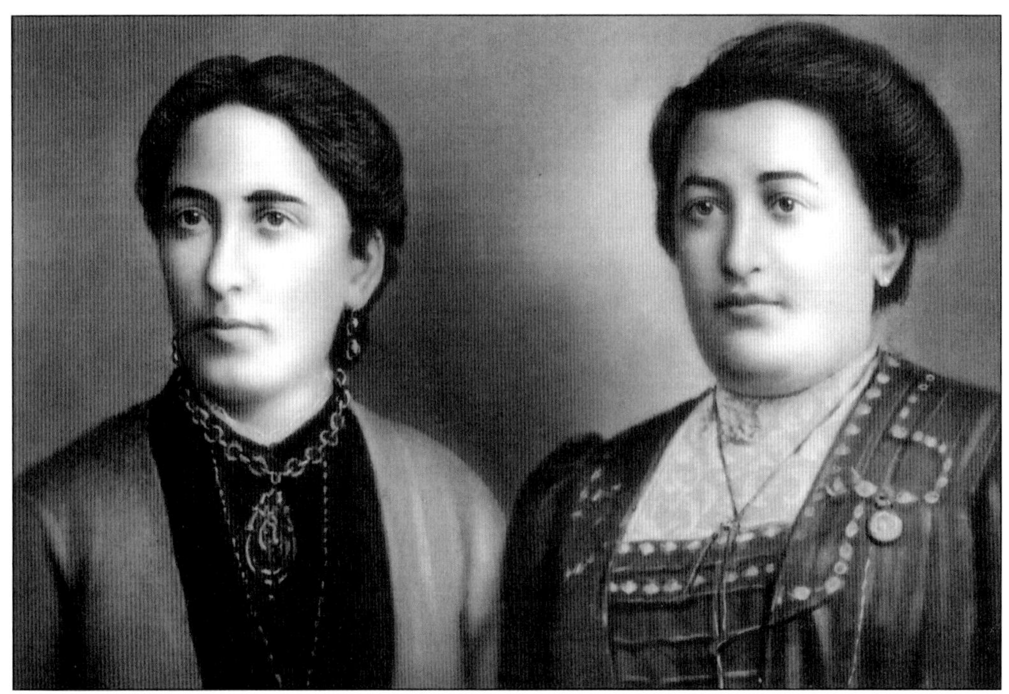

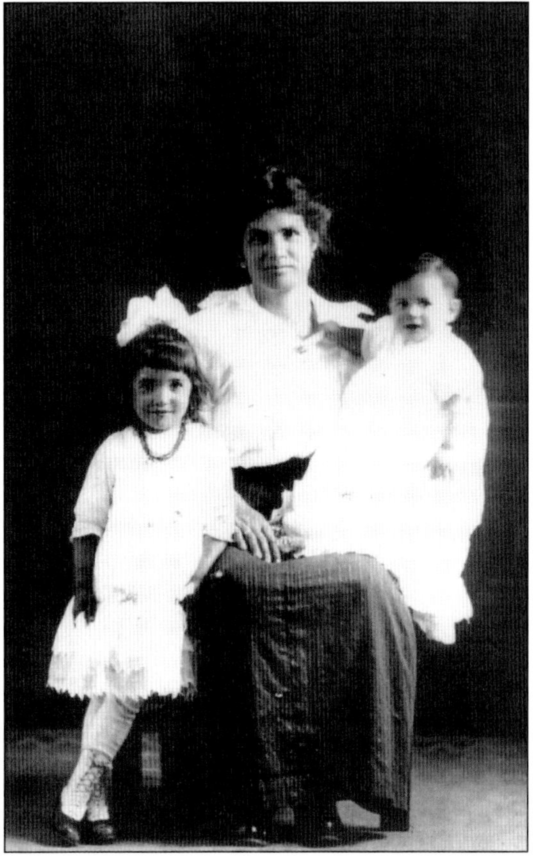

Marietta and Lucia Ventimiglia (above), daughters of Salvatore Costanzo Ventimiglia and Speranza Bruno Ventimiglia, married and remained in Sicily after the death of their mother. Salvatore Ventimiglia took his six sons, Francesco, Orazio, Gaetano, Giuseppe, Antonino, and Salvatore, to America to fish in Black Diamond. At left, Mary Grace Mercurio holds two of her children. She was the sister of Rosalie Mercurio DiMaggio and died in 1939. Prior to her death, she had to deal with the pain of the loss of one of her sons, Joseph Ventimiglia, who was hit in the head with a baseball at Jack's Park in Monterey. He died of a subdural hematoma in the middle of the night. (Both, author's collection.)

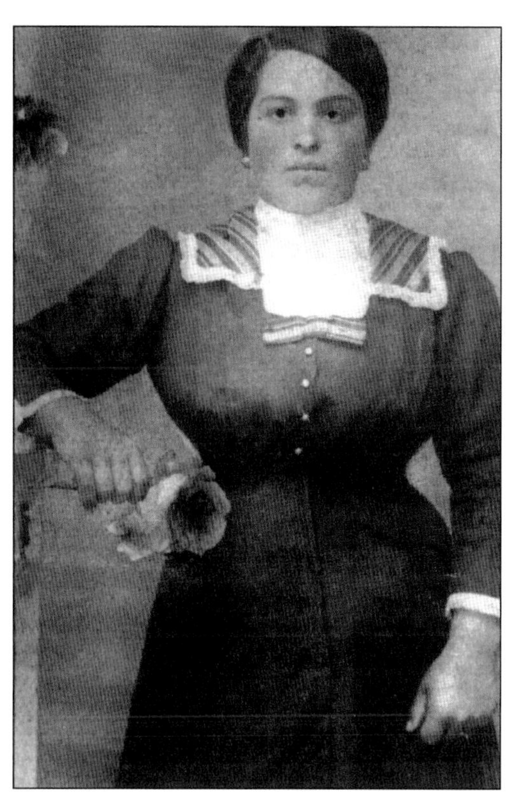

Mary Ventroni Iannotta (right), born in Curti, Italy, on May 12, 1892, was the mother of Florence Iannotta Ventimiglia, the wife of Mike Ventimiglia. Mike worked for Mariano Torrente, who married Mike's sister, fishing the waters of Monterey and Alaska during the years of the Silver Harvest. Pictured below on August 31, 1928, are Rose Enea and Louis Warren Hill, chairman and president of the board of the Great Northern Railway Company, shown here as judge for the costume contest during the Serra Pilgrimage Festival. Rose Enea (left), was one of the prizewinners. (Right, author's collection; below, courtesy of Monterey Public Library's California Historic Room.)

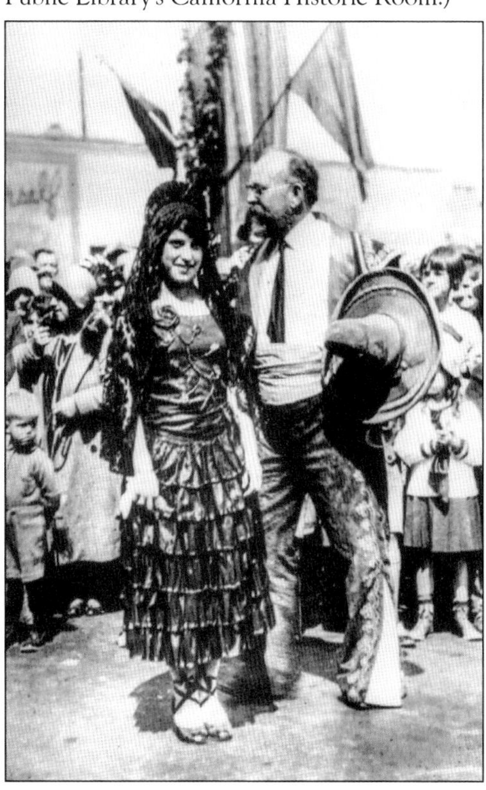

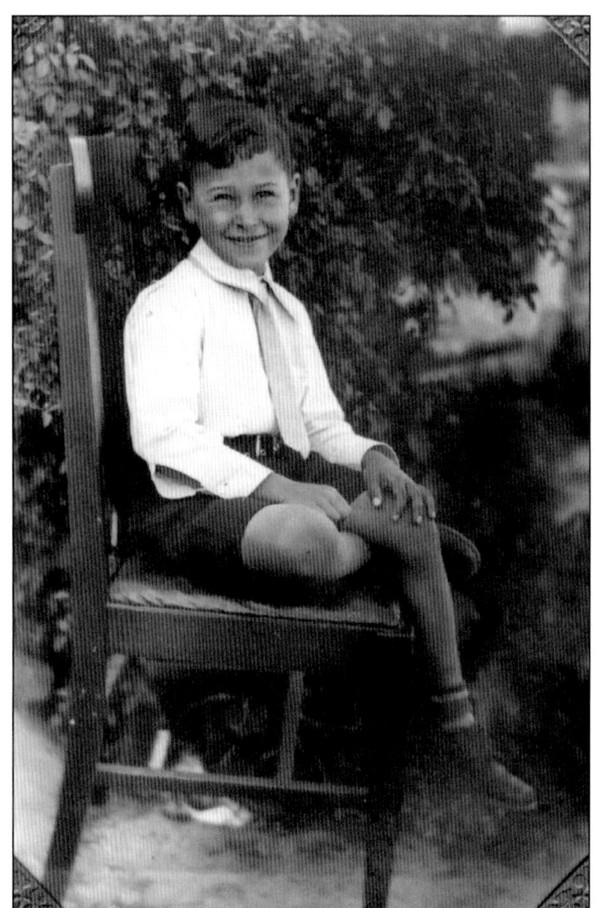

Salvatore Ventimiglia (left), whose father was also named Salvatore, was named under the Sicilian tradition of naming sons after the father and grandfather. Young Salvatore's father was a successful fisherman who owned a cannery on Cannery Row named California Frozen Fish Company. They canned fish under the brand names of New Hope and Mesa Del Rey and owned several fishing boats over the years, including the *New Hope*. Pictured below are Salvatore Ventimiglia (back row, second child from left) and his elementary school classmates. (Both, courtesy of Cathy Ventimiglia Gomez.)

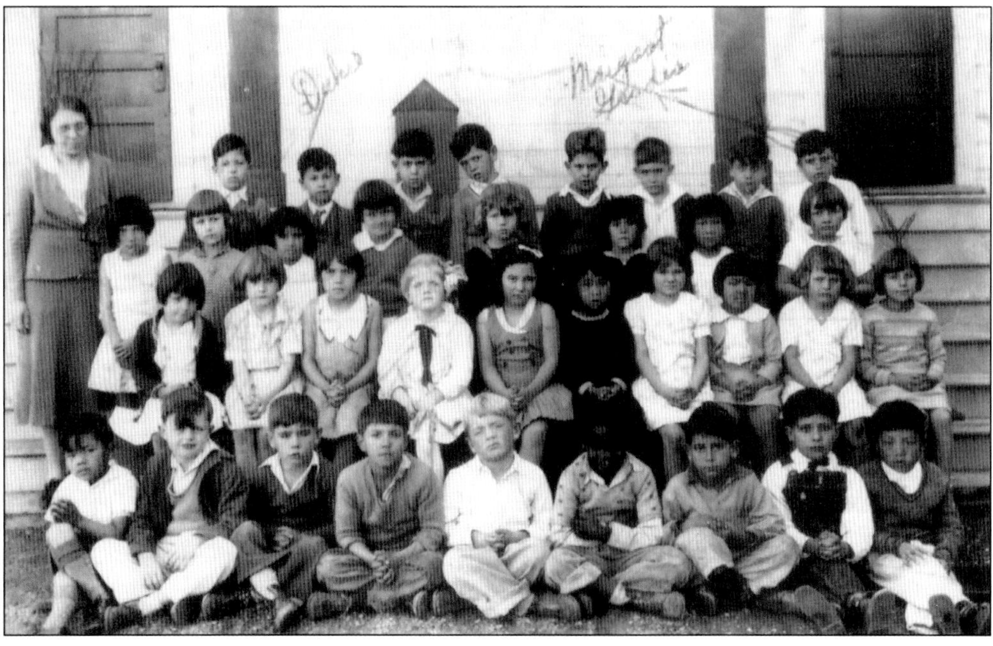

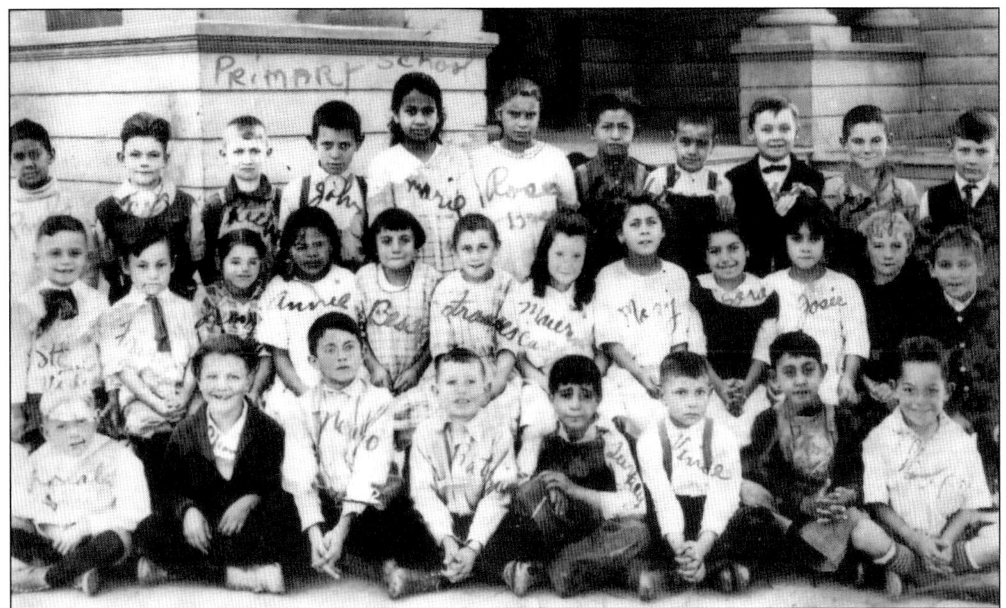

John Russo, fourth from left in the back row, is pictured above with his third grade class in 1922. John was between eight and nine years old and lived in Pittsburg, California, before the family moved to Monterey to fish. His father, Antone, was also a fisherman. Pictured below is the 1927 Monterey Merchants baseball team; in between fishing, the Italians enjoyed baseball. From left to right are (first row) Frank Cefalu, Phil Calbrese, unidentified bat boy, Phil Balesteri, Ted Rebello and Pop Warner; (second row) Louis Goldstein, Barry Salmeri, Frank "Ike" Ventimiglia, Tommy Lucido, Derby Minafo, Cookie Vargas, unidentified, and Mike Ventimiglia. (Above, courtesy of Mary D'Agui Wells; below, author's collection.)

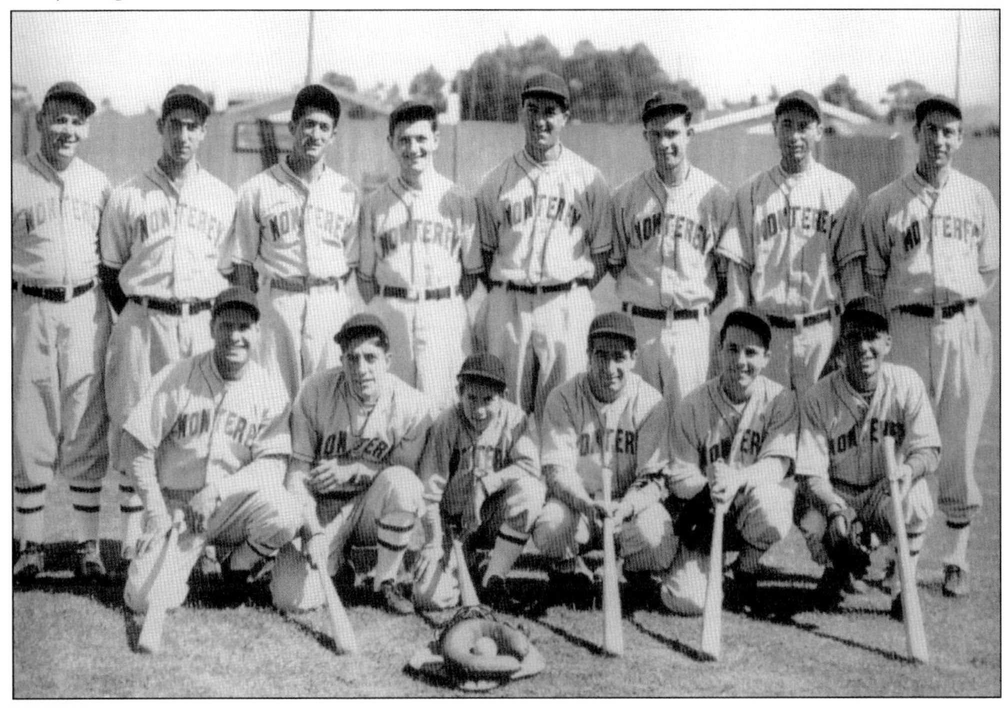

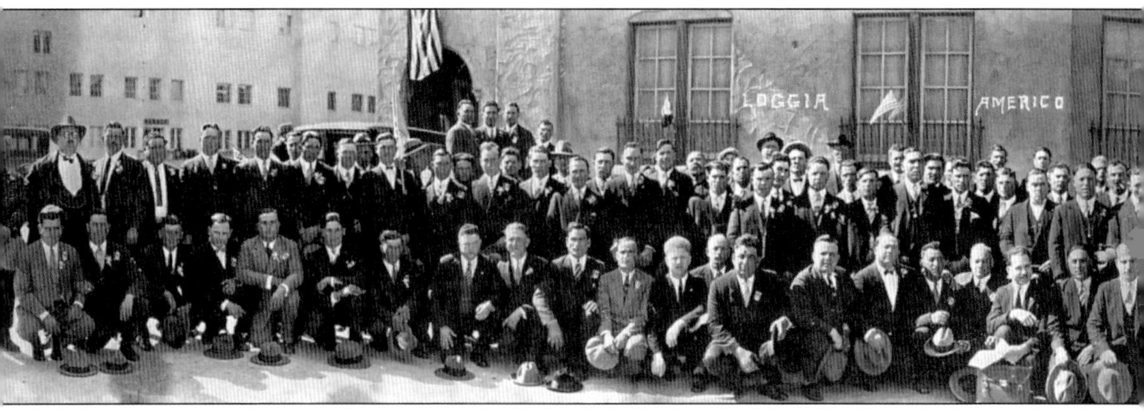


Pictured above and below, fishermen belonging to the fishermen's union pose for a group photograph on February 27, 1927. This was a proud moment for the Sicilian Italian fishermen, who came together only 15 months earlier and united, forming the Monterey's Fishermen's Protective Union. The union gave the fishermen greater power when negotiating with the local canneries on fish pricing. The unionization was a giant step for migrant fishermen, who came to the realization that there is strength in numbers. The union also negotiated with the Alaskan canneries, firming up on prices for salmon to the point that if the price was not fair, the union would tell the fishermen to stay home. (Both photographs by Heidrick, courtesy of Monterey Public Library's California Historic Room.)

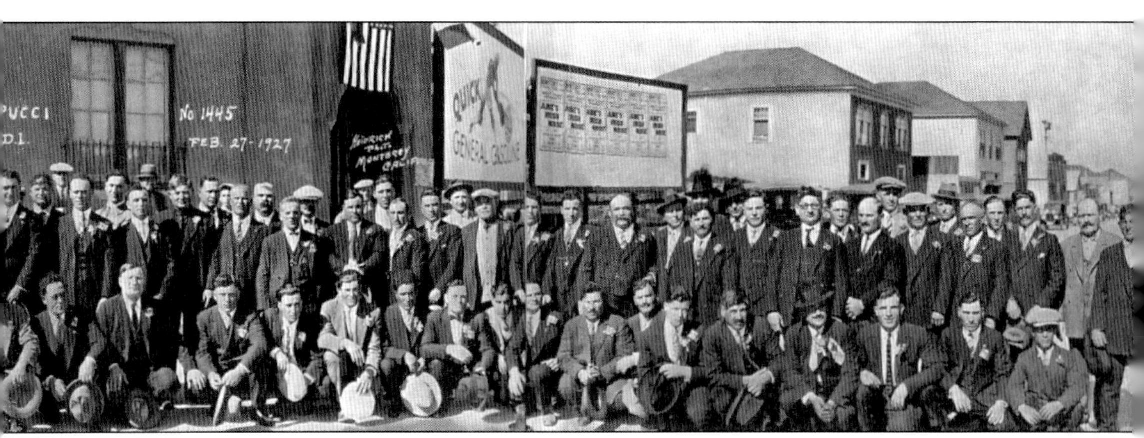

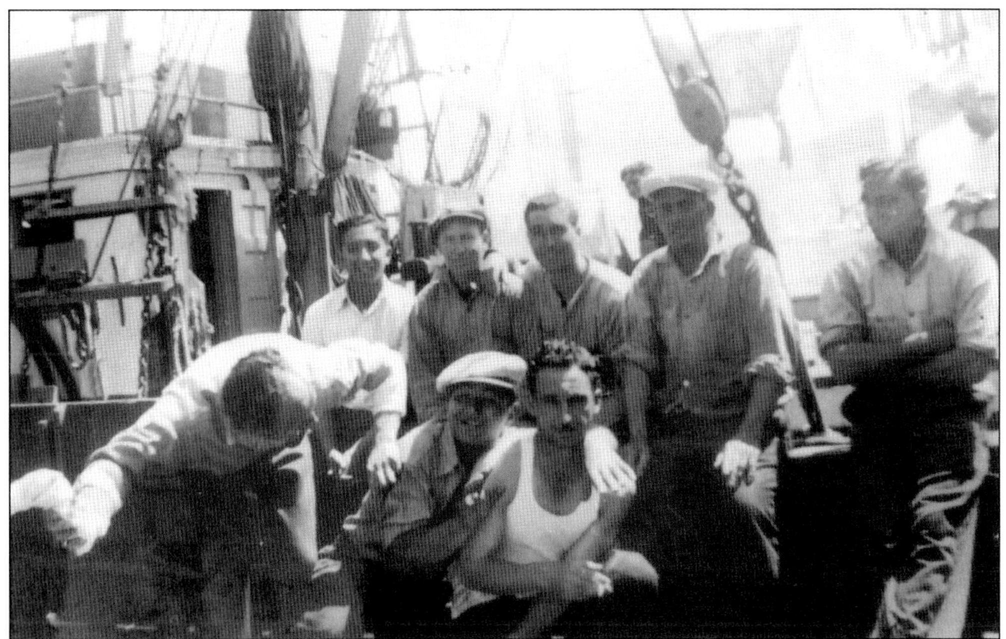

*New Admiral* crewmembers pictured above in 1930 are, from left to right, (first row) Horace Ferrante (captain), Vito Pomilia, and Tony Ferrante; (second row) four unidentified and Joe Ferrante. The boat was owned by brothers Horace, Tony, and Joe Ferrante. Additional crewmen included Pietro Teresa (advisor), Su Giovanni Aliotti, Frank "Buckets" Russo, Joe Criecu, John Lomanto, and one Japanese man called "Moonie." Pictured below is Anastasia's fish market in 1950; from left to right are Joseph Anastasia Sr., Jennie (his wife), and sons Phillip and Joseph. The market is now the home of Old Fisherman's Grotto Wharf I. (Above, courtesy of Vince Ferrante; below, courtesy of Angela Anastasia McCurry, Shades of Monterey, Monterey Public Library's California Historic Room.)

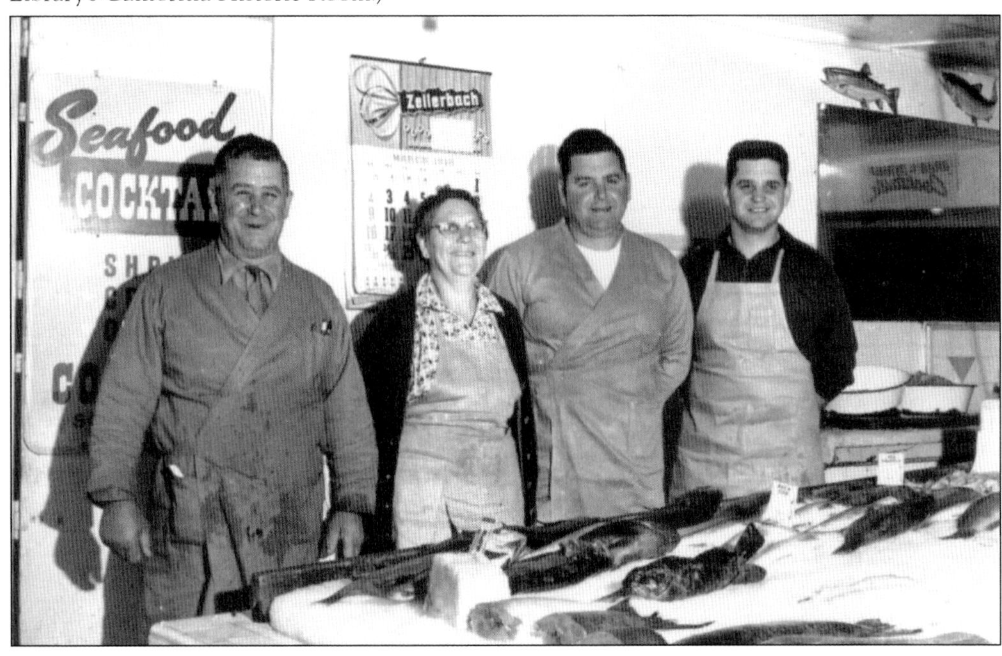

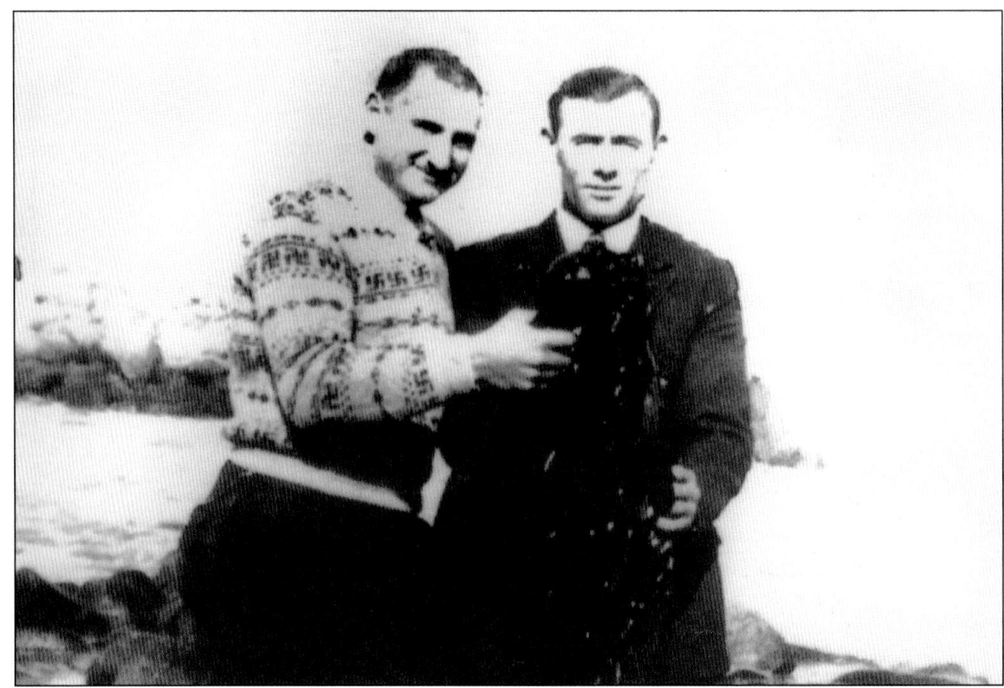

Pictured above in 1930, Jack Aiello (left) and Paul Cutino pose off Ocean View Avenue in Pacific Grove. The two were hunting for sea urchins (known in Sicilian slang as *reetzis*) in the tidal pools approximately where Hopkins Marine Station is now located. Regarded as something of a delicacy today, urchin roe was eaten raw in most Mediterranean cultures. Below, a group of Italian fishermen in 1932, with trunks packed, are headed for Alaska to fish for salmon for six weeks during June and July. They would fish on cannery boats, making a couple of thousand dollars, but work on the two-man boats was hard and dangerous. Local fishermen still fish the Alaskan waters, but it is not the same as the craft their forefathers practiced. (Above, courtesy of the Bert Cutino family; below, courtesy of Peter Torrente.)

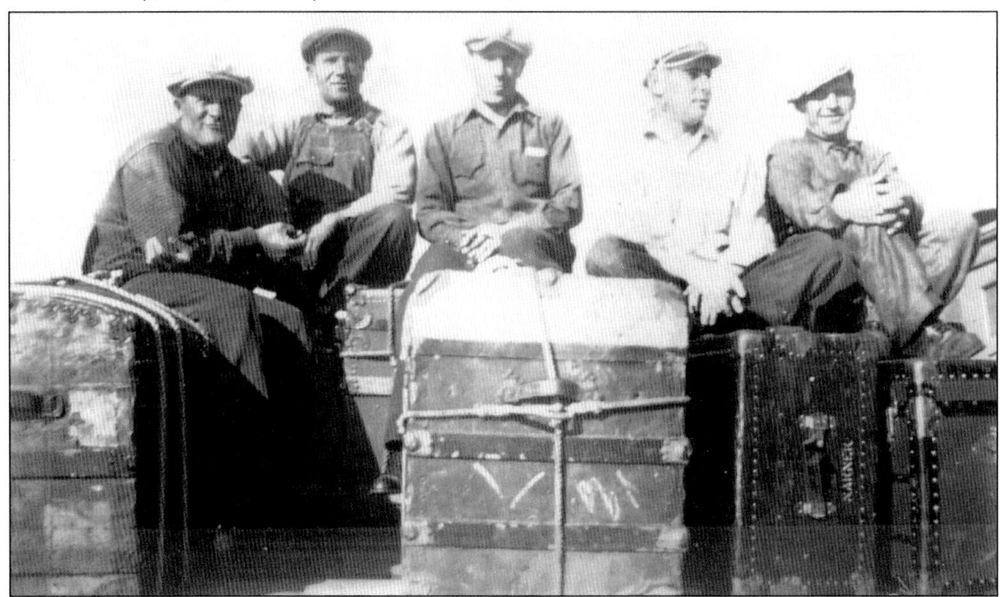

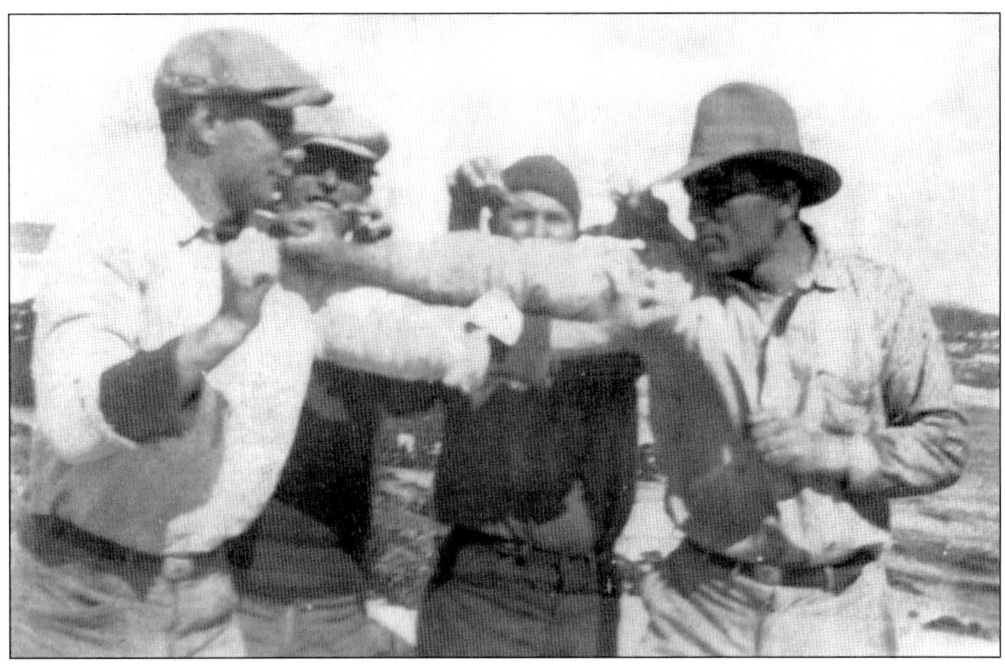

These fishermen are taking a break from fishing in 1936 during a full moon. Fishermen often took breaks from fishing during the full moon, as the reflection of the moon shines upon the water and the sardines cannot be seen. When the full moon is gone, the sardines shine in the water. Fishermen often visited Lover's Point in Pacific Grove with their family and friends during the day. Pictured above from left to right are Mariano Torrente, John Grammatico, Mario San Paolo, and Yago. Pictured below on the rocks at Pacific Gove beach are Mariano Torrente (left) and Mario San Paolo. Mariano has an apple in one hand and a bottle of red wine in the other. They would search for sea urchins, a Sicilian delicacy, and eat the roe. (Both, courtesy of Peter Torrente.)

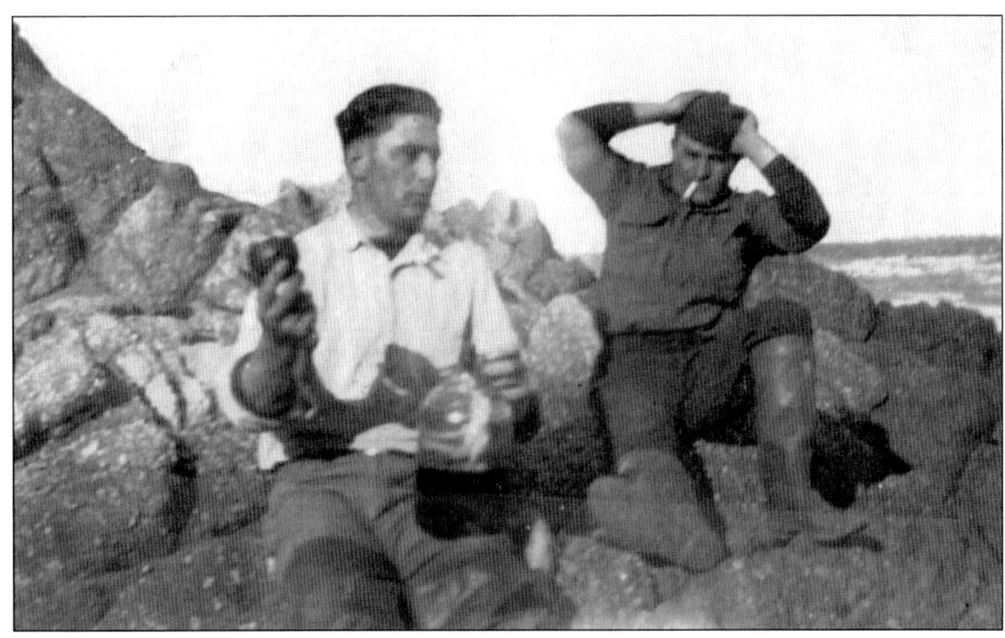

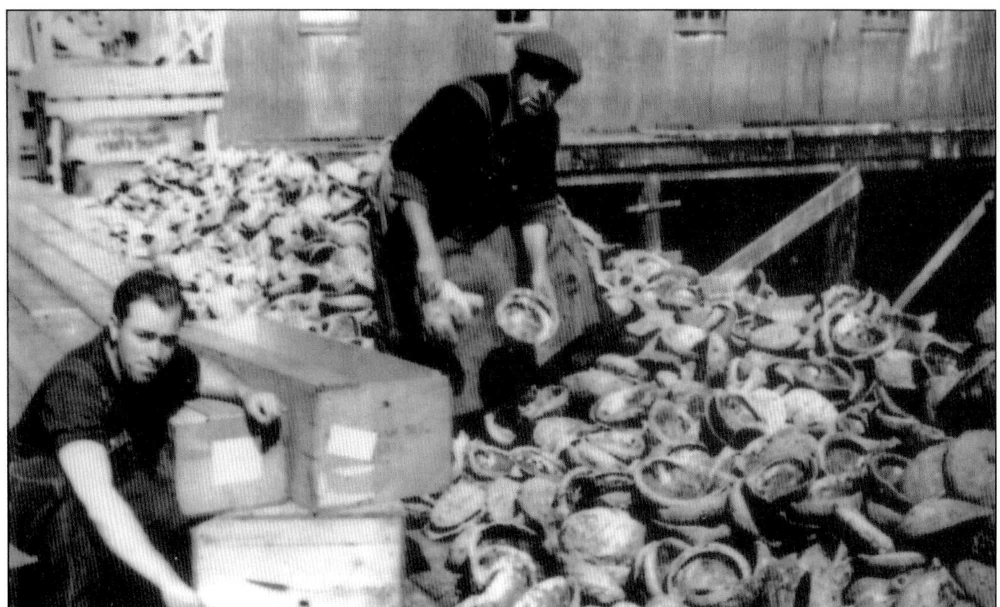

Pictured above at left, Cottardo J. "Monk" Loero worked as a manager in a fish market on Wharf II and lived at 80 W. Franklin Street in Monterey. The 1930 census lists his father, John, and mother, Estrella, as well as John, Cottardo and Josephine, Monk and his siblings. Frank Balesteri (right) lived at 574 Cortez Street in Monterey and worked for the San Francisco International Fish Company. Pictured below from left to right are Speranza Ventimigli Ernandes, daughter Catherine Marie, and Frank Ernandes. Speranza worked in the Booth Cannery as a floor supervisor when the sardines were flourishing in Monterey. Catherine, her daughter, would later marry Giuseppe "Joe" Cardinale, a successful fisherman and boat owner. Catherine would become a successful businesswoman and involved herself in the Italian community. (Above, courtesy of the Bert Cutino family; below, author's collection.)

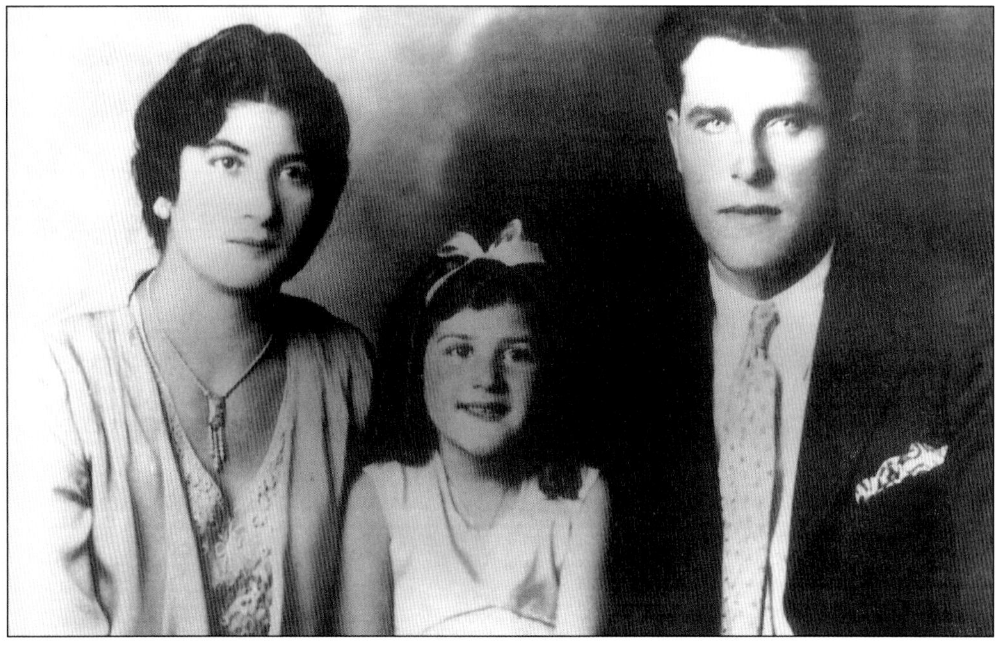

Pictured at right is the wedding portrait of Katherine "Katie" Aiello and Salvatore Colletto, a successful commercial fisherman. Below are Mario Lucido and Katherine "Kay" Russo on their wedding day. Mario was a commercial fisherman and lived at 258 Oliver Street in Monterey with his father, Neno, who was also a commercial fisherman. Mario and Kay were married at the San Carlos Cathedral in 1941, and after his return from World War II they lived at 281 Lighthouse Avenue and later moved to Hollister, California, in 1953. (Right, courtesy of the Bert Cutino family; below, courtesy of Katherine Lucido, Shades of Monterey, Monterey Public Library's California Historic Room.)

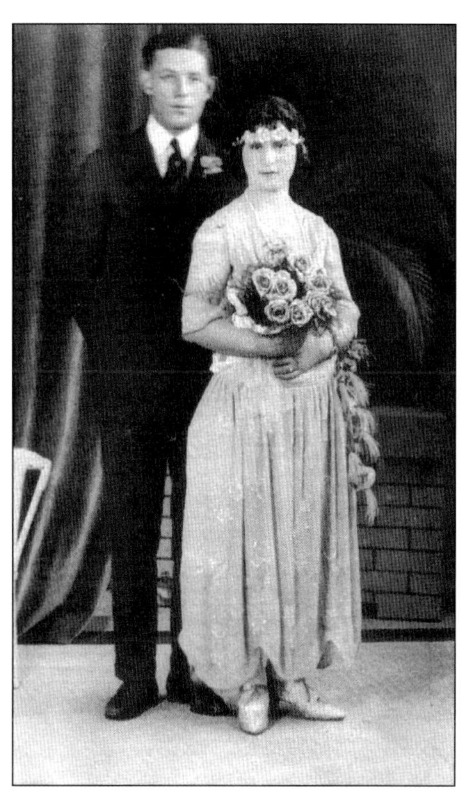

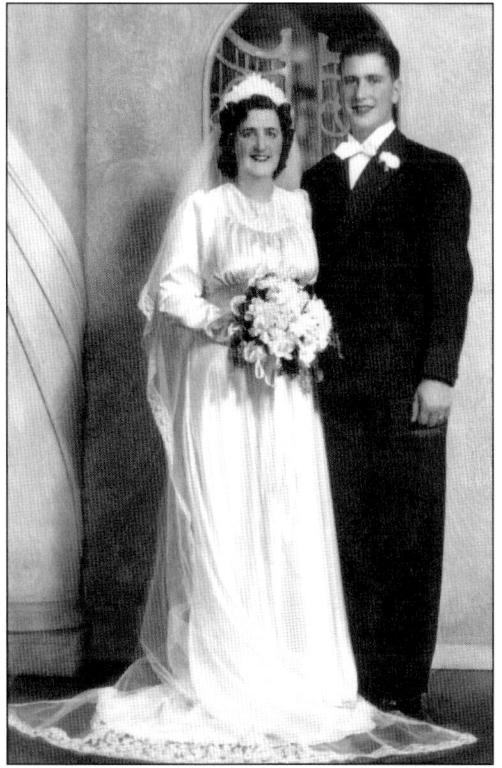

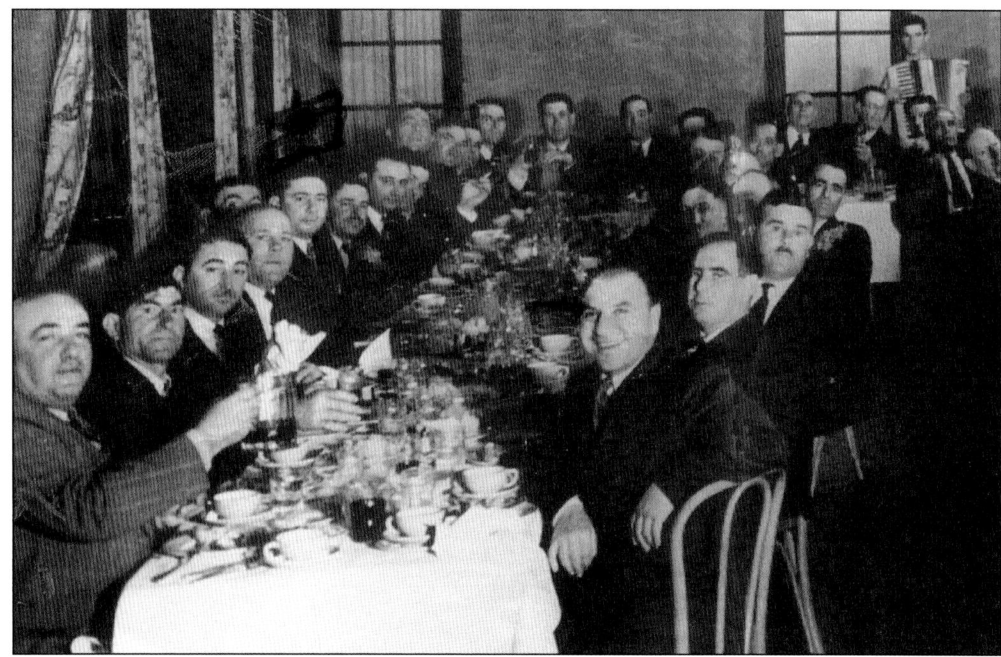

The 1939 Boat Owners Association dinner, hosted by the Monterey Sardine Industry Inc., was a special dinner to thank the boat owners for their contribution to the sardine industry. The annual dinner was a time for the owners to get together and celebrate their successes. Throughout the sardine fishing season, fish tallies in tons would be kept on each boat by the various canneries to determine the top skipper and top boat owner during that particular fishing season. The leading skippers earned bragging rights and also credit for their ability to run a boat. (Both, courtesy of Monterey Public Library's California Historic Room.)

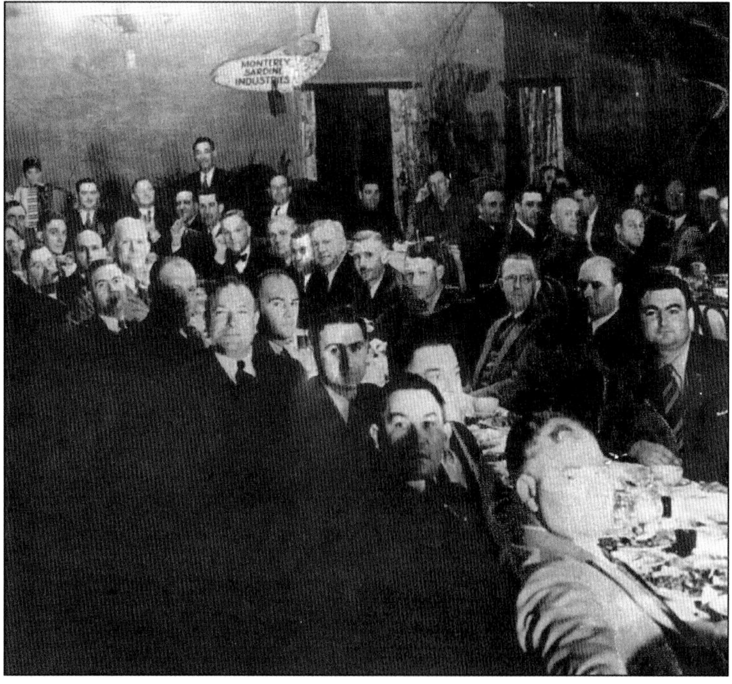

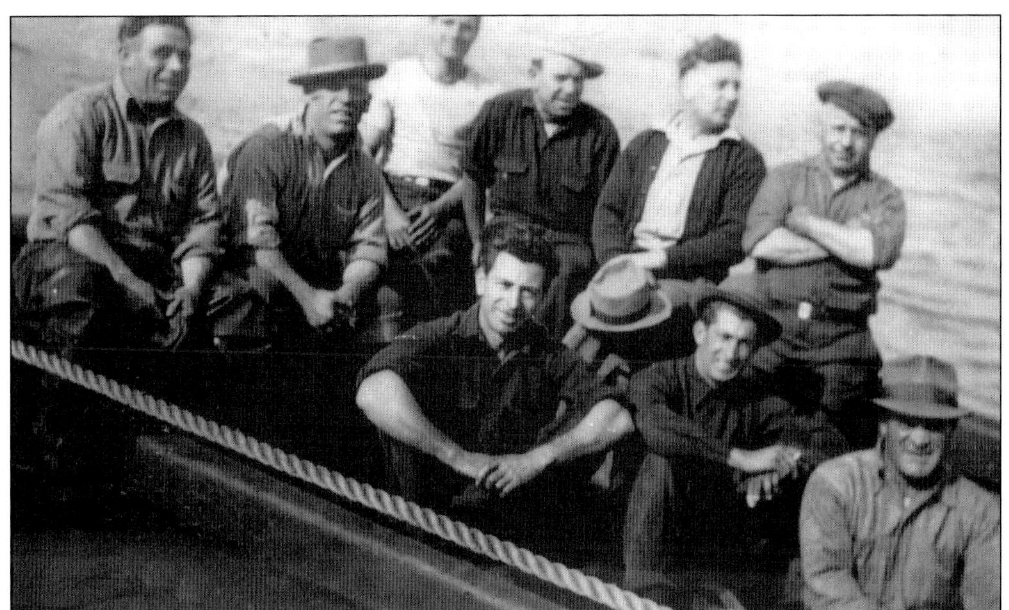

Pictured above are the crew of the *Vagabond*, a purse seiner owned by Mariano Torrente, about 1930; from left to right are (first row) Mike Ventimiglia, Frank "Ike" Ventimiglia, and Mario San Paolo; (second row) Peter Rocha, John Grammatico, Joe Cardinale, Sal Rombie, Capt. Mariano Torrente, and unidentified. Pictured at right is Salvatore Castaldo, who was born in Pazzallo, Sicily, on May 12, 1880. He was a rigger in a shipyard in Alameda, California, before moving to Monterey with his family. Salvatore often fished in Alaska in the off season, and he was lost at sea. (Above, courtesy of Peter Torrente; right, courtesy of Anne Castaldo Jay.)

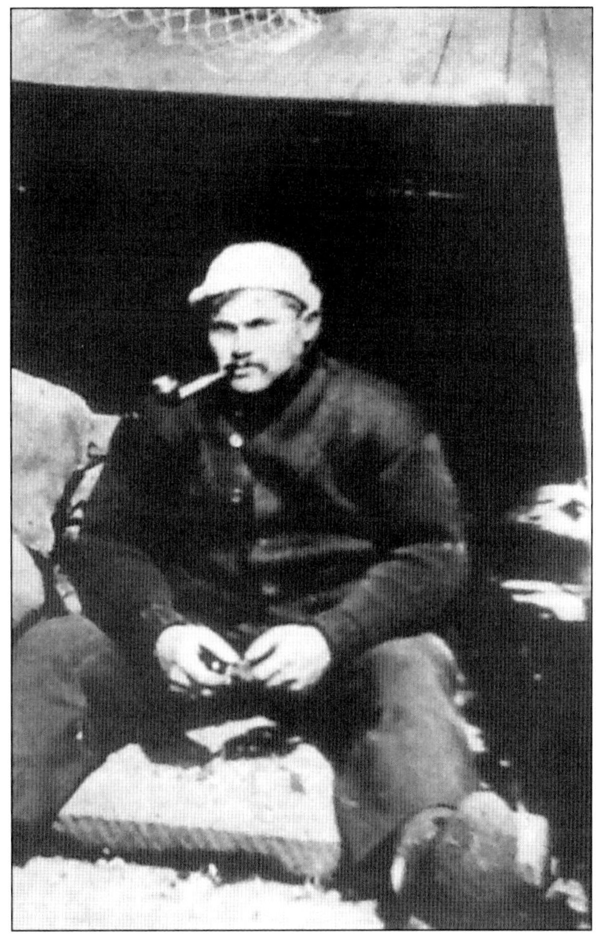

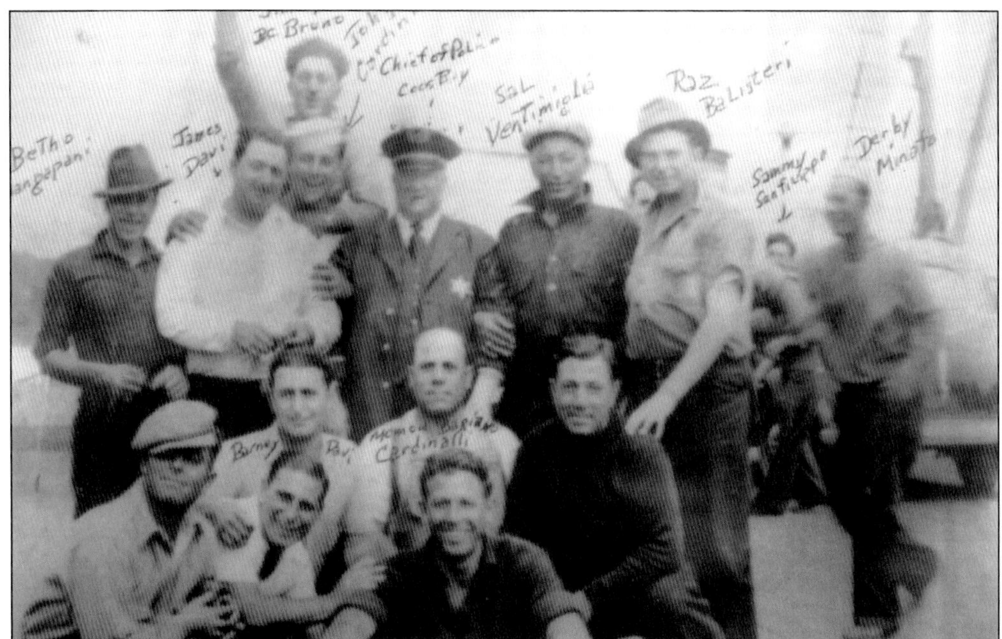


Above, fishing in Coos Bay, Oregon, from left to right are (first row) unidentified, Sparky Enea, and Dan Ventimiglia; (second row) Barney Davi, Momou Bariao Cardinalli, and Frank Minafo; (third row) Betho Mangapani, James Davi (Coos Bay chief of police), Salvatore Ventimiglia, Raz Balesteri, Sammy Sanfilippo, and Derby Minafo; (fourth row) John Cardinalli; (fifth row) Jimmy "BC" Bruno. Pictured below is the crew from the *New Rex*, fishing the waters off of Coos Bay in 1935. The introduction of the purse seiner boat allowed fishing boats to travel farther up and down the coast for fish, as the boat was equipped with amenities smaller boats did not have. (Above, courtesy of the Amici Club Monterey; below, courtesy of Peter Torrente.)

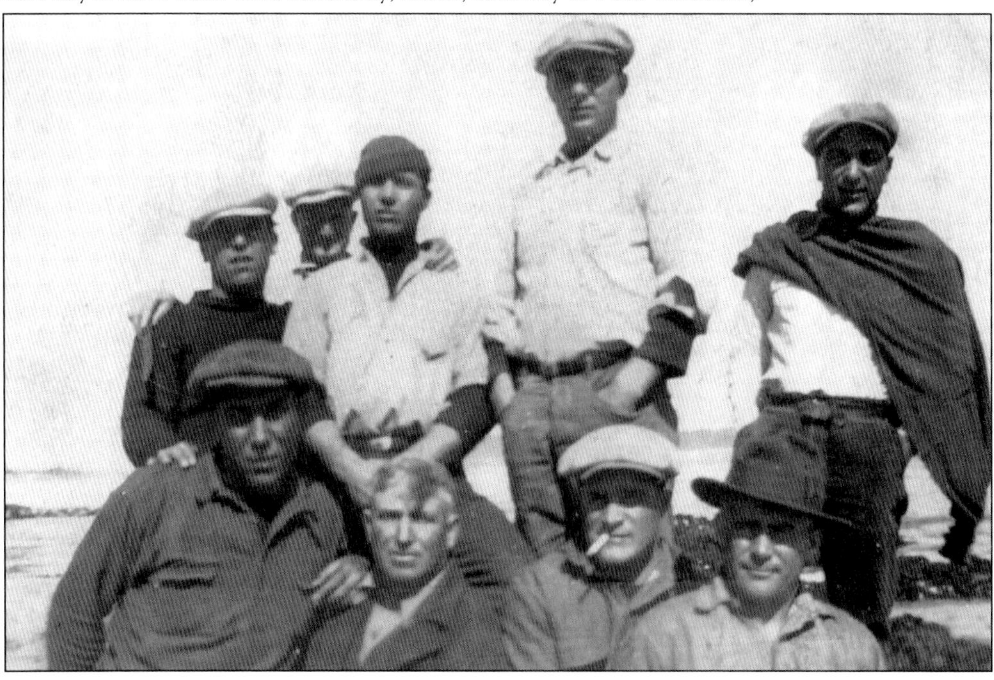

In 1935, John Cardinalli (right) was born into a fishing family; his father followed the fishing seasons, fishing in Pittsburg, the San Francisco Bay area, and Monterey. He joined his father-in-law, Salvatore Ventimiglia, and continued to fish in Monterey and Alaska. In 1963, he purchased the Yellow Cab Company and became a successful businessman for over 48 years. He was an active member in the community and belonged to various organizations, including the Italian Catholic Federation, Moose lodge, Knights of Columbus, and the American Legion. Pictured below is Frank "Sarley" Cefalu practicing his batting swing in 1936; baseball was a favorite pastime for Italians when not fishing. (Both, courtesy of Cathy Ventimiglia Gomez.)

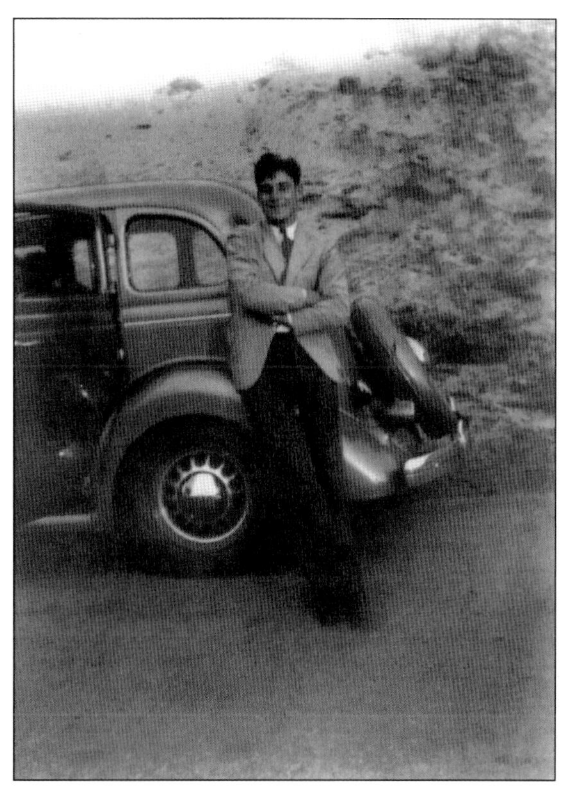

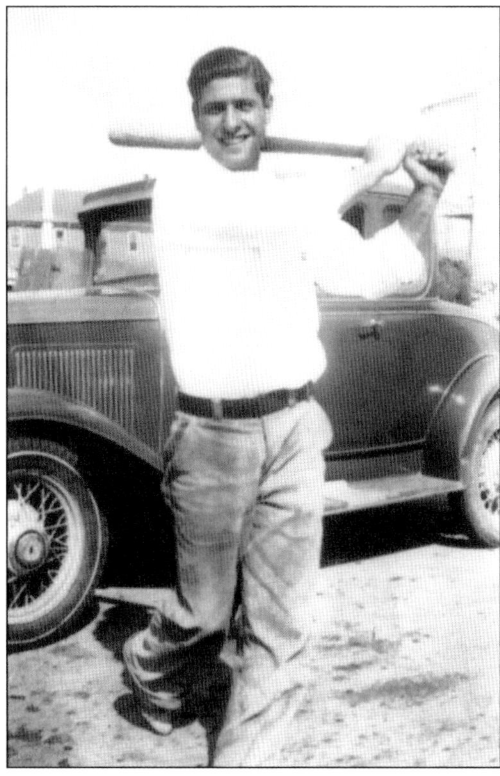

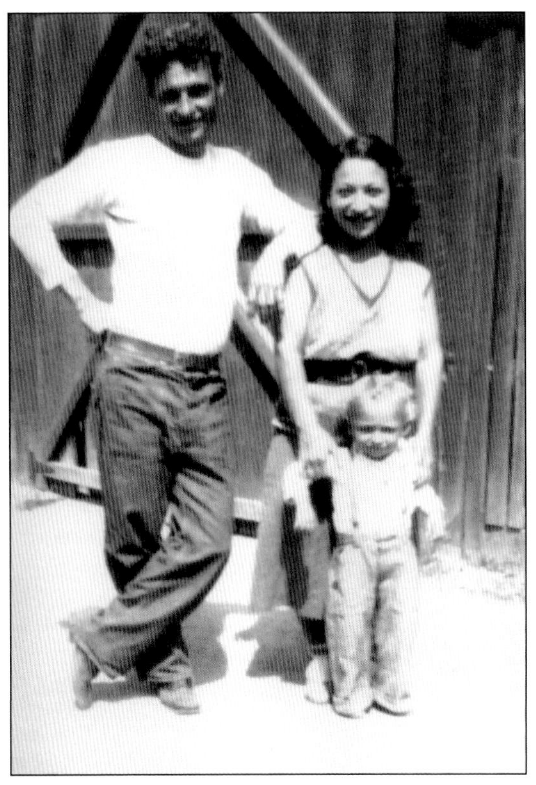

Pictured at left from left to right are Chinto "Charles" Roncarati, his wife, Mary Calabro Roncarati, and their son, Eugene Roncarati, in 1937. Charles was a garbage distributor for the canneries, and his wife, Mary, was a fish packer. Their annual combined salary in 1939 was $731, according to the 1940 census. Pictured below are the Jefferson Street kids in 1941; from left to right are (first row) Tony Rappa and John Coniglio; (second row) Francesca Giaconda; (third row) Paul Giamona, Peter Cutino, and Frank Bottero. The kids grew up together and played neighborhood games. (Left, courtesy of Dr. Pamela Brown; below, courtesy of the Bert Cutino family.)

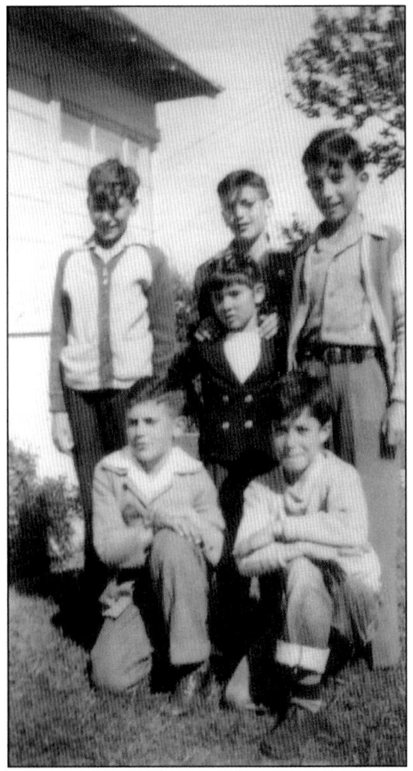

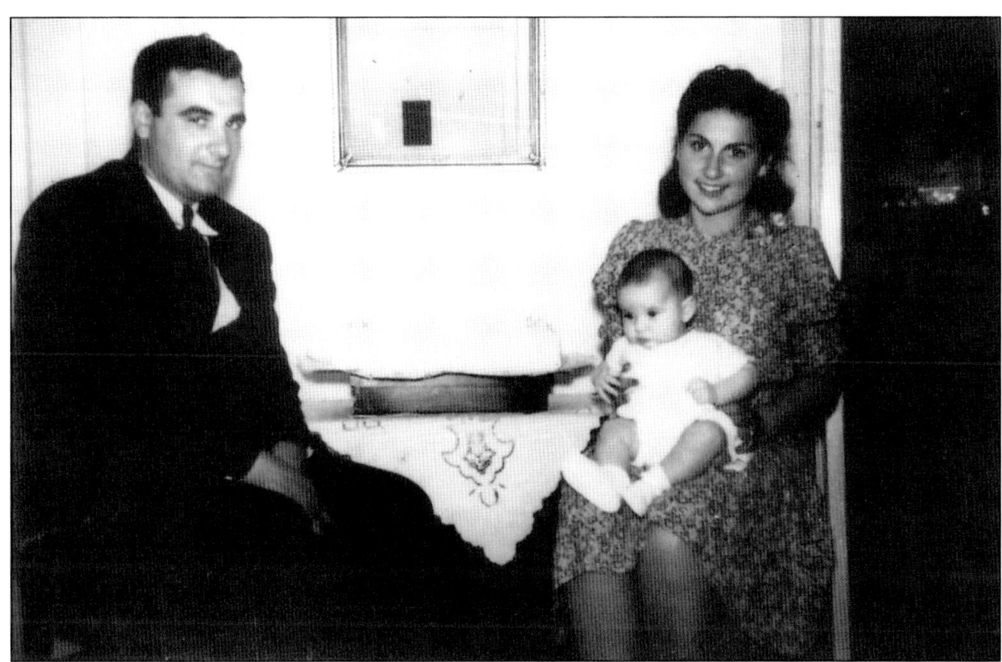

Above, godparents Joe Russo and Mary Lucido Stagi pose with baby John Russo, the son of John Russo, after he was baptized in 1941. To be asked to be godparents of a Sicilian Italian family was a great honor. Pictured at right in 1943, thirteen-year-old Peter Torrente stands with his father, Mariano Torrente, a successful fisherman who owned several fishing boats: the *Sea King*, *Vagabond*, *Vagabond II*, and the *New Rex*. (Above, courtesy of Mary D'Agui Wells; right, courtesy of Peter Torrente.)

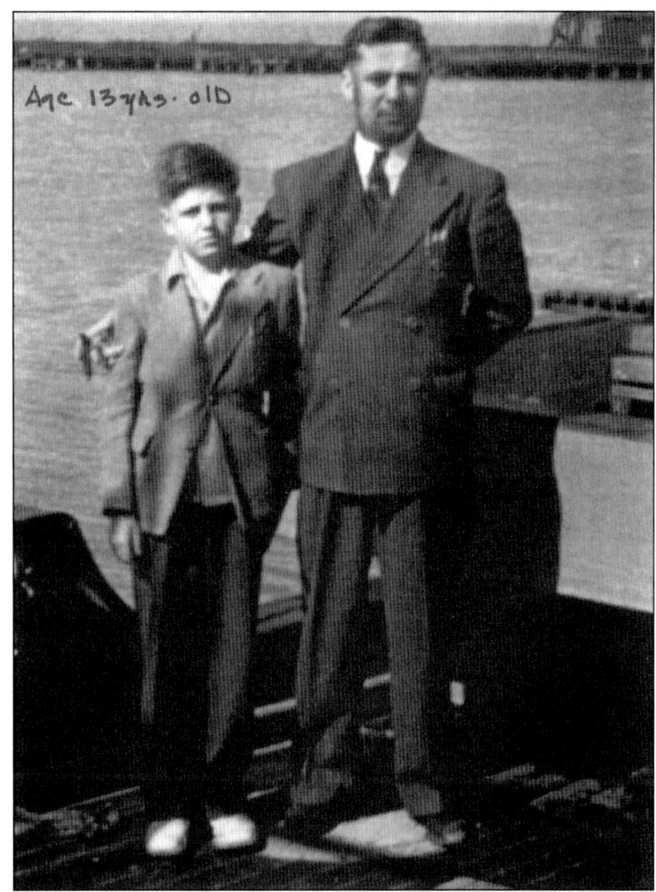

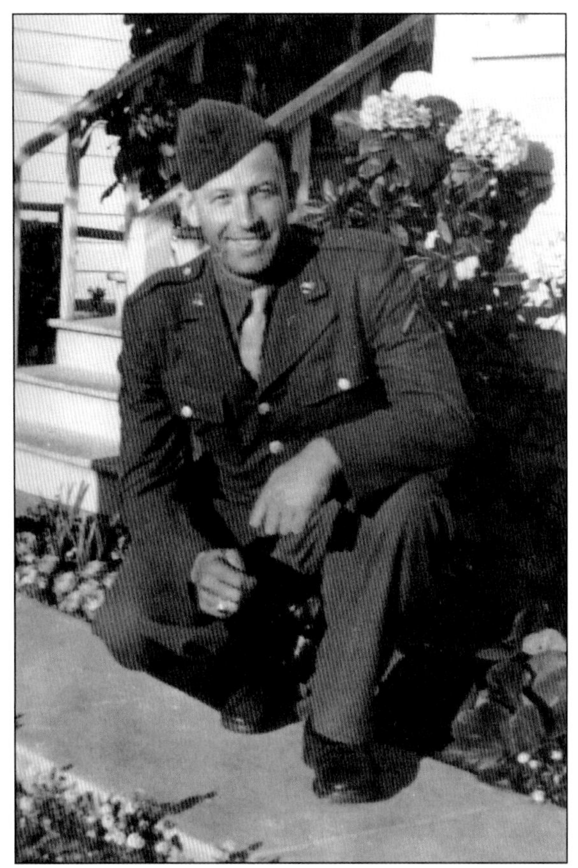

Salvatore "Dan" Ventimiglia (left) was one of many Sicilian Italians who served his country during World War II and paid the ultimate price; he was killed in action at Nettuno, Italy, on June 3, 1944. During the war, Italian Americans were being placed in relocation camps throughout the United States along with the Japanese Americans. In the town of Pittsburg, California, a monument was erected paying tribute to Italian Americans who were relocated. Pictured below is the wedding of Anthony Castaldo and Rose Favalora on February 27, 1943; from left to right are Joseph Battaglia, Rose Castaldo, Rose Favalora, Anthony Castaldo, Josephine Bruno, and John Favalora (Left, author's collection; below, courtesy of Anne Castaldo Jay.)

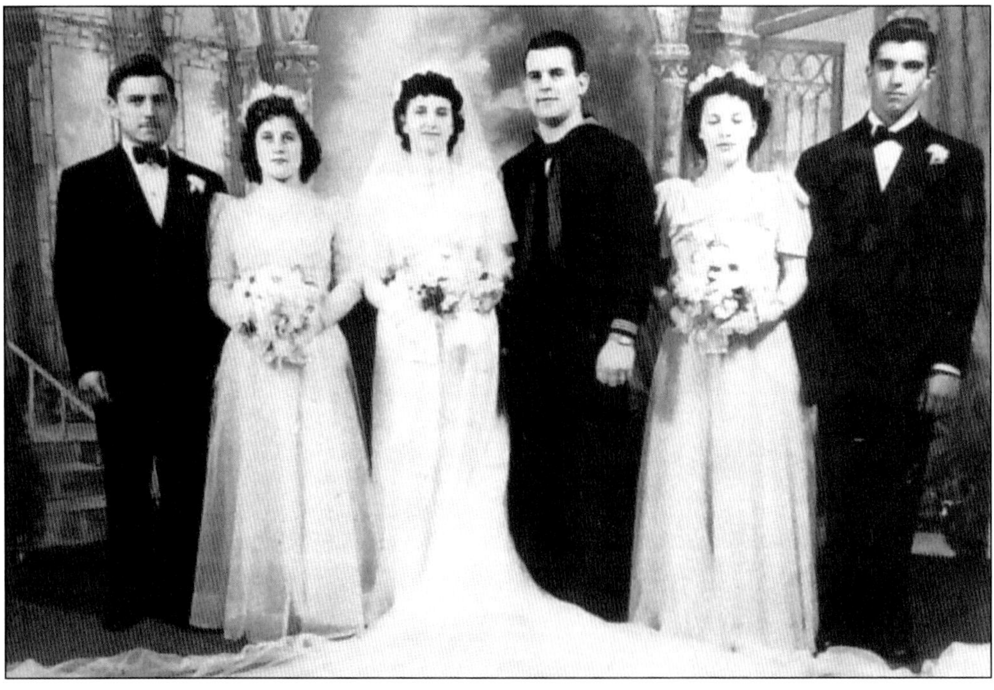

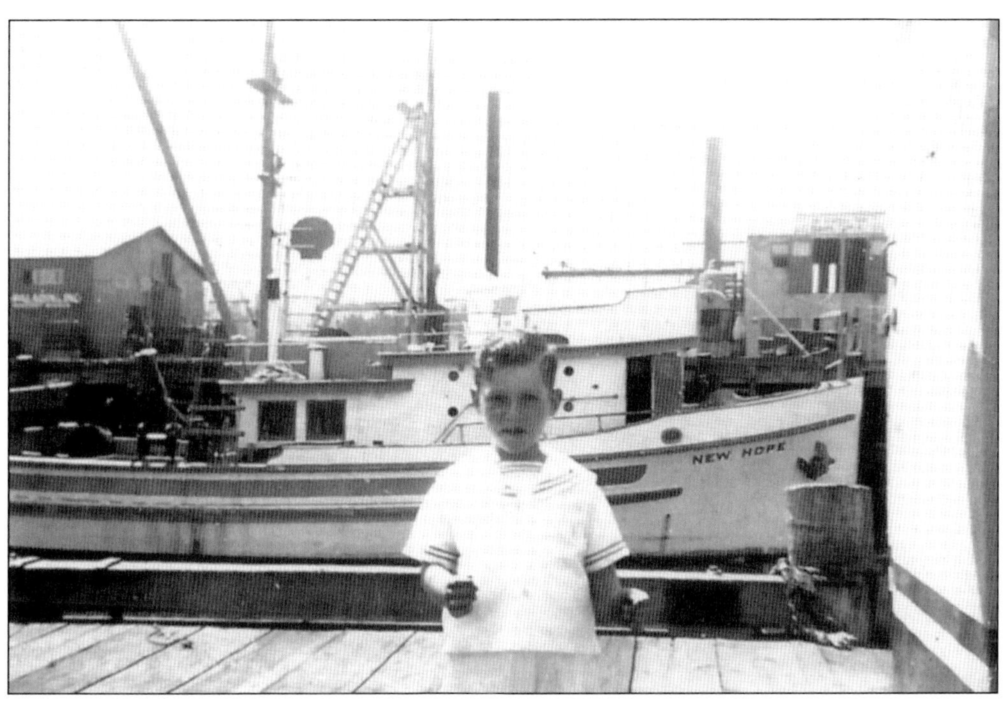


Above, Tommy Bruno, son of Dooley and Dorothy Jones Bruno, who lived at 150 John Street in Monterey in 1951, poses in front of the purse seiner *New Hope*. Tommy's father, Dooley, was a construction worker. At right in 1948 is the Cutino family; from left to right are young Bert Cutino (age nine), with his father, Paul Cutino, and his mother, Rose Aiello Cutino, at the christening of Paul's new boat, *Santa Rosalie*, in Sausalito, California. Young Bert Cutino would become a successful chef, businessman, and partner in Cannery Row Properties. (Above, courtesy of Marie Ventimiglia Person; right, courtesy of the Bert Cutino family.)

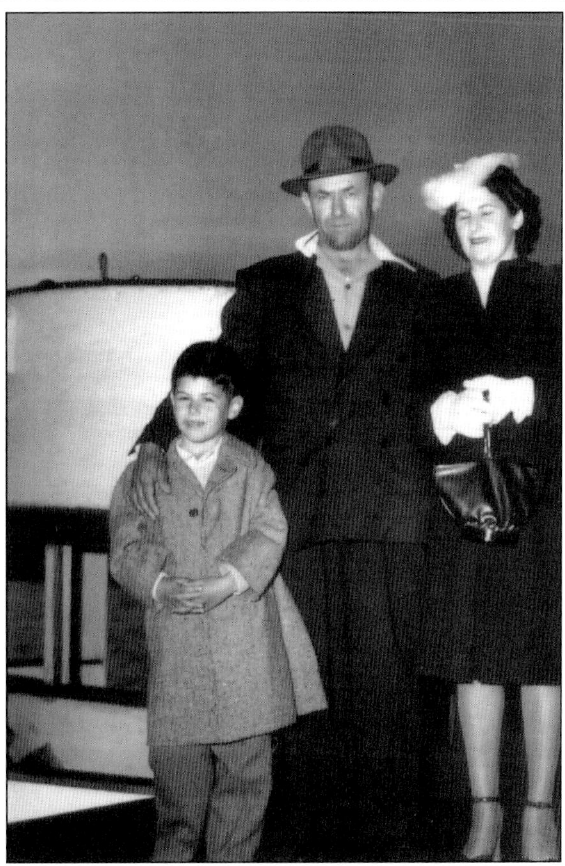

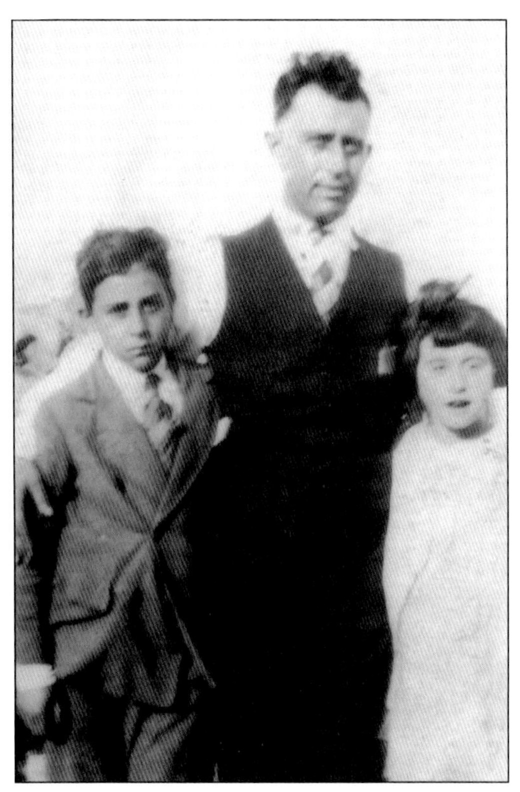

Pictured at left from left to right are Vincent Lucido, his father, Vincent Lucido, and sister, Sarah Lucido. The senior Vincent was born about 1894 and migrated to the United States in 1905. In 1930, they lived at 242 Lighthouse Avenue, where they rented a house for $35 a month. He was employed as a superintendant at one of the fish canneries on Cannery Row. Below is Salvatore Ventimiglia, a successful fisherman and cannery owner. He came to America in 1907 at the age of 14 with two of his brothers and fished in Martinez, California, with his father and other brothers. He purchased his own boat at age 26 and was one of the youngest captains, as most boat captains were in their 50s. (Left, courtesy of Mary D'Agui Wells; below, courtesy of Cathy Ventimiglia Gomez.)

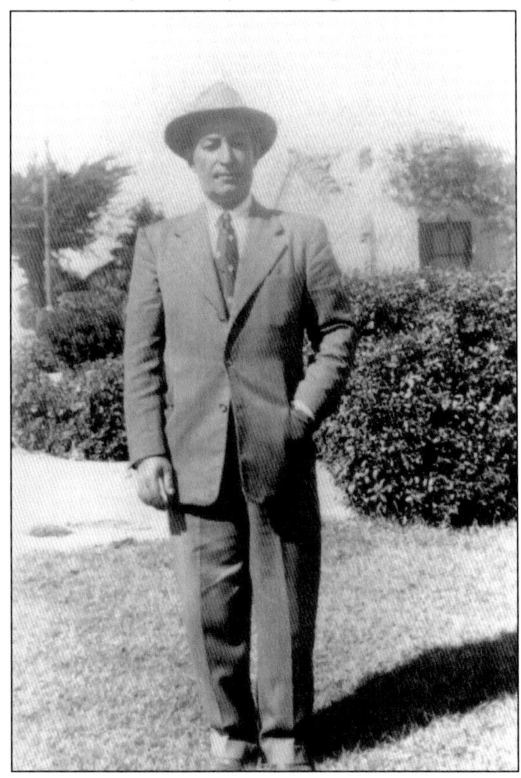

Orazio Ventimiglia (right) was listed as a business agent for the C.I.O. Fishing Union in the 1940 census report; he fished for most of his adult life and resided at 508 Abrego Street in Monterey. Orazio and his wife, Mary, reared nine children before Mary's death in 1939. Until his death in 1969, Orazio could be found at downtown Monterey's Red's Donut Shop in his business suit dunking his donuts in his coffee. Pictured below is the Castaldo family in 1950; from left to right are Anne Castaldo Jay, Anthony Castaldo, and Constance Castaldo Salmeri, posing for a milk commercial at the end of Wharf II. (Right, author's collection; below, courtesy of Anne Castaldo Jay.)

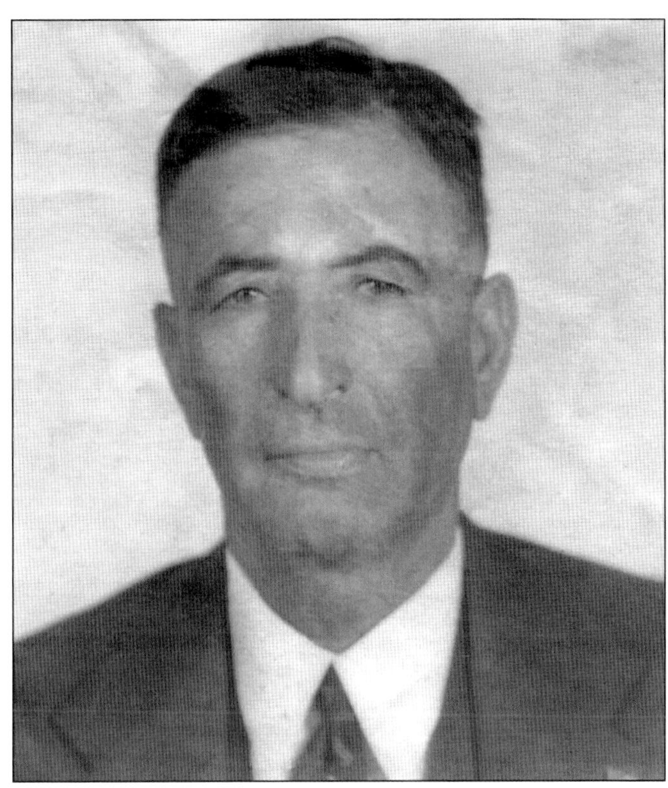

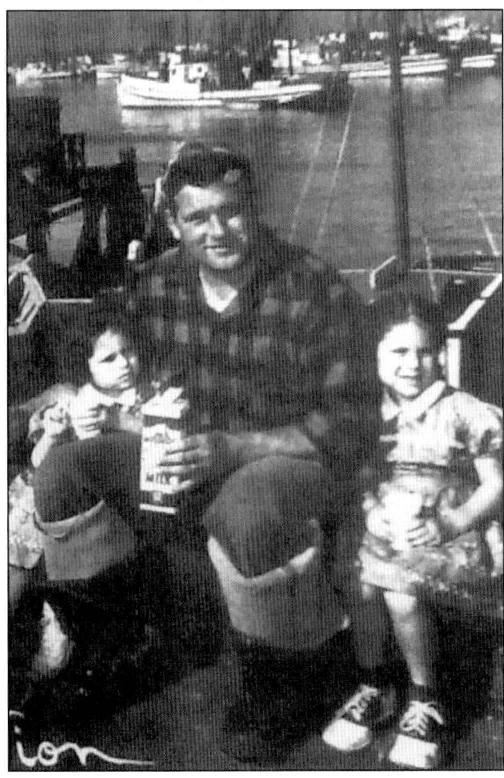

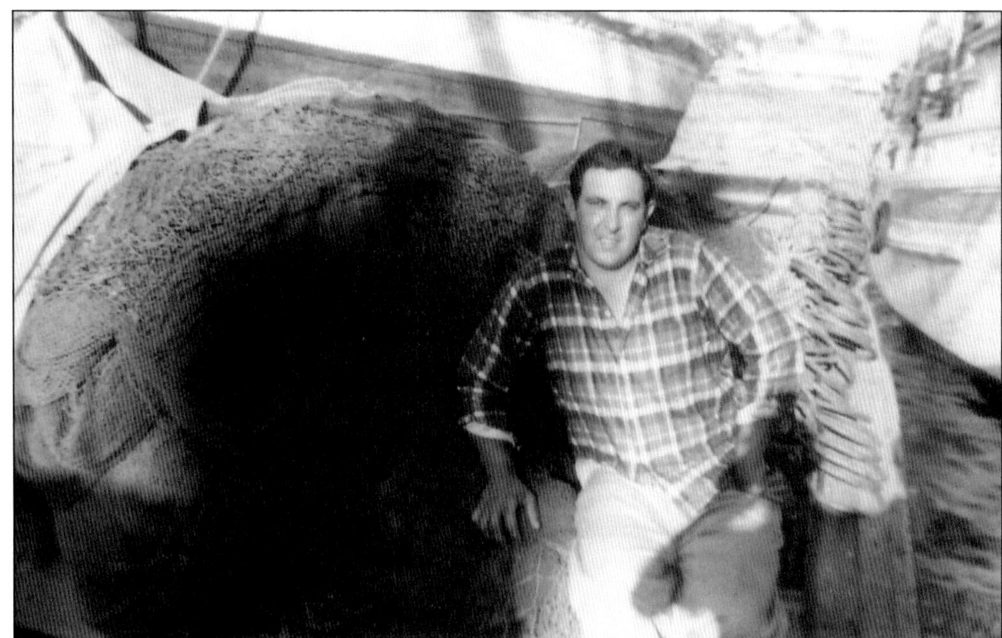

John Crivello (above) fished on the *Twin Brothers*, and the boat was owned by Salvatore Maiorana, who fished for California Packing Corporation in the 1930–1940 fishing season. When the sardine industry dwindled, John opened a small restaurant on Wharf I and provided for his family. Pictured below is Frank Sardina standing and mending fishing nets, preparing for the next time they head out to sea. The fisherman sitting and helping with the mending. Net mending was essential and had to be done correctly; if the mend did not hold, the entire catch could be lost under the weight of the fish. (Above, courtesy of the Amici Club Monterey; below, courtesy of Sardina family.)

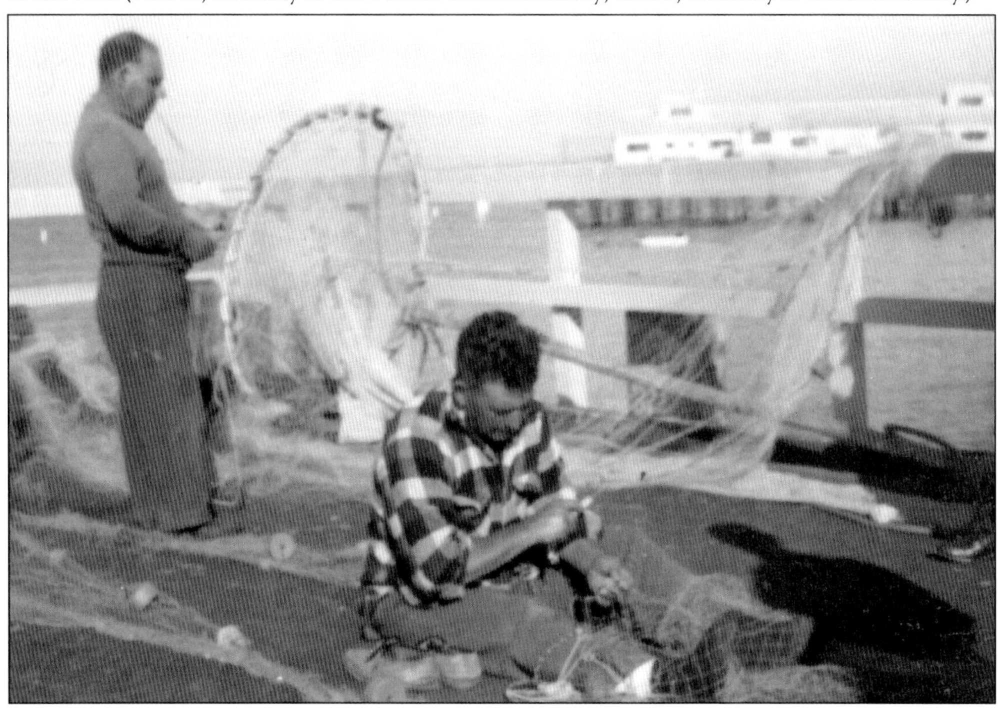

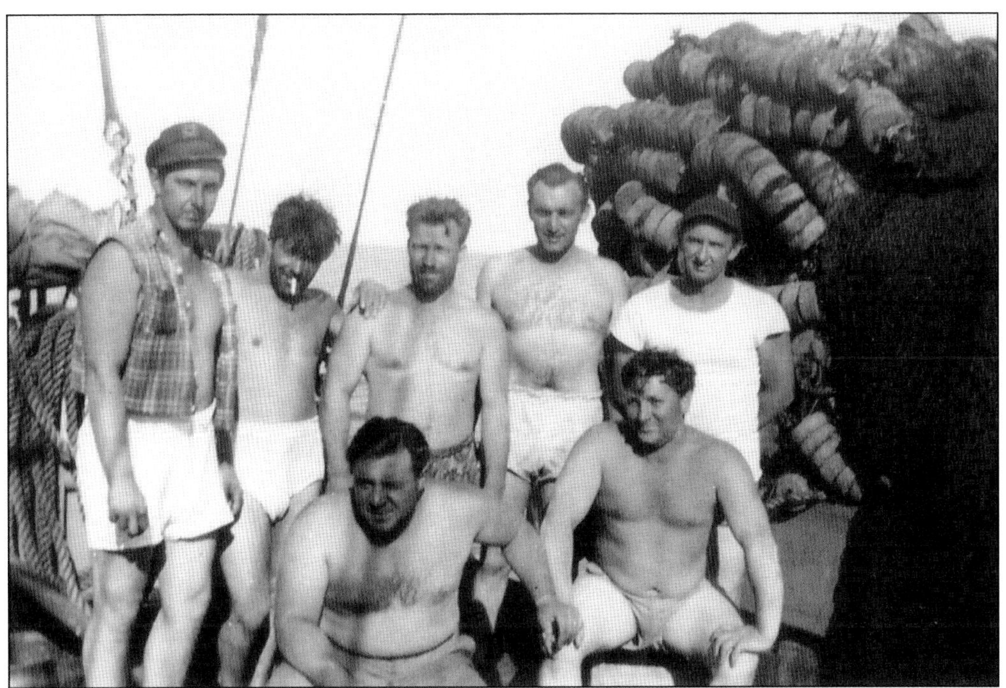

Giuseppe "Joe" Pennisi (among those pictured above) started fishing with his father when he was 16 years old. Over the years, the family has owned several boats, including the *San Giovanni*, *San Giovanni II*, and the *Diana*, and run the Royal Seafood Market on Wharf II. Pictured below fishing for squid in 1946 is the crew from the *Peter Boy* owned by Paul Cutino. Identified crewmen are, from left to right, (first row) Paul Cutino, Joe Azaro, Pepe Lione, and four unidentified; standing in the back is Sam Catania. The net would be set around the school of squid and pulled in by hand, and the squid would be scooped out of the net. (Above, courtesy of the Amici Club Monterey; below, courtesy of the Bert Cutino family.)

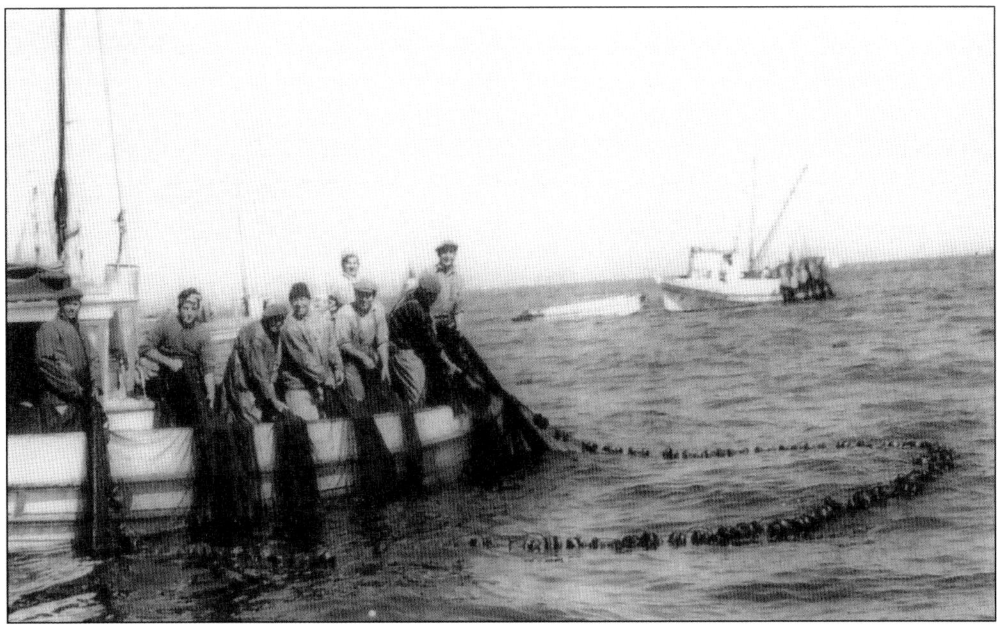

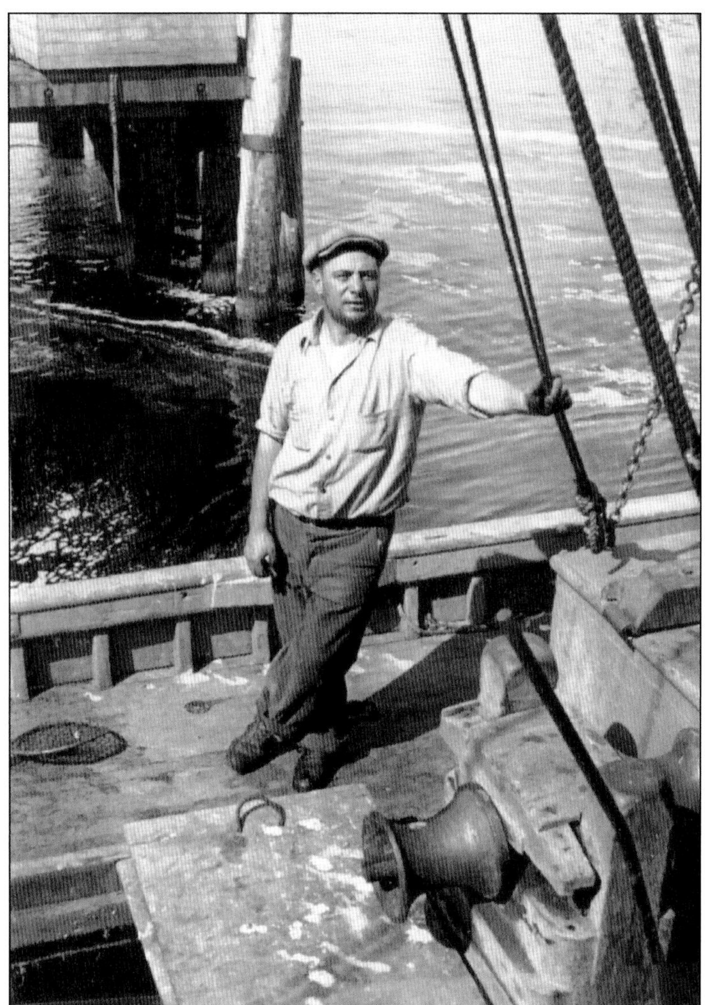

At left, Mariano Torrente poses with his first fishing boat, the *Sea King*, a lampara boat. Pictured below shortly after the end of World War II, several of the local Italians who were quite good at the game of golf worked as caddies for the Cypress Point Golf Course at Pebble Beach, California. This was an exclusive private club not open to the general public. From left to right are Peter Enea, Sammy Belleci, Turk Archdeacon, Sam Muniz, Trixie Balesteri, and Frank "Ike" Ventimiglia. (Left, courtesy of Peter Torrente; below, courtesy of Marie Ventimiglia Person.)

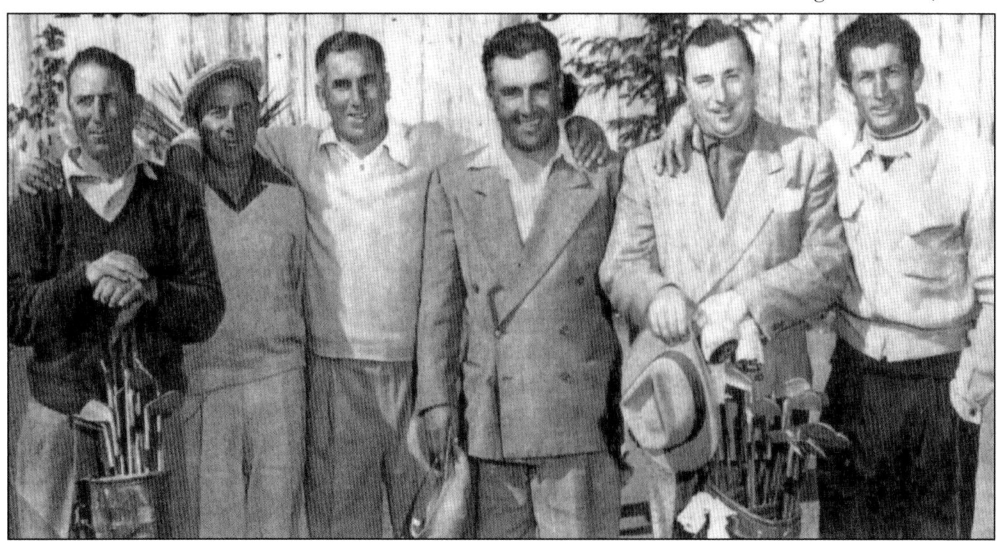

At right, Frank and Bessie Sardina pose in front of their home. Frank continued to fish after the sardines left Monterey Bay and provided fish to the commercial markets with his small boat. Pictured below are Mariano Torrente and his wife, Girolama, dancing at their son Peter's wedding at the Del Monte skating rink, where the wedding reception was held. Italians love weddings and events that allow them to bring family and friends together; the attendance at this wedding was over 500. The young man in the white tuxedo at right is author Mike Ventimiglia, who was ring bearer. The young lady in the white dress is JoAnn Rucello, flower maiden. (Right, courtesy of the Sardina family; below, courtesy of Peter Torrente.)

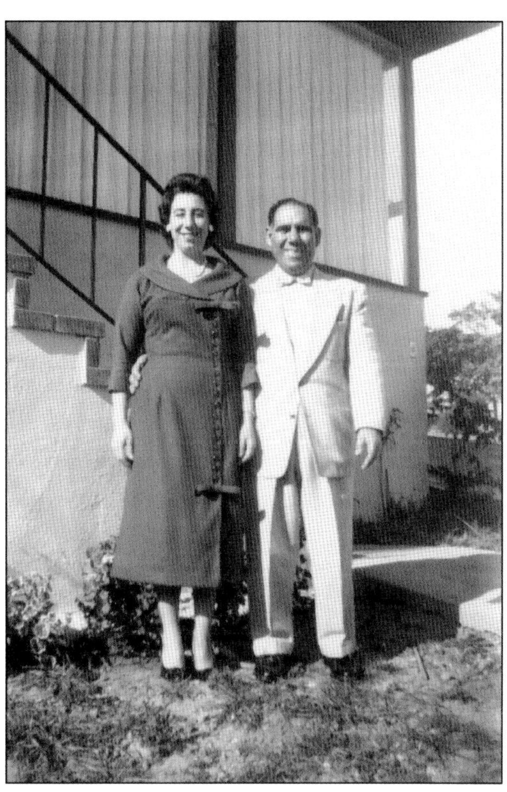

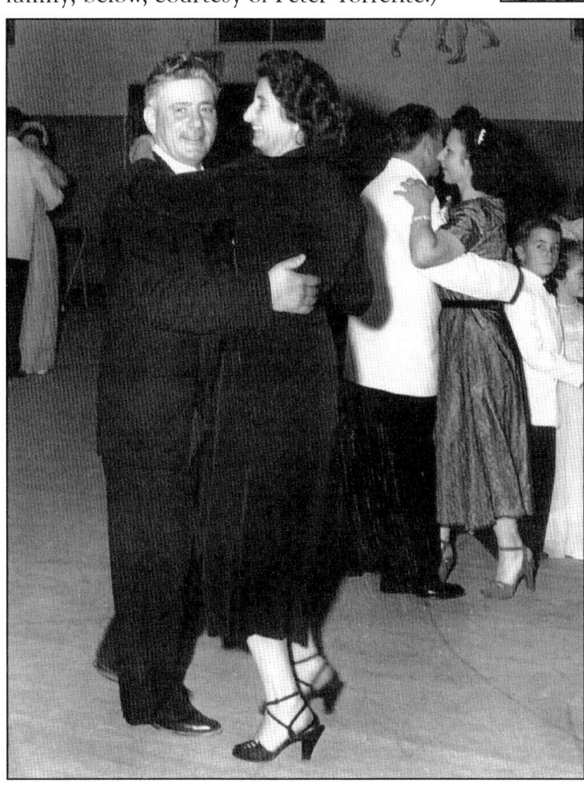

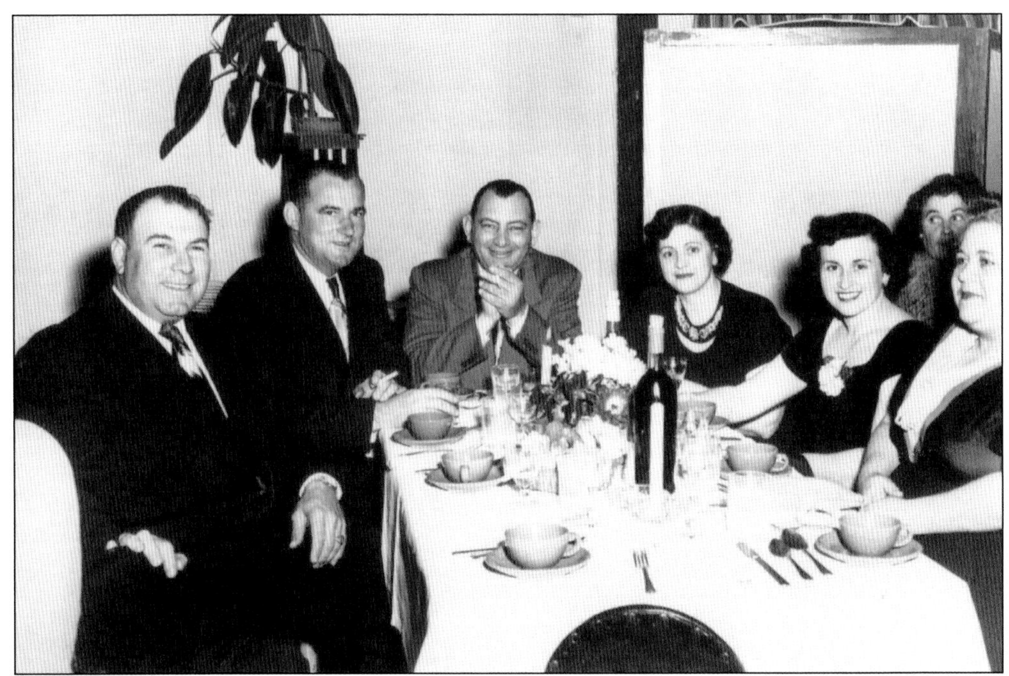

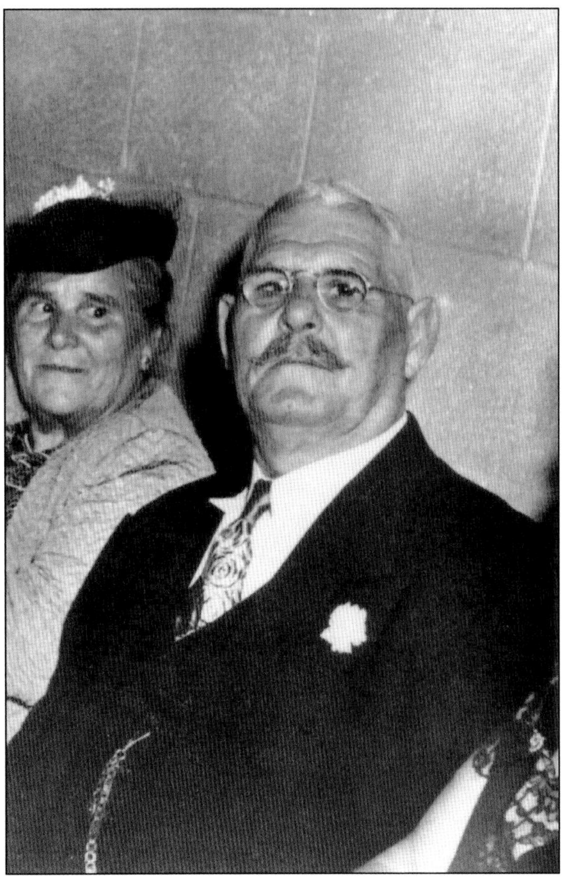

Above, partners in the fishing boat *Star of Monterey* enjoy a night out for dinner. Seated from left to right are Roual Bruno, John Russo, Tom DiMaggio, Antoinette DiMaggio, Sarah Russo, and Mary Bruno, no doubt celebrating another successful year of fishing. At left, Josephine Russo Aiello and Bartolo Aiello attend a wedding at Pittsburg, California. Monterey Italian and Sicilian community have close family ties in both Pittsburg and Martinez, as many family members left these areas to begin fishing for sardines in Monterey during the Silver Harvest years. (Above, courtesy of Mary D'Agui Wells; left, courtesy of the Bert Cutino family.)

At right, Salvatore Aiello (left) and Peter Cutino pose near 680 Jefferson Street in Monterey, about 1942. Peter or "Pete" as his friends would call him, would make his mark as head water polo coach for the University of California at Berkeley for 26 years. Pictured below are, from left to right, (first row) Rose Lucido Borrelli, Joan Giamona, Ada Giamona, Sarah Russo, Mary Lucido Stagi, Rose Davi, and Frances Lucido; (second row) Neno Bruno, Joe Russo, John Russo, Sal Costanza, Tony Bruno, and Neno DiMaggio. (Right, courtesy of the Burt Cutino family; below, courtesy of Mary D'Agui Wells.)

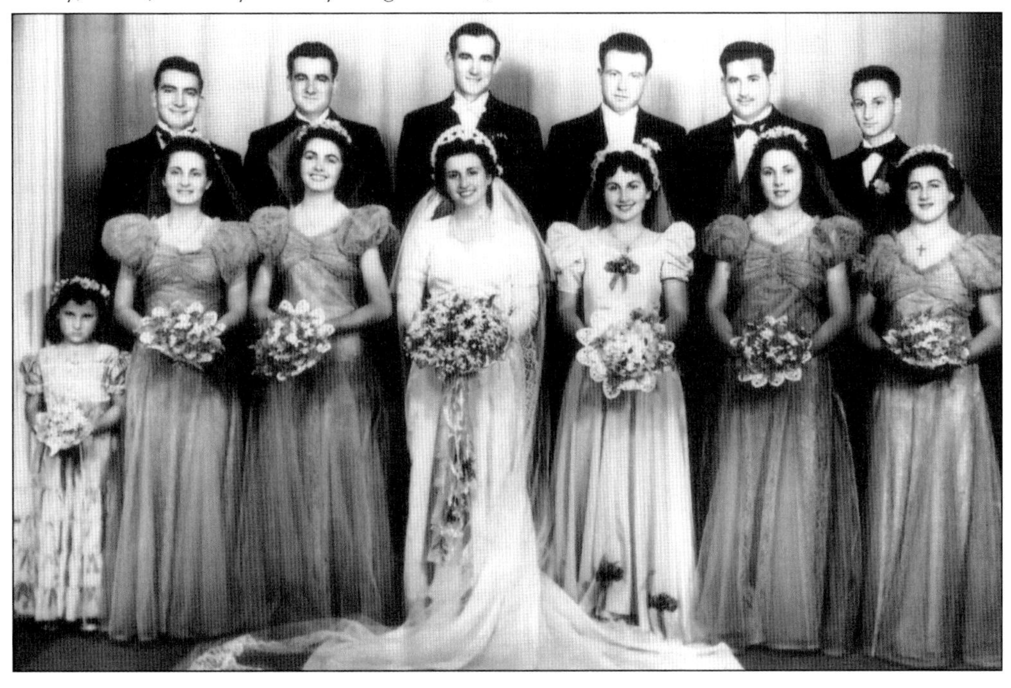

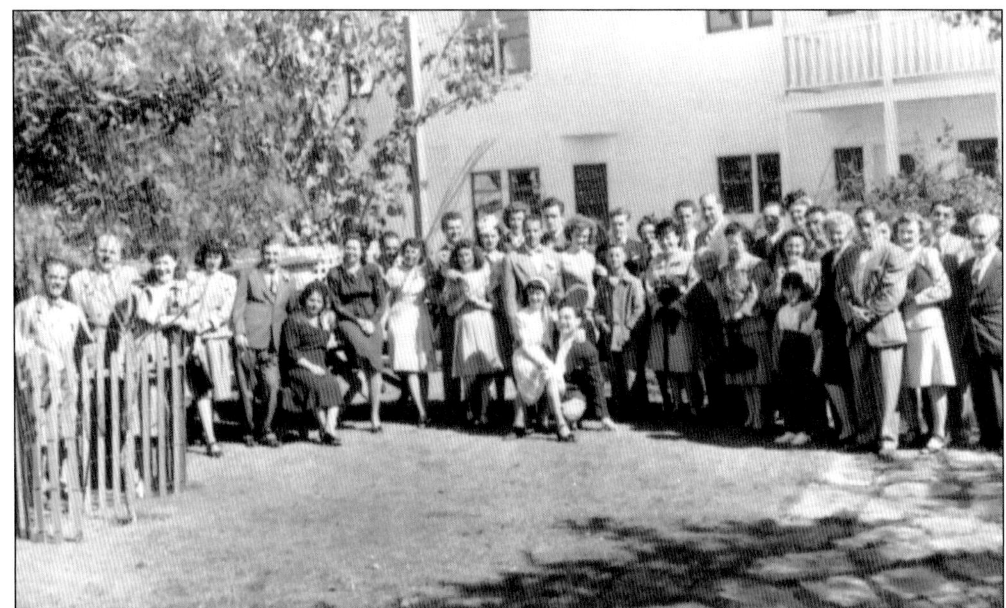

Above, a backyard gathering at Nick Marotta's home celebrates the wedding of Manny DiMaria and Murtice Murray around 1941. Those in attendance, in no particular order, were Lois Murry DiMaria, Angelo DiMaria, Vito "Tito" Marotta, Dutch and Carmen Quefurth, Dolly Chappell, Willard and Mary Branson, Murtice Murray DiMaria, Phil and Mike Marotta, Forney Murray, Billy Chappell, Nick Marotta Sr., Florence Murray Marotta, Jim and Mary Chappell Frank, Anna Bruno, and Emma Marotta Coopersmith. Below, the crew of a large purse seiner are in the process of mending the net prior to treating it at the tanning tanks. (Above, courtesy of Laurie Hambaro, Shades of Monterey, Monterey Public Library's California Historic Room; below, courtesy of Monterey Public Library's California Historic Room.)

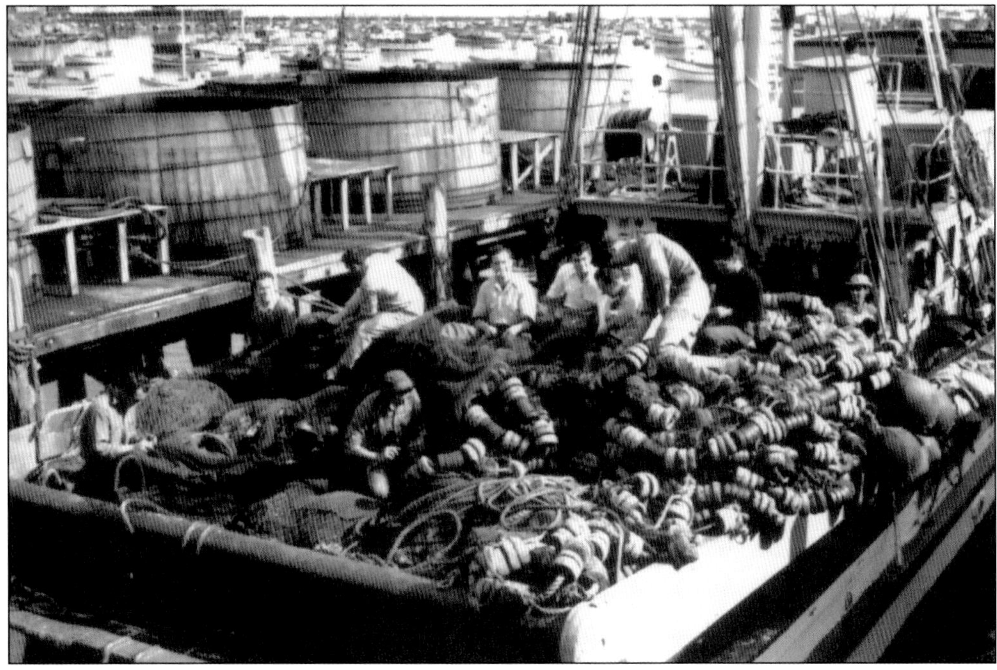

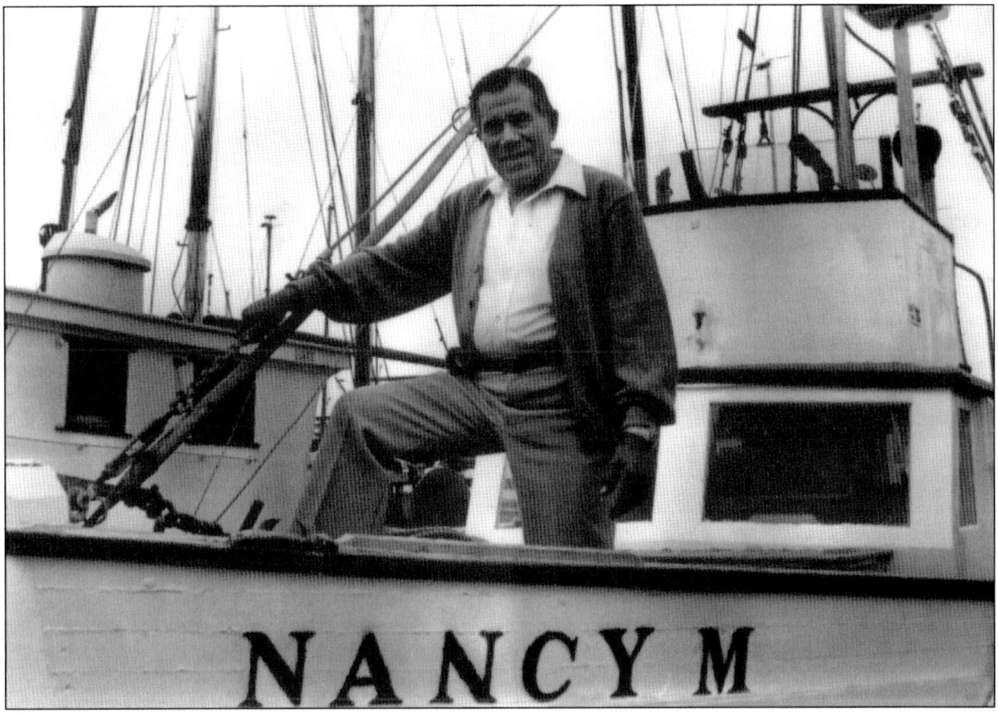

Above, standing on the deck of his boat, the *Nancy M*, is Albert Mangiapane. He named his boat after his wife, Nancy. The 1940 census shows the family with their son, Peter, living at 574 Cortez Street in Monterey. The image at right is from Dick O'Kane's warehouse and carousel, which in the 1950s was located at Prescott and Wave Streets, now the home of the Cannery Row Brewing Company. Eugene Roncarati (far right) would later become a firefighter for Monterey and refine the process for breading calamari, owning Calamari Specialties in Monterey. (Above, courtesy of the Bert Cutino family; right, courtesy of Dr. Pamela Brown.)

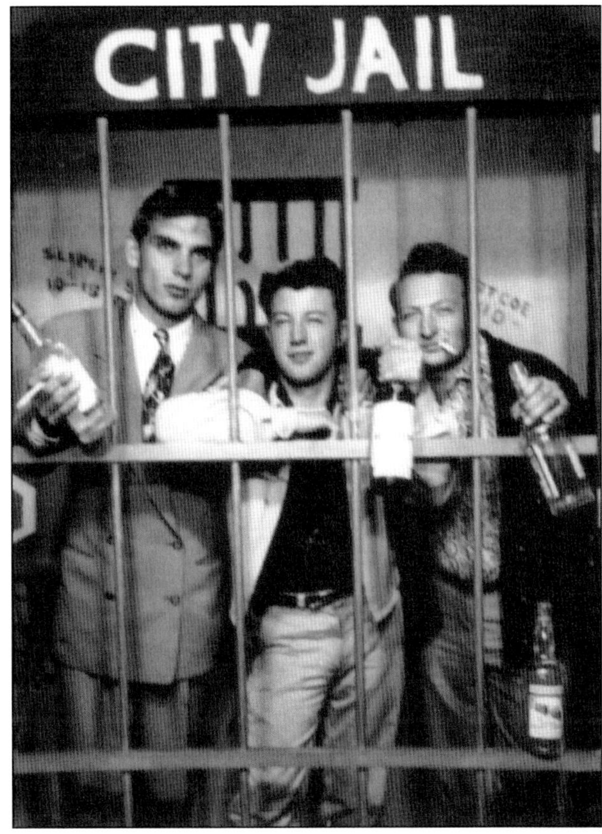

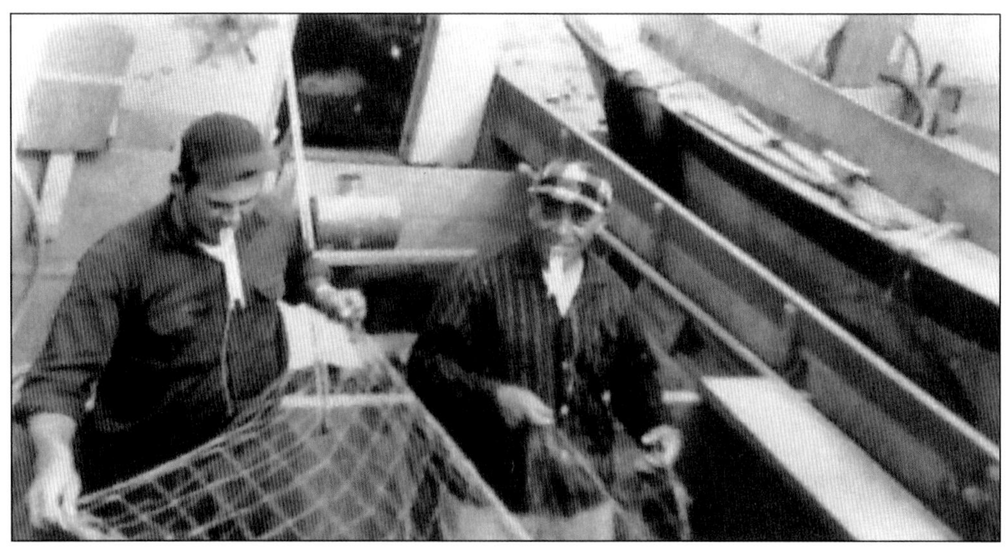

Above, Anthony Castaldo (left), alongside an unknown crewmember, is mending a fishing net. Both are holding the mending needles in their mouths as they search through the net for holes that need to be repaired. It was essential that all holes be mended, as a small hole could cost them their entire catch. Pictured below is John Russo's family gathering. From left to right are (first row) Bessie Russo DiMaggio and Salvatore "Sheik" Russo; (second row) Mildred Russo DiMaggio, Rose Russo Amo, John Russo, Catherine Russo, Josephine Russo Balesteri, Joe Russo, and Dora Russo Lucido. (Above, courtesy of Anne Castaldo Jay; below, courtesy of Mary D'Agui Wells.)

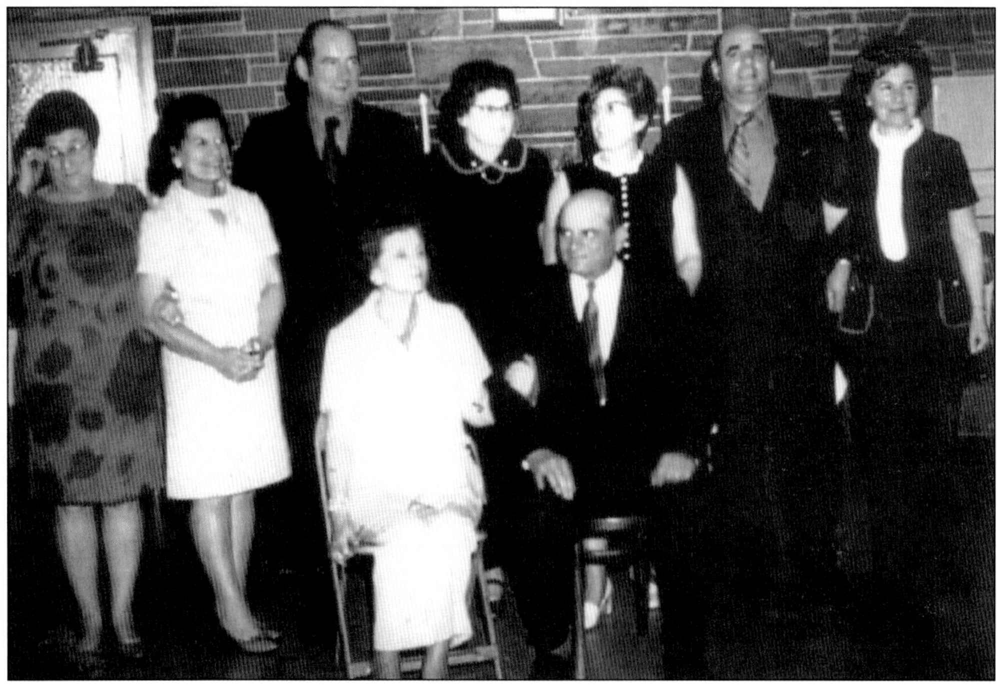

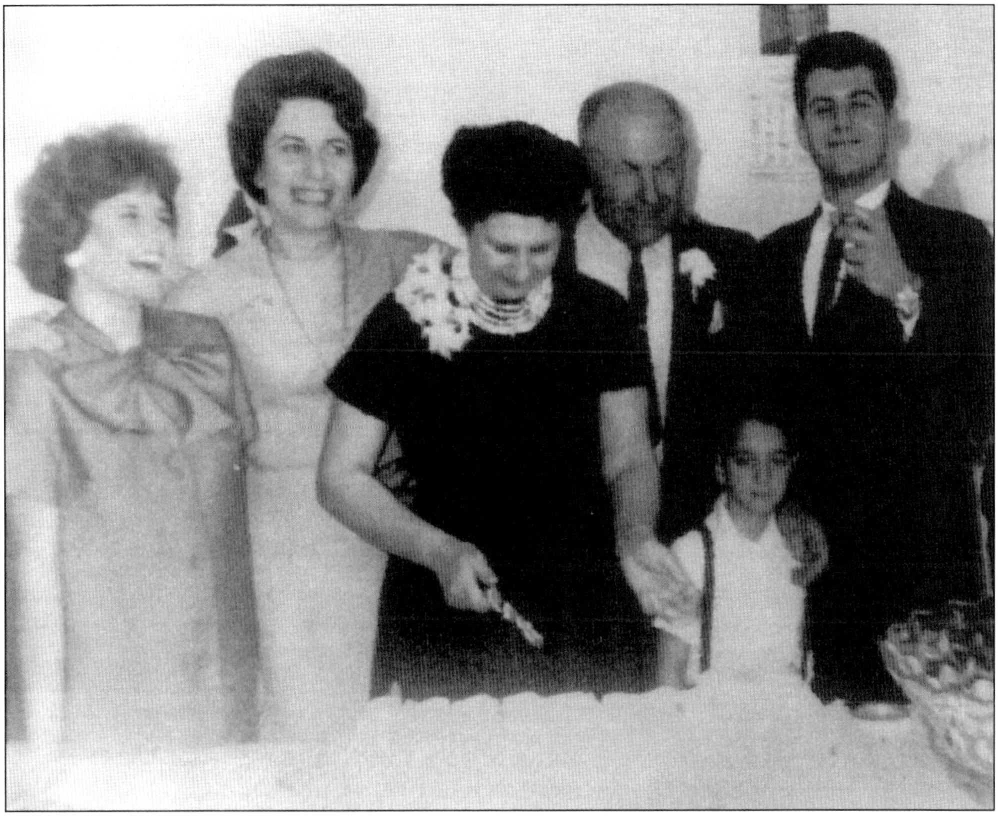

Pictured above in 1962 celebrating the 30th wedding anniversary of Paul Cutino and Rose Aiello Cutino are, from left to right, Josephine O'Neil, Rose Marie Topper, Rose Cutino, Paul Cutino, grandson Paul Cutino, and Bert Cutino. At right is Peter J. Cutino; in his 26 years as head water polo coach at the University of California, Berkeley, he was the all-time winning coach in US water polo history and is the author of several books on the subject. His teams won eight NCAA titles. In 1999, the Peter J. Cutino Award was established in his honor by the San Francisco Olympic Club. It is presented annually to the top American male and female collegiate water polo players. Pete passed away in 2004. (Both, courtesy of the Bert Cutino Family.)

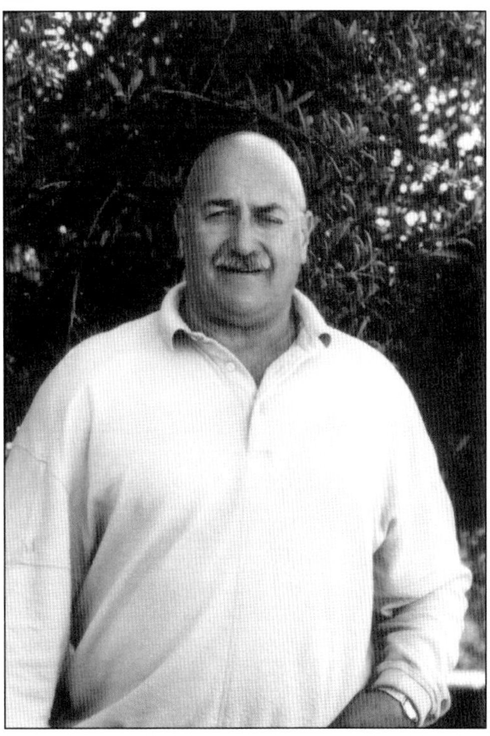

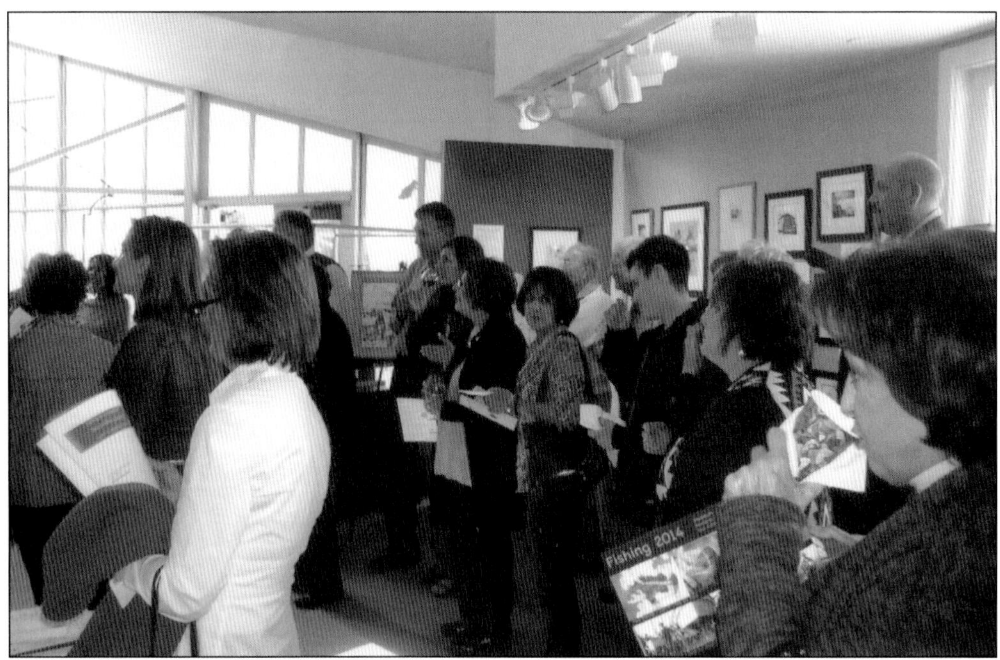


The Italian community comes together in 2014 to dedicate a special wall at the Stanton Museum in downtown Monterey honoring the Sicilian Italian fishing community. The display is a permanent part of the museum, showing early fishing photographs, canning implements, and biographies of fishermen. This was a special moment for the Sicilian Italian community, to have their story placed on display, capturing the years of the Silver Harvest. The Italian wall displays the flag of the fishermen's union, organized on November 27, 1925, as well as artwork, family biographies written by family members, and many more such items. Facing the camera is Gasper Cardinale. (Both, author's collection.)

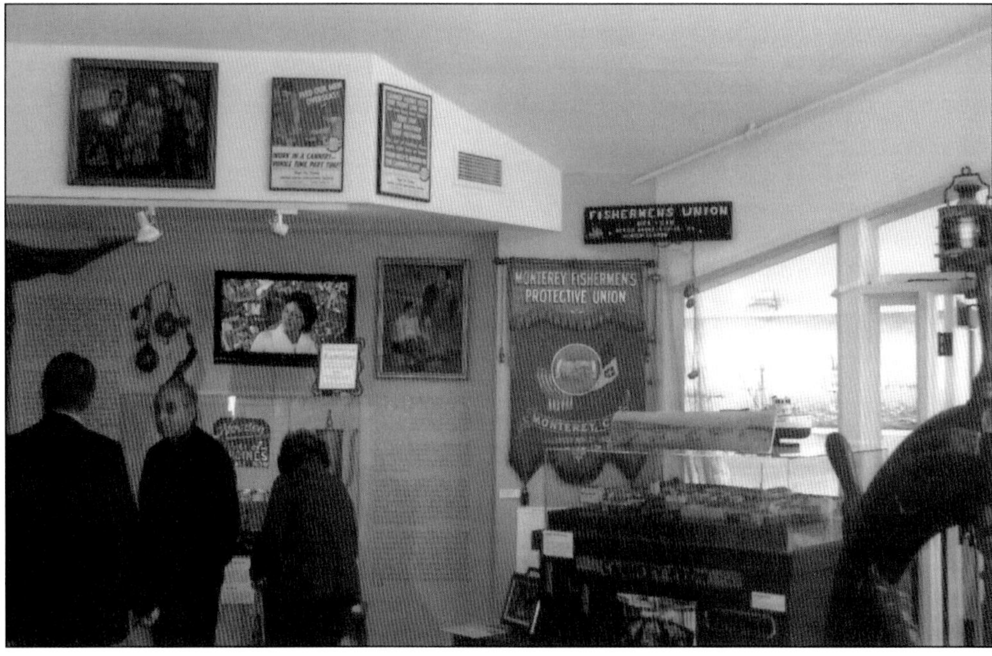

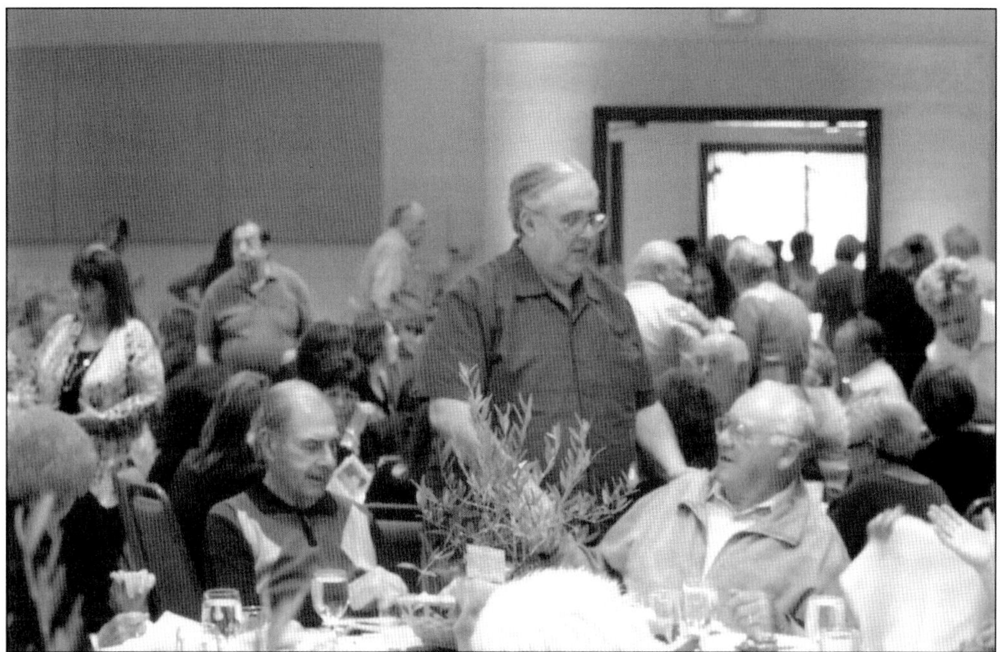

The John "Spud" Spadaro Annual Memorial Dinner was hosted on June 28, 2014, at the San Carlos Parish Hall. Donations are given to families in need of help. The John "Spud" Spadaro Foundation was established to continue John's legacy of generosity and service to the community. Seated at the center of the table above in jacket and white shirt is Salvatore "Coach" Cardinalli. Pictured below, a donation is given to the parents of three-year-old Renzo Lombardi, who was diagnosed with cancer and underwent six months of treatment. Making the presentation from left to right are J.R. Shake, Crystal Ventimiglia Lombardi, Vito and Providence Mineo Spadaro, Vince Lombardi, and Mike Bruno. (Both, author's collection.)

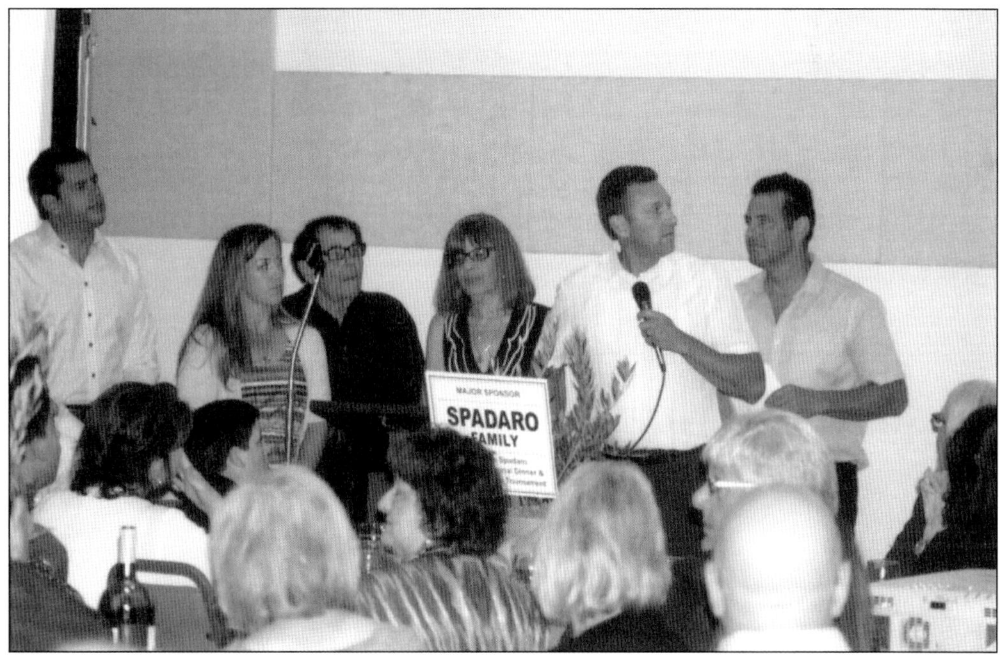

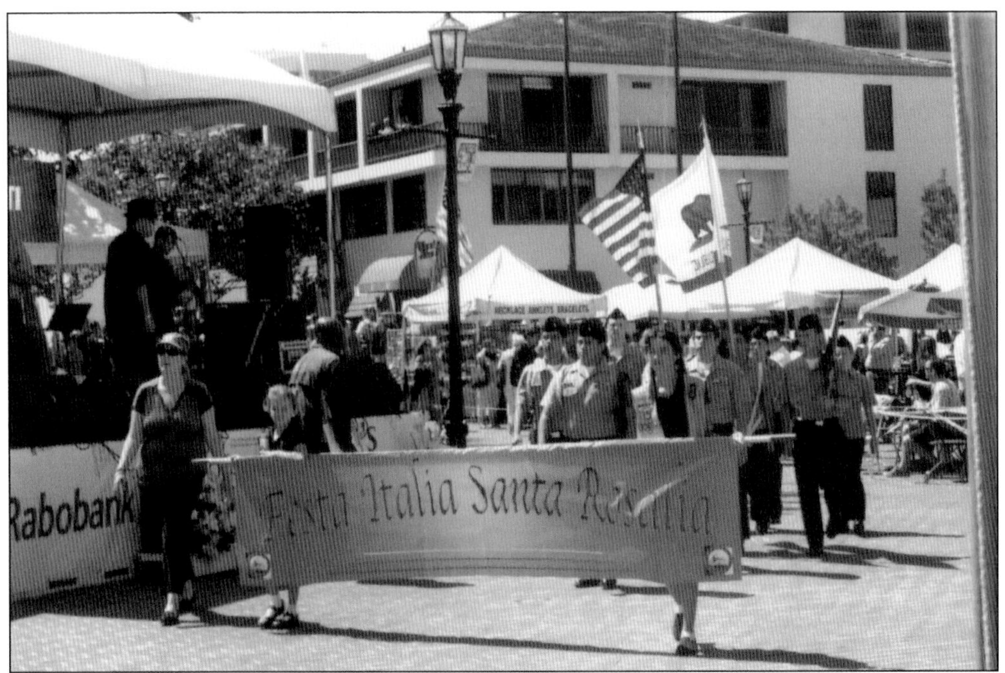


The Festa Italia and Santa Rosalia Parade ends at the plaza in downtown Monterey, where hundreds of onlookers of Italian descent and spectators have an opportunity to enjoy the Italian culture. This event draws thousands of people from around the state and provides opportunities for local Italians to reconnect with their relatives. The event has grown over the years into a three-day festival. Pictured below, the float *Johnny Boy* is pulled through the streets carrying children and future fishermen who can share their experience with the next generation. (Both, author's collection.)

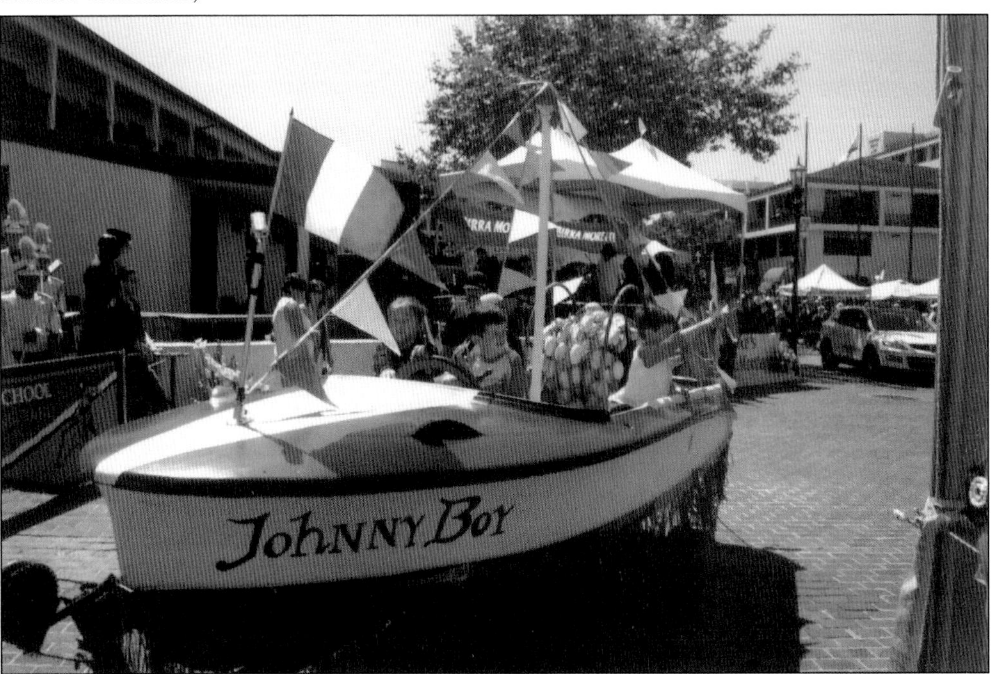

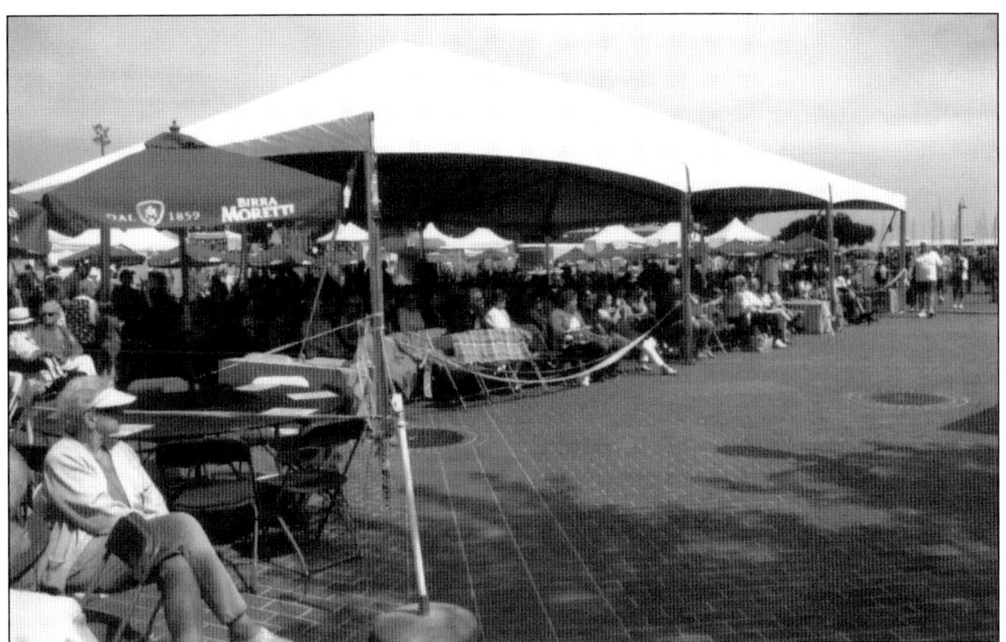


Above, a large shade tent is set up to protect the young and elderly from the hot sun so they may enjoy the Festa Italia and listen to the many bands and singers who perform over the three days. The event is free, and all monies made from food sales go to the festival to support the community. Pictured below are, from left to right, Phil Speciale, Domingo Alvarez, Gaspar Spadaro, and Kenn Morrison, who are working one of the many food booths. The Italian community over the last 100-plus years has bonded with the local community, and for the most part, provides a wide range of charitable and community involvement for people of all nationalities. (Both, author's collection.)

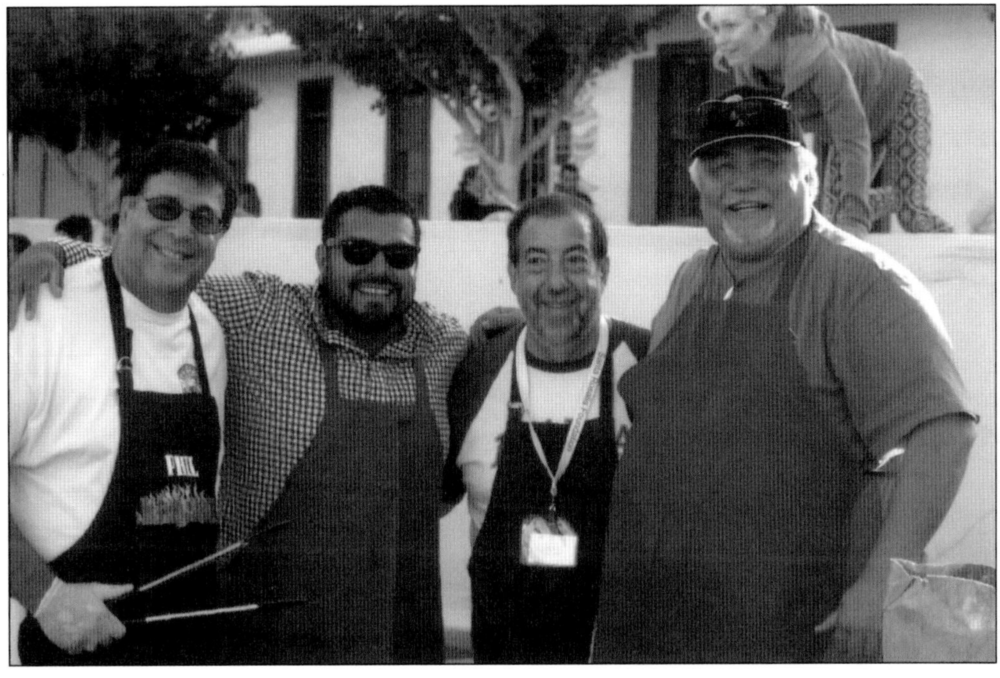

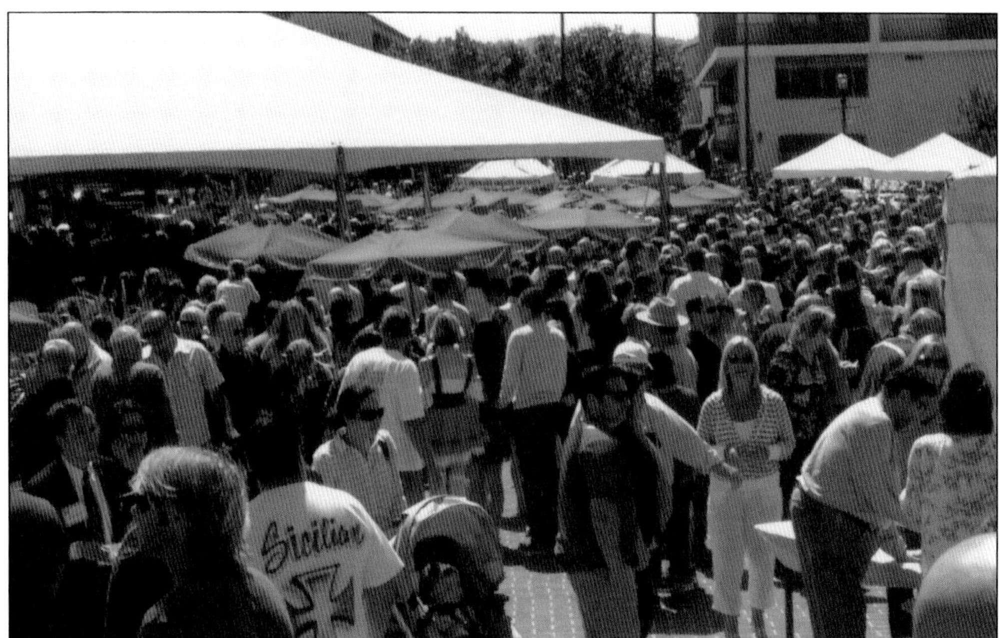


Pictured above and below are the crowds that this event attracts from different parts of the state and the country. They have an opportunity to taste some of the best Sicilian Italian food, including meatballs, pasta, sausage, calamari, and cannoli. Vendor space is also rented out, providing interesting fashions and jewelry, the sale of which aids in providing revenue for the Festa Italia Santa Rosalia Parade. Festa Italia distributes donations to various organizations in the community. Past generations provided much of the money to host the event through donations, but the younger generations have created a venue that is profitable and will be here for future generations. (Both, author's collection.)

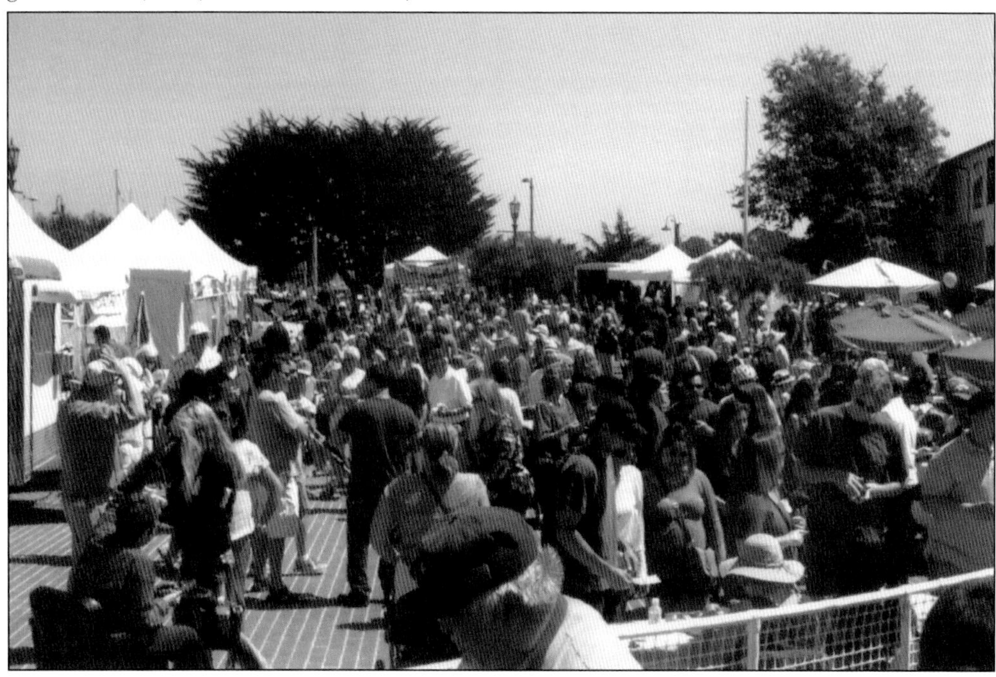

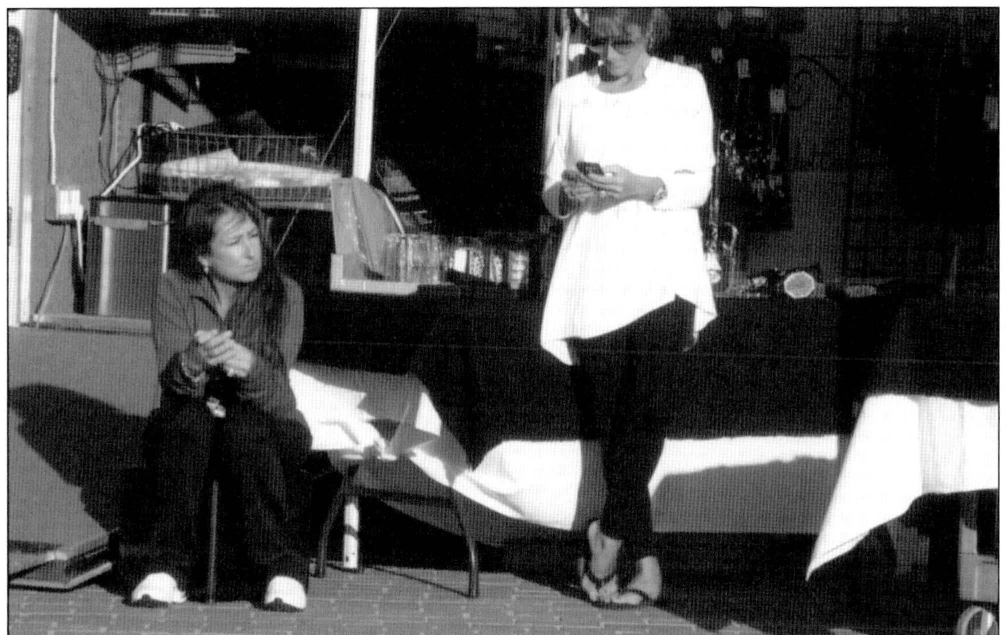

Above, Nina Asaro Leavenworth (left) and her sister Francesca Asaro Aiello tend their fashion and jewelry booth. Both women are very active in the community, working fundraisers and serving on community nonprofit boards. Francesca is part of the committee of the Festa Italia. Their father, Salvatore Asaro, was a commercial fisherman for 57 years, fishing for sardines and salmon in the waters of Monterey Bay and Alaska; he loved mending fishing nets. Pictured below from left to right are Turie Cavaliere, Rick Russo, and an unidentified person enjoying an opportunity to reconnect with family and friends they do not normally see from day to day. (Both, author's collection.)

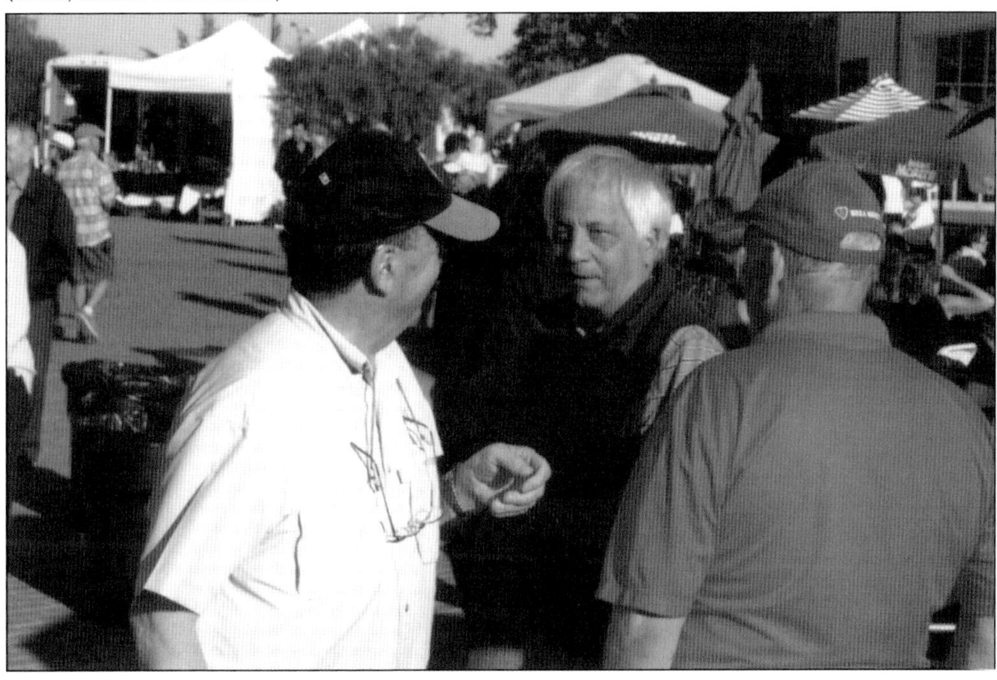

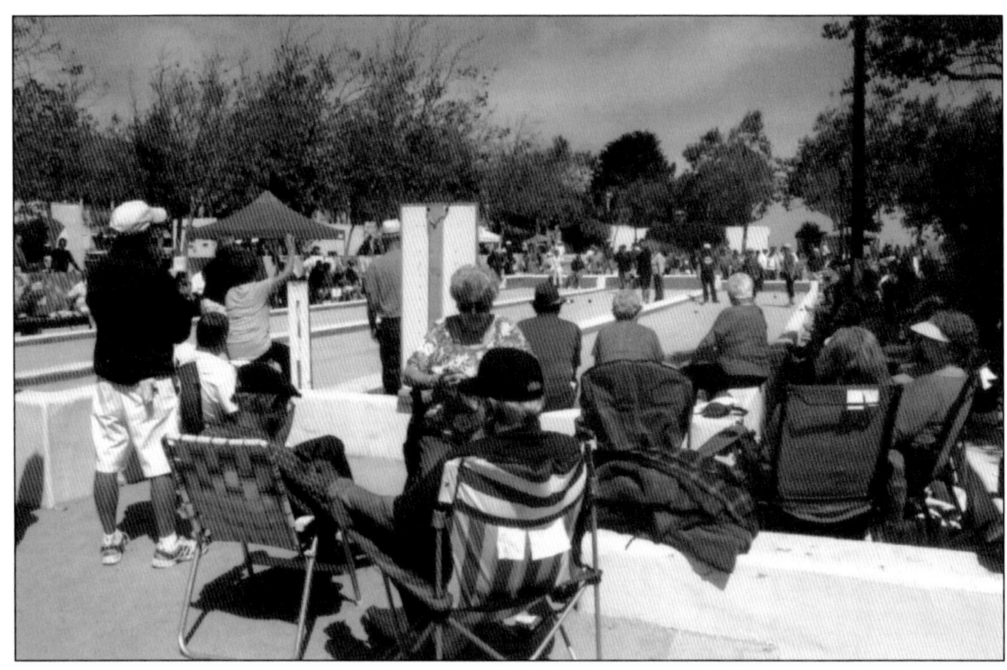

Pictured above and below is bocce ball, a game that has come to flourish in the United States after being carried over from the old country. There are only four strong local teams in Monterey, but during the Festa Italia, 36 teams come here to compete to be called the best. Most of them come from Contra Costa County in California, in which Pittsburg and Martinez are located. (Both, author's collection.)

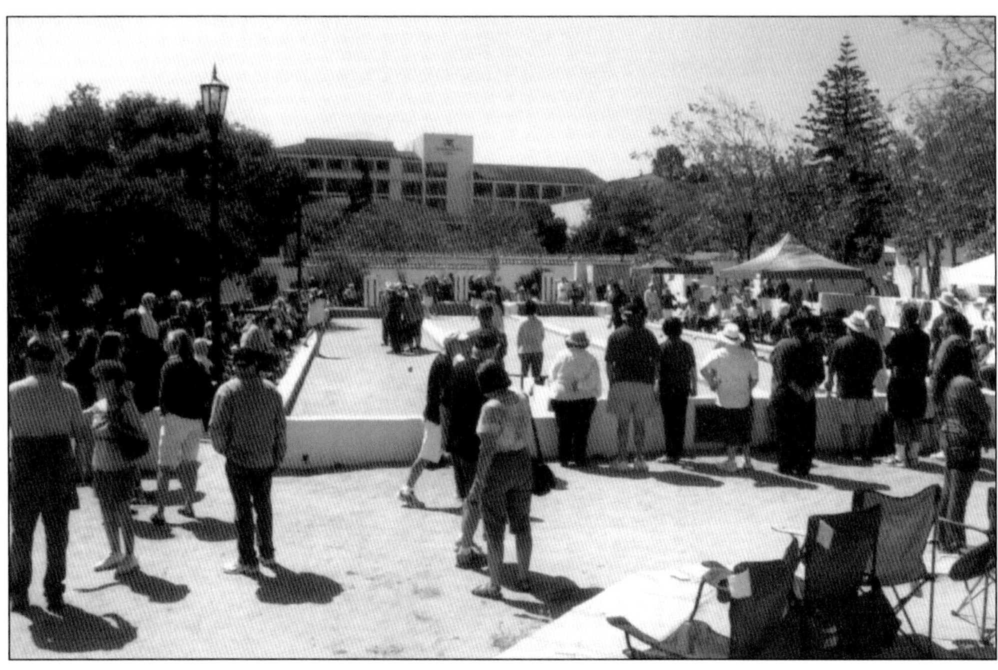

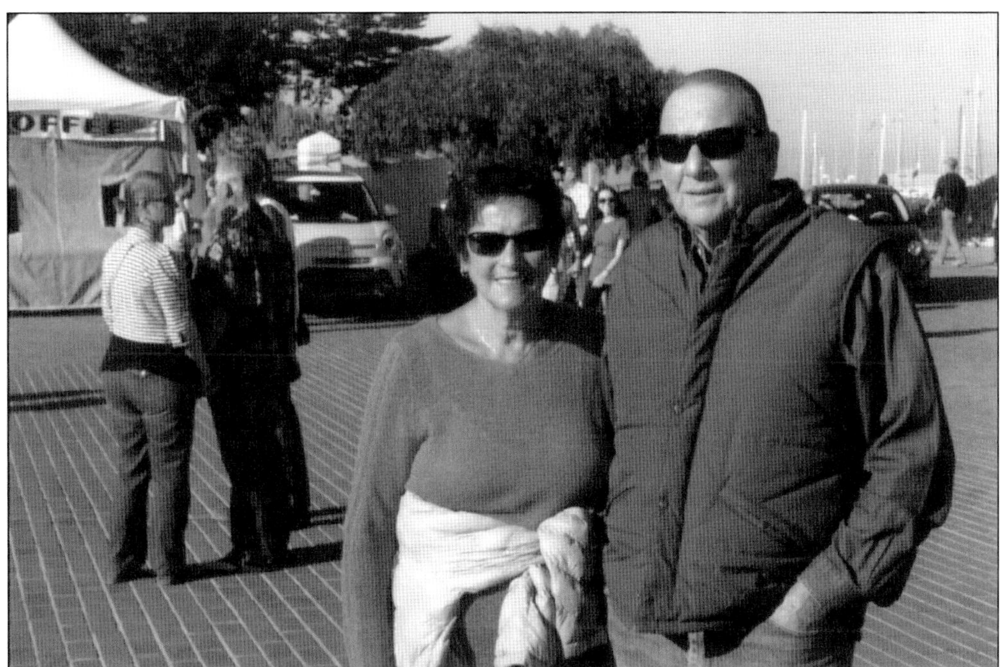

Above, Mary D'Agui Russo Wells and her husband, Roger, enjoy the Festa Italia. Mary's father, John Russo, fished for sardines in Monterey and was captain of the *Star of Monterey*. The Russo name is one of the most common Sicilian Italian names in Monterey. Pictured below at center with sunglasses and checked shirt is Jeff Cecilio, speaking with his hands in true Italian fashion to his many friends. Jeff is a successful businessman in the community and a city councilman in Del Rey Oaks; he supports community functions and is active in the local community. (Both, author's collection.)

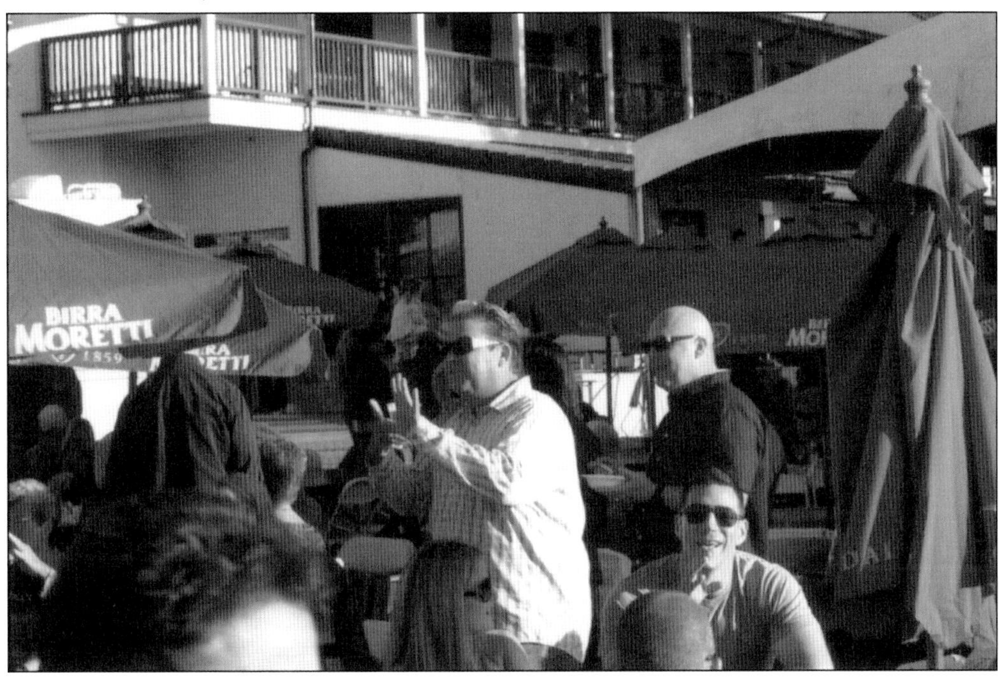

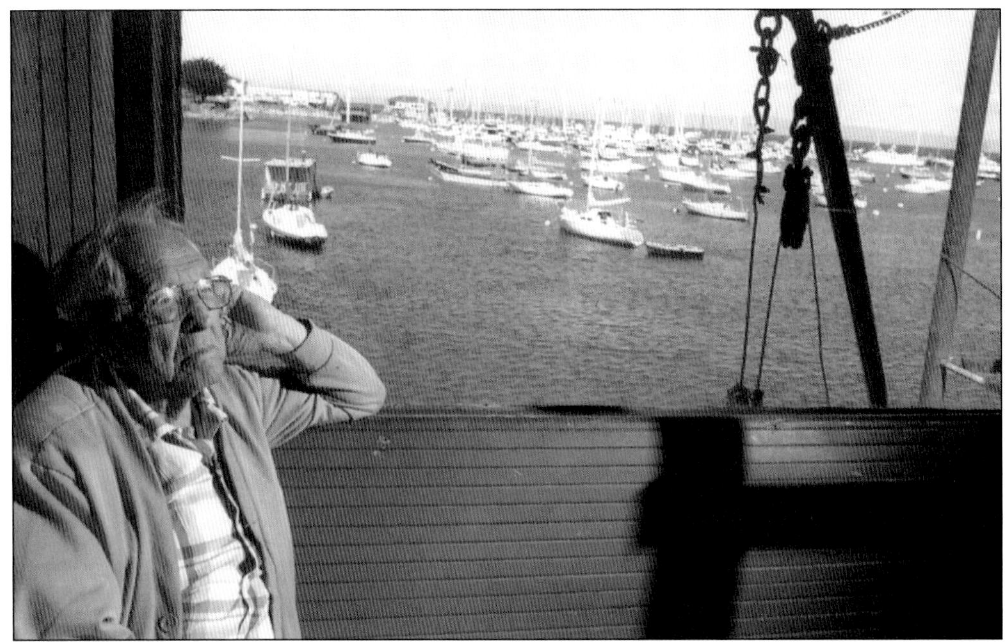

Pictured above and below is Angelo R. DiGirolamo, one of Monterey's and Fisherman's Wharf's most notable personalities. Angelo died unexpectedly on September 21, 2014. He owned the Wharf Theater and was born in Somerville, Massachusetts, the son of Sicilian immigrants. He came to Monterey at the age of 16 and spent the next 77 years in and about the wharf. Angelo and his brothers opened a successful restaurant in 1945 called Angelo's on Fisherman's Wharf. Angelo always had a love for the dramatic arts, and in 1975, along with his family, constructed the New Wharf Theater, known today as the Bruce Ariss Wharf Theater, named after his longtime friend. (Both photographs by Nic Coury, courtesy of *Monterey County Weekly*.)

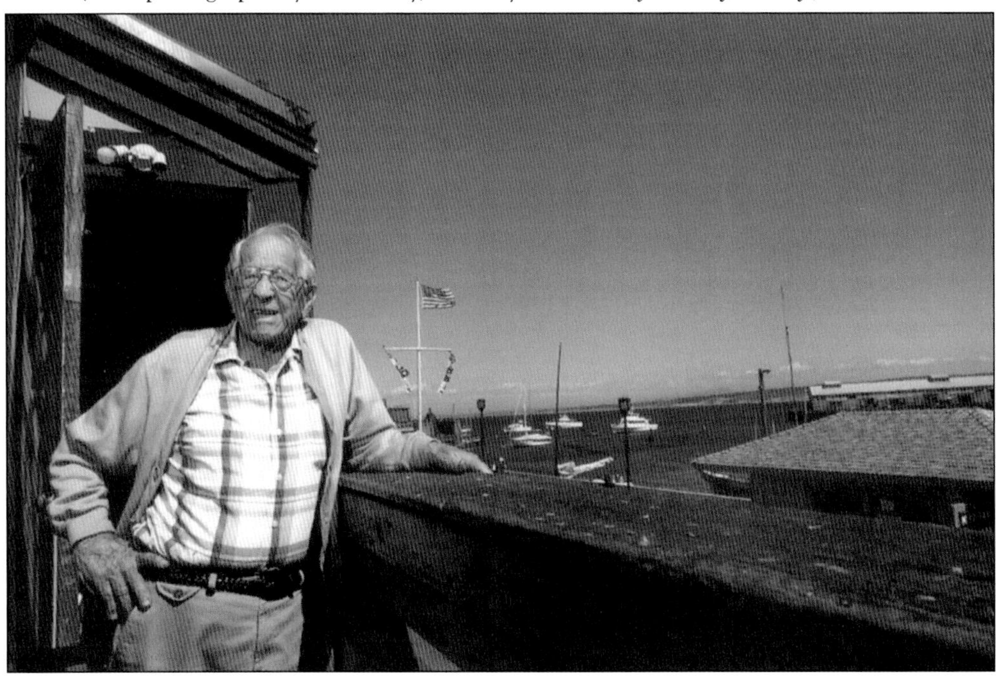

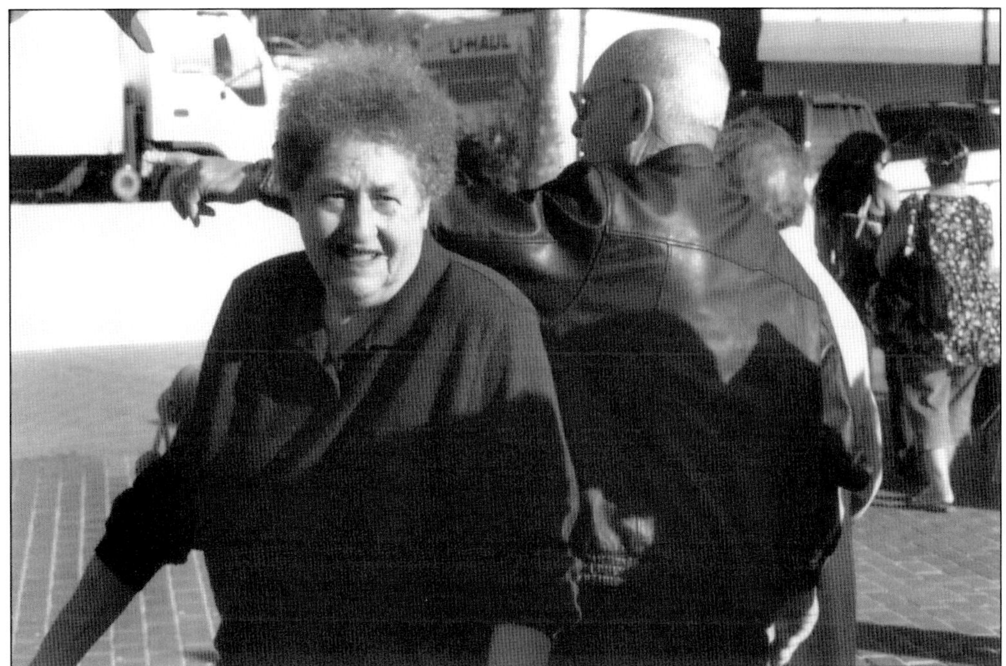

Katherine "Kay" Russo, pictured above at the 2014 Festa Italia, was formerly the Monterey recreation director, and spent years building the youth recreational programs. She had oversight of the Monterey Sports Center, a city-operated fitness center, which has been a success story. Kay spends time at the event reuniting with friends and relatives. Below, Bob Massaro looks over the activities at the festival; he sits on the committee that operates the event. Bob is an active businessman in the community and offers his services to various organizations and special events like Whalefest, which takes place on Old Fisherman's Wharf. (Both, author's collection.)

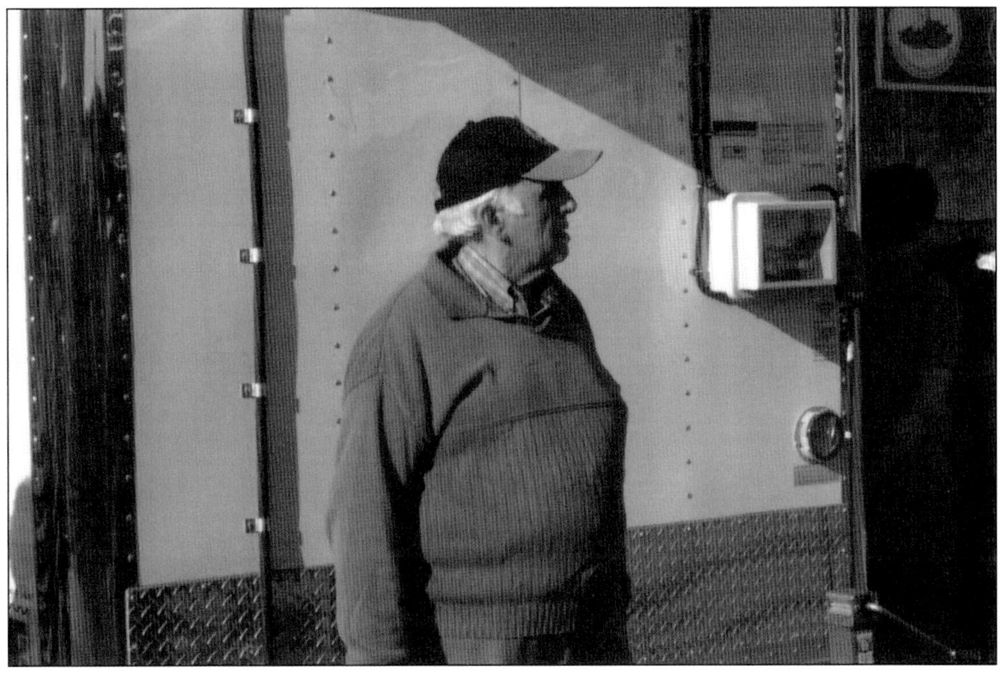

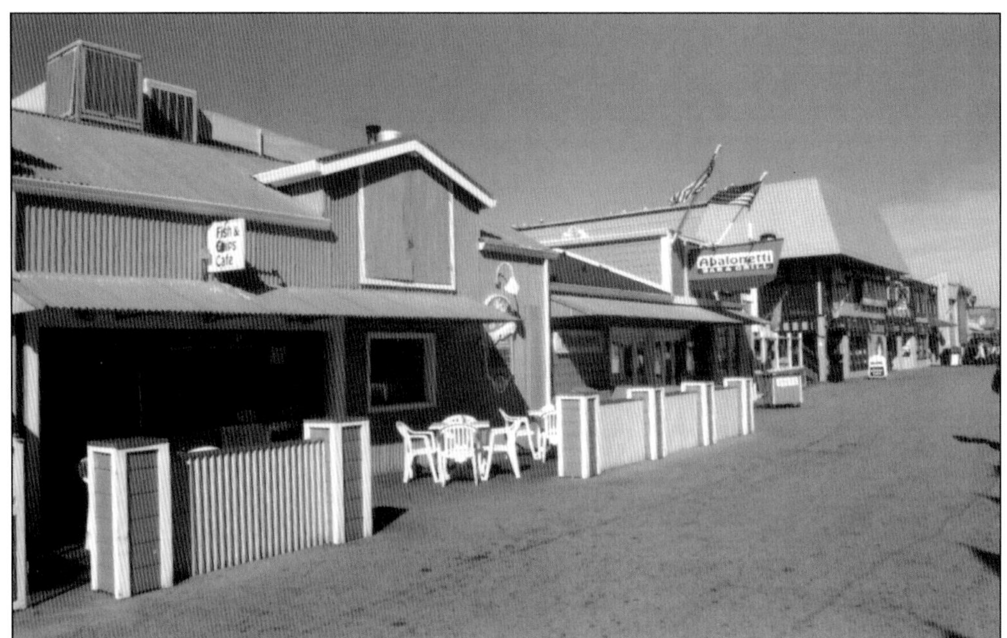


The Old Fisherman's Wharf of today is a far cry from the days of long ago. The wharf is the home of destination gourmet restaurants and shops, which attract thousands of visitors each year. Gone are the many fish markets that lined the wharf in the days of the Silver Harvest, and although the businesses have changed and the wharf has redefined its image, it is still a high revenue generator. Pictured below are the inner harbor and the beginning of Cannery Row, where luxury hotels have replaced the 19 canneries that were operating during the years of the Silver Harvest. Just like Old Fisherman's Wharf, Cannery Row has redefined itself and provides revenue to the city through metered parking and transit occupancy tax. (Both, author's collection.)

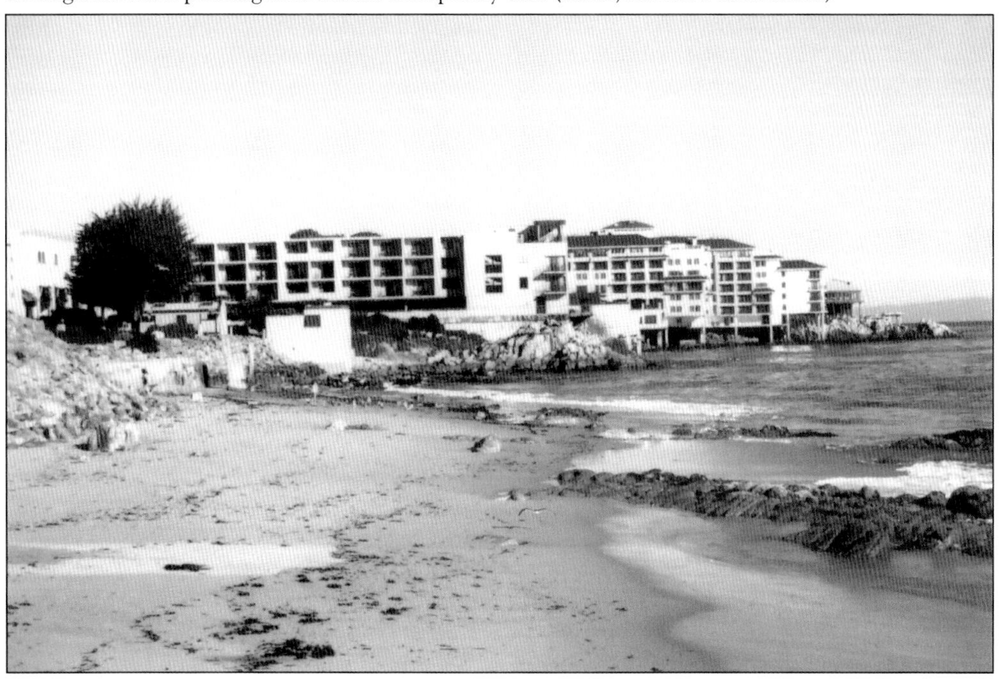

# INDEX